May Days in Hong Kong

May Days in Hong Kong

Riot and Emergency in 1967

Edited by Robert Bickers and Ray Yep

Hong Kong University Press
The University of Hong Kong
Pok Fu Lam Road
Hong Kong
https://hkupress.hku.hk

© 2009 Hong Kong University Press

ISBN 978-962-209-082-8 (*Hardback*)
ISBN 978-962-209-999-9 (*Paperback*)

All rights reserved. No portion of this publication may be reproduced or transmitted in any form or by any means, electronic or mechanical, including photocopying, recording, or any information storage or retrieval system, without prior permission in writing from the publisher.

British Library Cataloguing-in-Publication Data
A catalogue record for this book is available from the British Library.

Digitally printed

Contents

	List of contributors	vii
1.	Studying the 1967 riots: An overdue project *Ray Yep and Robert Bickers*	1

Section I: Strategy and History   19

2.	The 1967 riots in Hong Kong: The domestic and diplomatic fronts of the governor *Ray Yep*	21
3.	The 1967 riots: A legitimacy crisis? *Lawrence Cheuk-yin Wong*	37
4.	On not being Macao(ed) in Hong Kong: British official minds and actions in 1967 *Robert Bickers*	53
5.	A historical perspective: The 1967 riots and the strike-boycott of 1925–26 *John M. Carroll*	69

Section II: Policies and Legacies   87

6.	'Hong Kong headaches': Policing the 1967 disturbances *Georgina Sinclair*	89
7.	The banking and financial impact of the 1967 riots in Hong Kong *Catherine R. Schenk*	105

8. The riots and labour laws: The struggle for an eight-hour day for women factory workers, 1962–1971　　127
　　David Clayton

9. Learning from civil unrest: State/society relations in Hong Kong before and after the 1967 disturbances　　145
　　Alan Smart and Tai-lok Lui

Section III: Testimonies　　161

1967: Witnesses remember　　163
　　Robert Bickers and Ray Yep

Notes　　181

Bibliography　　207

Index　　215

Contributors

Robert Bickers is Professor of History at the University of Bristol, and a co-director of the British Inter-university China Centre. He is the author of *Empire Made Me: An Englishman Adrift in Shanghai* (2003), and *Britain in China: Community, Culture and Colonialism* (1999), and editor or co-editor of a number of volumes including *The Boxers, China and the World* (2007) with R. G. Tiedemann, and a volume on British communities across the globe for the *Oxford History of the British Empire Companion Series* (forthcoming). His other recent work has focused on the history of the Chinese Maritime Customs service and the early phase of meteorology in China. He is director of the 'Historical Photographs of China' project at the University of Bristol (http://chp.ish-lyon.cnrs.fr/).

John M. Carroll is Professor of History at the University of Hong Kong. He is the author of *Edge of Empires: Chinese Elites and British Colonials in Hong Kong* (2005) and *A Concise History of Hong Kong* (2007). He has also published articles in *Modern Asian Studies*, *Twentieth-Century China*, *Chinese Historical Review*, *Journal of Oriental Studies*, and *China Information*. Carroll is currently working on a book on the role of Westerners in the making of modern China.

David Clayton gained his PhD from the University of Manchester in 1994. His doctorate dissertation was published as *Imperialism Revisited: Political and Economic Relations between Britain and China, 1950–54* (1997). He is now Senior Lecturer in the Department of History at the University of York, where he teaches Asian and global history. He has done extensive work on the economic, social and political history of post-war Hong Kong, most of which has been published in specialist, peer-reviewed journals. He is currently examining the evolution of trademark law in Hong Kong and various aspects of industrial relations in post-war Hong Kong. He is also working with economic and cultural historians at York on histories of radio broadcasting in the British Empire.

Tai-lok Lui is Professor of Sociology at the University of Hong Kong. He has written extensively on social class and the changing class structure in Hong Kong, economic restructuring in Hong Kong and Singapore, and the formation of the middle classes in East Asia. He is also a regular columnist contributing to leading newspapers and magazines in Hong Kong and China. His recent publications include *Hong Kong: Learning to Belong to a Nation* (2008), *Consuming Hong Kong* (2001), *The Dynamics of Social Movement in Hong Kong* (2000), *City-States in the Global Economy* (1997), and a number of books on Hong Kong society in Chinese. He is currently completing a book on Hong Kong as a Chinese global city.

Catherine R. Schenk, FRHS, is Professor of International Economic History at the University of Glasgow. Her previous posts were at Royal Holloway, University of London and Victoria University of Wellington, New Zealand. She has published widely on Hong Kong's banking and monetary history in international academic journals and is the author of *Hong Kong as an International Financial Centre: Emergence and Development* (2001) and editor of *Hong Kong's Monetary and Exchange Rate Challenges: Historical Perspectives* (2009). In 2005, she was Visiting Professor at the Department of History, the University of Hong Kong. She was Research Fellow at the Hong Kong Institute for Monetary Research in 2005 and 2008. Her current research explores how a range of developing economies, including Hong Kong, made decisions about their exchange rate regimes in the early 1970s.

Georgina Sinclair completed her PhD at the University of Reading in 2002 and has since held lectureships in history at both Reading University and Leeds University. She is currently Research Fellow with the European Centre for the Study of Policing at the Open University, working on an inter-disciplinary project that considers the internationalization of British law enforcement. She has a substantive interest in British colonial policing, the cross-fertilization of British and colonial models of policing as well as British police/military relations from the nineteenth century until the present day. Her publications include a monograph, *At the End of the Line: Colonial Policing and the Imperial Endgame* (2006). A co-authored book (with Chris A. Williams), provisionally entitled *Global Cops: The Internationalisation of British, Colonial and Postcolonial Policing, 1920–2007,* will be published in 2010.

Alan Smart received his PhD from the University of Toronto in 1986. He is Professor of Anthropology at the University of Calgary. His research has focused on urban political economy, housing, cross-border flows of labour and capital, and social change. His research includes studies of Hong Kong's squatter areas and the impact of regulatory changes on them, Hong Kong investment in China and the social change in the areas where this investment is concentrated, and the politics of urban development in Calgary. He is the author of *The Shek Kip Mei*

Myth: Squatters, Fires and Colonial Rule in Hong Kong, 1950–1963 (2006) and *Making Room: Squatter Clearance in Hong Kong* (1992), and co-editor of *Petty Capitalists and Globalization* (2005). He has also published in journals including *American Anthropologist, Annual Review of Anthropology, Urban Anthropology, Cultural Anthropology, Critique of Anthropology, International Journal of Urban and Regional Research, Society and Space,* and a variety of edited volumes.

Lawrence Cheuk-yin Wong completed his MPhil on the 'Chinese Communist Movement in Hong Kong and Sino-British relations in the Cultural Revolution' at the University of Hong Kong in 2001. After graduation, he worked as a research member in the China-ASEAN Project at the Centre of Asian Studies, the University of Hong Kong. From October 2003 onwards, he has been a PhD candidate of the Graduate School of Asia-Pacific Studies at Waseda University in Japan. He is carrying out research on the Japanese military occupation of Hong Kong and Singapore during 1941–45. He is now teaching at the Open University of Hong Kong.

Ray Yep is Associate Professor in the Department of Public and Social Administration at City University of Hong Kong. He has written extensively on the political economy of market reforms and rural development in post-Mao China. He is the author of *Manager Empowerment in China: Political Implications of Rural Industrialization in the Reform Era*. He has also published articles in leading journals, including *China Quarterly*, *Pacific Review*, and *Public Administration Review*. He is currently working on a book about the domestic and diplomatic aspects of the 1967 riots.

1
Studying the 1967 riots:
An overdue project

Ray Yep and Robert Bickers

The 1967 riots are understudied, but the events which began in May 1967 in Hong Kong led within a year to 51 deaths, 4,500 arrests, and a campaign of bombings which threatened to destabilize the colony. What began as a strike at an artificial flower factory became a major anti-colonial movement led by local leftists, which was eventually countered by a full range of emergency and security measures instituted by the colonial administration. The press and the education system became areas of conflict, and the impact of the events spilled over into Sino-British relations more broadly, and to outbreaks of violence in London, Shanghai and Beijing. By any objective standards this was a major crisis. However, while the public memory of the event is still alive, the public representation of these months of conflict is muted — there is little mention of them in the Hong Kong Museum of History, and most works on post-war history of Hong Kong allocate no more than a few pages on this subject.[1]

Despite the paucity of analysis, accounts of the event contrast sharply. Notwithstanding the poor working conditions and appalling state of welfare provision in Hong Kong during the 1960s, John Cooper argued that 'whatever the causes of this unrest were, they could in no way be sufficiently sound to justify the "reign of terror" which was to characterize the daily life of the Colony throughout the long summer of 1967'.[2] His indictment focused on the violence of the political campaign instigated by the communists who started 'with the assumption that the Colony would bend under pressure as easily as Macao had done'.[3] Cooper's view finds resonance in an unexpected source; Jin Yaoru, a local communist boss in charge of propaganda work in the 1960s, voiced similar views on the influence of external sources on the unfolding of disturbances almost three decades later. In his book on Chinese Communist Party's Hong Kong policy, he argues that the anxiety of the local party leadership to prove its loyalty to the radical movement in Beijing was the main impetus behind the campaign.[4] Hong Kong's 1997 reunification with China seems to have emboldened a segment of the left-wing camp to talk about the events, and more work on the issue has been published in recent years.

Gary Cheung's collection of interviews with several key players in the communist camp adds further ammunition to Jin's argument.[5] While not disputing this basic argument, the account by Zhou Yi, former deputy chief editor of *Wen Wei Po*, provides a more nuanced analysis of the involvement of leftists in the confrontation. By contextualizing the event against the background of the unabated persecution of leftist organizations and individuals by the colonial administration in post-war Hong Kong,[6] Zhou portrayed the turbulence simply as an explosion of anger fuelled by grievances at the persecution endured by the communist sympathizers over the years, and the violence unleashed as self-defence in the face of colonial ferocity. On the other hand, with the benefit of access to the now-open Foreign Office files, Liang and his colleagues have made a very important contribution to the general understanding of the matter by bringing in the views of the British and colonial governments. Based on the official records of communications between London and Hong Kong during that period, their analysis offers invaluable access to the thinking and calculation of the 'British' side and thus constitutes an important supplement to the various left-wing accounts mentioned above.[7]

This project is a response to the renewed interest in the 1967 riots. Despite the 'mini-boom' in publications on the event over the last few years, most analyses remain journalistic or partisan. This book aims at revisiting two fundamental questions. First, what had really happened during the riots? By this, we do not mean simply the chronology of events (which is well documented) but aim at uncovering the dynamics and logic of the interaction between the different parties concerned.[8] Second, we wish to explore the importance of these events. Were they a turning point in Hong Kong history or is that an exaggeration? Was it really a legitimacy crisis, just a storm in a colonial teacup, or a test as argued by former colonial officials? 'How fatuous the whole thing was,' reflected former governor Sir David Trench in 1987, '[t]here was no issue between us and the people who were rioting except that they wanted to riot and we didn't want them to.'[9] So, do they in fact belong to the obscurity that has mostly enveloped them? Were the social reforms of the post-riots years simply inevitable even without the turbulent explosion in 1967? We aim here to look beyond narratives of confrontation and the parochial dimensions of the event by placing our analysis in a wider context. We conceive the events in 1967 in a wider historical perspective and focus on how the previous experience of local disturbances in the colony had shaped and influenced its responses and perceptions of the challenge faced in the 1960s. We also try to place the analysis in the wider context of the late British Empire as the unfolding of events was determined not only by the concerns and anxiety of the colonial state during the Hong Kong emergency, but also by calculations of the British government that concern higher national interests, such as the diplomatic relationship with China, and strategic imperial planning.

In the following sections, we will present an overview of the main concerns of this collective effort. Specifically, the contributors intend to uncover four major issues in our analysis: historical continuities and the potency of the China factor, the importance of the riots, the capacity of the colonial state, and the relationship between the colony and the sovereign power. Before we proceed to this discussion, three key points about the background of the events need to be elucidated.

Heroes or villains?

First, we need to consider whether it is appropriate to use the term 'riots' to describe what happened in 1967. The Hong Kong and British governments quickly adopted 'confrontation' as their formal term for the events that unfolded from May 1967 onwards. The prisoners' issue, which continued until 1972, was usually referred to in Foreign and Commonwealth Office parlance as one concerning 'confrontation prisoners'. We might understand more fully the response of British official minds if we remember that they viewed the events at the time as a 'confrontation', that is, a formal contestation of British power, involving popular internal as well as external forces.[10] The related term that was used, though less frequently, was 'emergency'. This had practical and technical consequences. 'I believe that it would be wise,' suggested General Sir Michael Carver, Commander-in-Chief Far East, after his visit in July 1967, 'to recognize that Hong Kong faces a situation which, although not styled as such, is in effect an emergency, and to adjust the methods of all concerned accordingly.'[11] When debating the colony's response to the escalating bombing campaign in September 1967, diplomat Sir Arthur Galsworthy sketched the comparative experience of 'previous emergencies elsewhere', in 'the Malayan, Kenyan, Cyprus and Aden Emergencies', and in Rhodesia for good measure.[12] Hong Kong was, after all, one colony amongst others. Using the contemporary term would help focus attention on the wider context of the events, and help their placing within that broader context of late British Empire history and popular contestations of British colonial rule. Whilst there were clearly unique aspects to the 1967 events, such as its relationship to the Chinese Cultural Revolution, there were also commonalities in the response of the British to the situation which might be argued to help us better understand the events if we move away from the commonly used term.

The term 'riots' is, however, more commonly adopted by the local population in Hong Kong in both Chinese and English (and it is how retired British officials often label it). Publications relating to the events are catalogued under 'Riots, 1967' in the Hong Kong University Libraries, while they are usually indexed under 'Riots' in histories of Hong Kong. The term, 'riots' (*baodong*), carries negative connotations of violence, wantonness and destruction, as it does in English. Notwithstanding the leftist coinage, *fanying kangbao* ('anti-British and anti-violence campaign'), is commonly used by that camp and it characterizes leftist action as justifiable acts of self-defence against colonial oppression. The collective memory of the event as 'riots' reflects widespread popular contempt and condemnation of the disturbances that took place in 1967. Chinese public opinion was clearly on the side of the colonial administration in 1967. More recently, the public outcry provoked by the government's decision in 2001 to award the Grand Bauhinia Medal to Yang Jiang (Yeung Kwong), the former chair of the Hong Kong Federation of Trade Unions, is illustrative of this general sentiment. Many people who had gone through the long summer of 1967 found it hard to accept the bestowal of such an accolade on someone who presided over the All Circles Anti-Persecution Struggle Committee, the body nominally in charge of all left-wing activities during that period. In reality, the events of 1967 alienated the left-wing from the local society and drove it into marginality. For much of Hong Kong popular opinion these were ultimately 'riots'. Xu Jiatun, who came to Hong Kong to take over the post of director of the New China News Agency in 1983, recalled that 'when I first arrived, some local cadres told me that after the riots, there was a general fear of Chinese officials in Hong Kong. Local people even dared not go into Chinese product department stores. Our cadres had to hide their official affiliation. Most people treated us with contempt and called us the leftist (*zuozi*) behind our back.'[13] The title of this volume includes both key terms, riot and emergency, with neither privileged. In the chapters, however, except where used in quotations, the contributors mostly use the term 'riots'. This should not be taken to indicate that we agree with this characterization of the events above any other; rather, adoption of this term simply reflects our respect for the sentiment of the generation who have witnessed the episode, and the resilience of the label in popular usage.

A Crown Colony

Hong Kong was part of Britain's contracting imperial patrimony. It is in fact easy to forget that Hong Kong was a colony, and that it was one amongst others, however uniquely placed (while the overall number of colonies was steadily shrinking).[14] It was, as John Darwin notes, a 'most unusual colony' on a number of counts, but there were few, if any, territories which matched the ideal template, and while we might agree that it was more unusual than most, the literature has for too long neglected to examine Hong Kong in its wider colonial context.[15] Two moments at which the colony might have reverted to Chinese rule — in 1945 and in 1949–50 — passed without incident, and it seemed that it was a colony which could not be shaken off.[16] Nobody wanted it 'back'. Meanwhile, in the decade preceding 1967, thirty British colonial territories had secured independence; the Gold Coast, Kenya, Straits Settlements, Nigeria, Cyprus, Western Samoa and Jamaica were among those states from which the British had withdrawn. The process continued: in summer 1967 an inglorious and bloody endgame was being played out in Aden.[17] The Colonial Office itself had been so denuded of its charges that it was merged with the Commonwealth Relations Office in 1966, and its increasing administrative overlaps with the Foreign Office presaged the merger of the two into the Foreign and Commonwealth Office in

October 1968. Nonetheless, Hong Kong remained a colony, with an administration recognizable 'instantly as "British" ', as Wm Roger Louis notes, and it was both a product of its colonial history and of its complete integration into the formal apparatus of colonial rule (not least the circulation of staff).[18] It was also integrated into the informal and insidious world of colonial assumptions and attitudes, not least about White British relations with non-white peoples.

Hong Kong's 1967 trial thus took place within the active sphere of British colonial policymaking, strategies and history. Its leading officials were men who had served in colonial administration across the world, and had done so during the heyday of the British Empire. Governor Sir David Trench was the Indian-born son of an engineer. His colonial service career had begun twenty-nine years before May 1967, and he had served in the Solomon Islands and in Hong Kong.[19] Colonial Secretary Michael Gass first served on the Gold Coast in 1939, and thereafter in Gold Coast/Ghana, the West Pacific and in Hong Kong.[20] Philip Rogers, who chaired the Cabinet's Defence Review Working Party on Hong Kong, joined the Colonial Office in 1936, serving in Jamaica as the governor's private secretary. Trench and Gass may have adapted themselves and their assumptions to the realities of cold war Hong Kong, but they brought to their posts, as did many of their more junior officers, assumptions and experiences from elsewhere in the pre-war and post-war empire. This was not simply a matter of administrators and their attitudes, but was fully structural. Georgina Sinclair's account of late-colonial policing, for example, places the Hong Kong police firmly within this networked and circulating colonial world.[21]

We also need to remember that, as on many other occasions in Hong Kong's past, there were divergences and disagreements between British colonial policy and diplomatic policy. There were also discrepancies between the viewpoints of the Hong Kong colonial government and those of the British embassy in China.[22] The former was par for the course of metropolitan/colonial relations within the British Empire. Men on the 'spot' administered their territories within the realms of practical local politics, balancing central instructions and requirements with realities (as they saw them) on the ground (and they usually felt that they saw them rather more clearly than the men behind desks in Whitehall). Hong Kong was not alone in having an administration which could frustrate London's instructions and evade its requirements. The latter situation — which prompted what were in effect at times competing and contradictory foreign policies with central or regional power in China — was more unusual. The Foreign Office line was always ultimately the dominant one, and the diplomats were consistent in their efforts to remind the Colonial Office that British China policy was only partially concerned with Hong Kong.

The Hong Kong emergency also took place in other contexts — in the Chinese Cultural Revolution, and the Cold War, and it took place while the experience of the establishment of the People's Republic was still fresh in planners' minds — British firms and interests, and British nationals had effectively been held hostage as the new regime took over the Chinese economy and drove out foreign interests.[23] It also took place as the colonels consolidated the April coup in Greece, the Wilson government applied to join the Common Market on 11 May, Israel launched the six-day war on 2 June, the Federal Army mutinied against the British in Aden later that same month, and the Biafran war began in July. Hong Kong struggled to keep a place in UK headlines over the year. A bomb or two is news, but 1,778 of them were a statistic that failed to maintain the headlines in the face of such competition. British policymakers had a wide range of issues to confront in early 1967. More widely, although Harold Wilson's first government had asserted a commitment to maintain a strong British military presence in the 'East of Suez', longer-term thinking about Britain's world role and the economics of his second term were forcing the radical rethink that was to lead to the January 1968 announcement of the intention to withdraw forces from Southeast Asia and the Gulf.[24] As the workers at the San Po Kong Artificial Flower Factory clashed with the Hong Kong police, the British state was intensely discussing how far its responsibilities should stretch.

No dinner party in Hong Kong

Regardless of the causes of the confrontation or its labels, the disturbances which started in 1967 were strikingly violent. Table 1.1 provides a succinct account of the intensity of violence during this turbulent period.

The disturbances started as a labour dispute in an artificial flower factory in Kowloon in April 1967. The row between police and the defiant factory workers on 6 May marked the beginning of violent confrontation. The intervention of the communist-dominated Hong Kong Federation of Trade Unions two days later signalled the politicization of the events. The turning point, however, was the involvement of the Chinese Ministry of Foreign Affairs on 15 May 1967. A protest statement was passed to the British chargé d'affaires in Beijing, which was followed by anti-British demonstrations in the capital and in Guangzhou, accompanied by sympathetic editorials in the *People's Daily*.[25] The local leftists took note of these developments and formed an All Circles Anti-Persecution Struggle Committee (*Gangjiu guojie tongbao fandui gangying pohai douzheng weiyuanhui*) in Hong Kong the next day. This heralded the full-scale mobilization of local communists into the territory-wide anti-colonial campaign.

The leftists pursued the campaign with a multi-front approach. The struggle after May 1967 entailed the following.

Demonstrations. This was the most common tactic deployed in the early stage of the events. Union members, students and supporters were called to the street to make their voices heard. Thousands of protesters were mobilized to challenge colonial authority by rallying outside the Governor's House in mid-May 1967. Such gatherings of left-wing supporters outside government premises and court houses

Table 1.1
Statistics of disturbances in Hong Kong, 11 May 1967–1 June 1968

Casualties	
Killed	51
Injured	848
Prisoners	
Arrests 4,498	
Convicted	2,077
Property damage	
Buildings	122
Vehicles	164
Ammunition expended by police	
No of occasions gas used	90
No of ball ammo. used	87
Bombs	
Explosions	253
True bombs	1,525
Hoax bombs	4,917
False alarms	2,645

Source: TNA, FCO 40/53, Serial No. 115, June 1968.

clutching the Little Red Book in their hands characterized the first two months of the confrontation.

Strikes. A 'general strike' was called in late June with more than twenty trade unions responding to the appeal. While the impact of the four-day event was less significant than leftists' expectations of it, the strong presence of left-wing unions in transport services and public utilities (see Table 1.2) suggests that their actions caused considerable interruption of normal life.

Propaganda. Propaganda was a key battlefield between communists and the colonial administration during the confrontation. For left-wing activists, the nine pro-Beijing newspapers in Hong Kong provided moral support and encouragement, ammunition against imperialism, cues for action and major means for mobilization and propaganda. These titles, with daily circulations totalling more than 400,000,[26] contributed about a quarter of the total newspaper circulation in Hong Kong. The papers were flooded with rhetorical attacks on the 'atrocities and repressions' of the colonial government and with personal abuse of the governor, Sir David Trench. They reprinted editorials and articles from *People's Daily*, and the leftist's

Table 1.2
Staff position of public transport and utility companies

Public utility company	Strength prior to disturbance (A)	Number dismissed after strike	Strength by the end of 1967 (B)	(B)/(A)
Star Ferry	590	590	456	77%
Hong Kong and Yaumati Ferry	1885	115	1828	97%
Hong Kong Tramways	1713	679	1522	89%
China Motor Bus	2360	1273	1756	74%
Kowloon Motor Bus	7194	4907	4505	63%
Hong Kong Electric	978	148	883	90%
China Light and Power	2745	709	2567	94%
Hong Kong and China Gas	548	334	407	74%

Source: TNA, FCO 40/52.

interpretation of the confrontations. Chinese members of the Hong Kong Police Force were singled out by the communist press for a consistent propaganda barrage. Intimidating messages warning Chinese personnel not to be the 'running dogs' of the British appeared regularly. In addition to the orthodox press, many 'mosquito', 'underground papers' were published by left-wing groups after the colonial administration tightened its squeeze on the communist papers in August.

Bomb attacks. The leftists resorted to a more radical armed strategy in the form of a campaign of bombing when large-scale arrest sweeps of radicals by police began in July 1967. While most of these 'bombs' were hoaxes, there were still nearly two thousand genuine bombs or attempted attacks. Government premises, police stations and public utilities were common targets of these incidents, but civilians were not immune to these threats. Normal life was severely affected and the colony was shocked by the death of two young girls as a result of an explosion in North Point on 21 August. The effectiveness of such tactics as leverage for the struggle against the colonial government is debatable, but it undoubtedly aroused a great deal of resentment from the general public, and perhaps more than anything indicated the alienation of the left from the populace and its general impotence. This wave of terrorism gradually faded out by the end of 1967.

The China threat. The most potent weapon available for the leftists, however, was the threat of a potential takeover of the colony by China. Local communists suggested throughout the campaign that they had clear and full endorsement of Beijing for their radicalism in Hong Kong. As a matter of fact, although Beijing's involvement was evident, it is debatable whether or not the local campaign was fully orchestrated by the Party centre. However, editorials in the *People's Daily*, mass rallies in major cities, financial donations to local trade unions and the Chinese Foreign Ministry's diplomatic pressure on the British camp were illustrative of high-level support for the radicalism in Hong Kong.[27] The attack on the premises of the British Mission in Beijing by the Red Guards on 22 August 1967 was a naked act of retaliation against the Hong Kong government's decision to close down the operation of three communist papers in Hong Kong. However, it was the clash at Sha Tau Kok in July 1967 that put the confidence of local population on the edge of collapse. The conflict between several hundred Chinese residents and Hong Kong police in the border on 8 July resulted in the deaths of five policemen and the mobilization of British military force.

The colonial administration under Governor Trench responded with no less determination. While observing a restrained approach in handling the crisis in the early weeks and hoping that the tension would soon subside — 'We tried to do it softly, softly,' he later reflected, '... without capitulating,' more assertive measures were deployed as it became evident that the disturbance had the capacity to persist for a protracted period.[28] Once clearance from London was granted, levers of state coercion were fully utilized in combating the radicals. The administration used a combination of new regulations and old-style force to strike hard at the leftists. The strategy involved the following components:

Raids of communist premises and arrest of left-wing leaders. As part of the strategy of disrupting the co-ordination of leftist activities, the police force resorted to large-scale arrests of trouble-makers through raids on communist premises. Based on intelligence provided by the Special Branch, searches of the offices of trade unions, communist schools and cinemas became more frequent after early July 1967. The most dramatic episode was the raid on the Qiaoguan Building in North Point on 4 August, where the alleged headquarters of the leftists was housed. Backed up by military force, teams of policemen landed at the roof of the building from helicopters and crashed into the premise. Members of the All Circles Anti-Persecution Struggle Committee were specific targets of these raids. Many were arrested in follow-up action and detained in the centre at Morrison Hill for interrogation.

Emergency legislation. The colonial government also brought in further emergency legislation to combat the rioters. These legal devices imposed new restrictions on activities such as making inflammatory speeches and displaying relevant materials (such as banners and posters), possession of dangerous goods and offensive weapons, and assembly. These measures widened considerably the powers of police to combat the emergency, but their immediate and their longer-term repercussions for civil liberties and the rule of law were evident.

Banning of pro-communist papers. Communist newspapers were always seen as the major pillar of the left-wing campaign, and Trench was determined to take the initiative in this area. After intensive exchanges with London, five editors and publishers of three pro-communist newspapers, *Tin Fung Yat Po*, *Hong Kong Evening News* and *Afternoon News,* were arrested on 9 August. The three papers were eventually suspended for six months and three of the prosecuted were sentenced to three years' imprisonment.

Closure of communist schools. Local communists had established a strong hold in local education in the immediate aftermath of the Second World War, given the colonial administration's general reluctance to involve itself in social welfare provision. The government certainly found little comfort in such development and a drive to close down schools without proper registration, many of them left-wing schools, was launched in the early 1960s.[29] The 'problem' of Chinese state or party-affiliated education was one of long-standing within British Asian possessions.[30] The fear re-emerged during the confrontation in 1967. An internal report of the colonial government in late 1967 reiterated that 'there is evidence of sustained and intense communist and subversive indoctrination'[31] within communist-controlled schools. In the evening of 27 November, an explosion was heard from Chung Wah Middle School. An injured teenage student was found with one hand and three fingers lost. The police found explosive powder and chemicals suitable for bomb-making as well as evidence of other explosions on the premises. Consequently, six people were arrested and the director of education closed the school until 15 August 1968.[32] Other communist schools were raided and searched in the following weeks and more than a hundred students and teachers were detained and arrested.[33]

Militarization of the response. British soldiers played a mainly back-up but nonetheless key role in confronting rioters during the riots. However, their presence had a key role in maintaining public confidence. For many, it was an important sign of British commitment to the colony. At the time of the disturbances, there were approximately four thousand British troops and five thousand Gurkhas in the territory.[34] As disturbances proliferated, the original plan for reduction of British forces outlined in the ongoing Defence Review was reversed. Instead, a further Gurkha Battalion arrived in late June 1967. The British battleship, HMS *Bulwark* also visited Hong Kong in May 1967 as a further gesture of commitment. In the use of combined and co-ordinated police and military force against the leftists lay one key to the success of the clampdown, but it was the loyal effectiveness of the police, and their garnering of widespread public support that maintained the important civilian character of the administration's response to the events.

'Winning hearts and minds'. Propaganda warfare is a common counter-insurgency activity as was demonstrated in the Kenyan and Malayan emergencies in the 1950s and 1960s.[35] A publicity committee headed by the deputy colonial secretary was formed in the early weeks of the disturbances. Both Hong Kong and London agreed that a more permanent base for 'psychological operations' was necessary in order to co-ordinate the efforts of Radio Hong Kong, the Government Information Department, the police, and other departments. Themes stressed in the materials disseminated by these units included the damaging effect of the Cultural Revolution on China and the importance of stability for the Hong Kong economy.[36] The Hong Kong Government Office in London initiated a new programme to 'project the image of the Hong Kong government' in the 'right perspective' to the Chinese community in Britain and more widely in Europe.[37] The operations and effectiveness

of the psychological warfare remain unexplored, yet it is undeniable that there was popular support for the colonial government during the riots, especially after the commencement of random bomb attacks by the leftists. Contemporary observers were not slow to assert that the government had failed in the ordinary course of events to communicate effectively with the population. Its public image needed a makeover.[38]

This sketch of the strategies deployed by both sides in the struggle outlines the tensions faced by the local population during the riots period and the interruption to social order they experienced. The unfolding of events is, however, primarily a reflection of the interaction and contestation between domestic and external forces that had a major stake in maintaining or reversing the status quo of the colony. The objective of this exercise to revisit the history of the 1967 riots is thus not simply to produce a more detailed narrative of the events; instead, the task here is to provide a more nuanced understanding of the nature of colonial rule in Hong Kong. To elucidate the point, let us look at the several issues that are central to the analysis in this volume.

Historical continuity and relevance of the China factor

'Policy makers are heirs before they are choosers', Richard Rose has argued.[39] Colonial governors learnt from their predecessors when it came to handling emergencies and contingencies, and there were also striking similarities in the perimeters of policy options between crises. As revealed in the chapter by Georgina Sinclair in this book, the circulation of personnel between colonies and centralized imperial thinking on specific issues such as policing models contributed to establishing common approaches to handling crisis and thus forging certain connections between historical episodes. Historical continuities can be expressed in temporal terms as well. John Carroll's comparison between the strike boycott of 1925–26 and the 1967 riots is illustrative of such an approach. The most obvious parallel uncovered in his chapter is the potency of the China factor and the extent to which events in mainland China could affect the colony. Carroll argues that despite the local social, economic and political conditions in the 1920s and 1960s, both disturbances could not have occurred without extensive support from within China. For the 1967 riots, the respective analyses of Wong and Yep also show how local developments resonated with the rise and fall of radical factions in Chinese politics. Radicalism in China and its spill-over appeared to be the regular source of instability in the colony, and return to normality in Hong Kong eventually came when the mainland government chose a change of direction. For colonial administrators, crisis management in the colony always needed to commence with informed guesswork about China's intentions. Bickers' chapter in this volume demonstrates how the confrontation in Macao, the so-called '12.3 Incident', which happened six months before the outbreak of violence in Hong Kong, shaped the course adopted by the colonial administration during the 1967 riots. The humiliation of Portuguese authorities in Macao shaped the template of British strategic planning for the colony and the cost of indiscriminate concessions to the communists was, as a result, deemed unacceptably high by segments of the policy community.

The historical continuity of the relevance of the China factor in colonial governance is demonstrated not only in the form of the 'export of revolution' or of violence, but also in terms of frameworks of reference used by Hong Kong people as well. Despite emotional attachments to the motherland, the mainland alternative also denoted instability and political radicalism in local eyes. The general uneasiness with the latter concerns, as uncovered by Carroll and Yep's analyses, ironically helped to reinforce colonial rule in Hong Kong during the crisis period. For people who lived through the 1967 riots, the choice of loyalty between the motherland and an alien rule was made easier in the face of the political reality of chaos and fanaticism in the Mainland. Perversely, troubles in China may have reinforced general contentment with, or acquiescence in, the second best option open to Hong Kong's populace: stable alien rule. This was one key to colonial governance in the territory and was central to the success of the colonial administration in securing public support on both occasions in the 1920s and 1960s. Basic services were maintained during the strike period as a result of the volunteer activity of many local people. Tung Wah Hospitals also provided a food service that helped minimize the impact of the disturbances. David Trench achieved no less a success in mobilizing social support in the 1960s. Hundreds of social and community organizations pledged support for the government during the first week of the events. 'This support for the colonial government during both disturbances certainly reflected the concerns to preserve order and, especially in the case of the business and professional elites, class interests', Carroll contends. The enthusiasm of Shouson Chow and Robert Kotewall during the 1920s and the loyalty of the Executive Council to the governor during the riots certainly confirmed such view. For these elites or the local community in general, the status quo, no matter how imperfect it was, was still more preferable to the alternative scenario of violence and uncertainty. After all, this was the reason why many had fled to the colony from the Mainland in the relatively recent past.

Capacity of the colonial state

A standard characterization of the colonial authority until the late 1960s is of a 'minimal state'. As Ian Scott argued, 'for much of its history, the activities of the colonial state in Hong Kong did not serve to distinguish the territory from other tropical, backward, disease-ridden, barely self-sufficient imperial acquisitions'.[40] Implicitly, therefore, Scott notes that it was, as it on the whole was, a fairly typical colonial state in terms of how it perceived its remit to engage with and shape local society. Indifference and distance were regarded as defining characteristics of governance of the colony. The resolve of the colonial state to posit itself as a proactive administration was further tested by the challenges to its legitimacy from the Chinese Communist Party across the border. Consequently, there was a general sense of insecurity and incomprehension concerning local society among colonial officials. Leo Goodstadt has suggested that officials 'never felt completely secure in their authority and were never entirely free from the fear that the public might desert them'.[41] The chapter by David Clayton in this volume certainly confirms this image of an indifferent, distant state. His analysis shows that despite growing pressure from London, colonial administrations under Robert Black and David Trench persistently declined to take concrete action to regulate industrial relations before the riots.

The reluctance to penetrate and engage with local society, however, should not be taken as equivalent to weakness. Comments of senior colonial officials deriding the riots as a 'storm in a teacup' as documented in Wong's chapter may be an exaggeration, yet the colonial state's success in withstanding the 1960s storm is vivid proof of its tenacity and capacity. As revealed by Catherine Schenk's contribution, the colonial authority's ability to maintain public confidence in financial institutions provided another key to its survival during this stormy period. Its fiscal strength also allowed uninterrupted support for the propaganda and law enforcement teams to counteract leftist activities. The colonial state also demonstrated its coercive capacity during the confrontations and its ability to call on wider imperial force. As described in Sinclair's chapter, its experiences in handling earlier disturbances turned out to be a blessing in disguise: the local police was well prepared for the task and performed admirably in disrupting the leftist network, arresting ringleaders and raiding communist premises. Reinforcement of the British garrison certainly helped maintain the confidence and morale of the police, yet it was the effectiveness and loyalty of this local civilian force that held the key to eventual success in containing the disturbances. Nonetheless, the events of 1967 prompted a rethink in the ongoing Defence Review discussions about the level of military commitment to be made to the colony. As a result, initial plans were changed and forces were redeployed permanently to Hong Kong from Southeast Asia (notably Royal Air Force helicopters and the Brigade of Gurkhas). It is tempting to see this significant enhancement of the military presence, especially when combined with the turn to a more proactive state, as representing nothing short of a formal re-occupation of the colony, one which lasted until the 1997 handover. The survival of the colonial state did not simply hinge upon its coercive capacity alone, however. In fact, the alien authority also demonstrated its symbolic capacity in winning the trust and support of local people during the confrontation. Gregor Benton has shown how the government's representative office set out, with some success, to engage systematically with the Chinese population in Britain, and build effective ties with community organizations.[42] For residents of the colony and their confreres overseas, as Carroll points out here, colonial rule ultimately was preferred as the law and order option against the political fanaticism and chaos offered by the leftist alternative. Such support, however passive in nature, did lay down foundations for the perpetuation of colonial rule.

Nevertheless, the most salient feature of the strength of the colonial state was revealed by its capacity to reform and revitalize itself after the riots. Unlike previous post-crisis reforms, such as the inclusion of Chinese members on the Executive Council after the strike-boycott of 1925–26 and the aborted proposals of the Young Plan in the aftermath of the Japanese occupation, the changes introduced after the riots were much more comprehensive and drastic. The so-called 'MacLehose years of social reforms' witnessed fundamental changes in policy concerning public housing, education, workers' rights, and medical services. They indicated a departure from the previous position of detachment and heralded a more proactive approach of colonial governance. Smart and Lui argue, however, that these changes are not merely responses to the crisis of the riots. For the British, the main lessons of the confrontation in 1967 were the vulnerability of Hong Kong and the dim prospects for British rule over the territory beyond 1997, these authors contend. Thus, they believe that when MacLehose took up his office, the governor found it important to boost public confidence and to secure hegemonic leadership before China raised questions concerning the future of Hong Kong. The social reforms were therefore part of the preparation work for the forthcoming negotiations with the Chinese.

Importance of the riots

Regardless of the motivation behind these social reforms, the 1967 riots have always been seen by many as the turning point of the history of colony. Ian Scott, for example, argues that the disturbances 'illuminated the weakness of the system and pointed to the need for change . . . and that a new political order and a new basis of legitimacy were urgent requirements'.[43] Authors in this book, however, offer a different view. The major argument forwarded by Smart and Lui is that while consenting to interpretations of the nature of the 1967 riots as a catalyst for social reforms in the 1970s, they contend that the changes in the aftermath of the event actually only make sense in the context of previous disturbances and the challenge that they posed to colonial authority. The MacLehose reforms were, therefore, products of reflections on the merits and demerits of various responses to a long list of challenges to the colonial regime: the Kowloon Walled City incident (1948), the Tung Tau Comfort Mission riot (1952), Double Ten disturbances (1956) and the Star Ferry riots (1966). Whereas the 1967 riots were seen as being externally provoked, all these confrontations stemmed from local problems that needed to be addressed and showed the limitation of responding with stop-gap measures. These incidents also exposed the vulnerability of the administration to local frustration and the necessity of capturing active support if the regime was to survive.

Clayton's work challenges the conventional wisdom that claims the 1967 riots as the turning point from another angle. Using the case of labour law on the eight-hour working day for women, Clayton argues that while the mass protests in the 1960s did provide ammunition for some benevolent bureaucrats in Hong Kong and London to circumvent business opposition to reform and justification for policy shift, the radicalism of 1967 failed to prompt fundamental change in the attitude of those who opposed state regulation of the economy. For the progressives, the year 1967 revealed workers' frustrations and signs of market failure, yet for the pragmatists, the fear of social revolution soon receded in the aftermath of the riots. For some, the loss of credibility of left-wing unions may have even emboldened their opposition to reforms as well. The 'watershed' argument probably needs to be refined.

Relationship between the colony and the sovereign

Scholarly works have highlighted the autonomy enjoyed by the colony, and argued that the governors were not always subservient to their superiors' opinions in London. Bickers' previous work reveals the Foreign Office's irritation with Hong Kong's pursuit of local diplomacy with the Guomindang authorities between 1917 and 1927, which directly defied London's instructions to Hong Kong to communicate with China only through the Legation in Peking or the Consul at Canton.[44] Colonial governors had also demonstrated repeated stubbornness in adeptly resisting reform initiatives from London when they found the latter's proposal inconvenient. Miners' case study of the abolition of *mui tsai* system, a disguised form of slavery, uncovered how local administration could defuse and resist the pressures and efforts of two foreign secretaries and the British parliament. Goodstadt attributes this 'informal devolution' to the remoteness of Hong Kong issue from the mainstream of British politics as the relevance of Hong Kong faded with the rapid shrinking of British Empire in the post-war period, but this is a common feature in colonial governance.[45]

Essays in this volume suggest that central to the dynamics of the relationship between the colony and the sovereign is their respective interpretation of 'British interests'. For the colonial governor, effective governance in the territory was the primary interest of the British Empire in Hong Kong. London, however, did not always concur. From time to time, the colony appeared to be dispensable in the light of larger strategic interests. Carroll's chapter reveals that there were occasions during the interwar years when British officials had considered surrendering Hong Kong as a gesture of British goodwill in the face of rising Chinese nationalism. Contributions by Bickers, Schenk and Yep in this volume also reveal that evacuation was an option seriously contemplated by London during the early weeks of the confrontation in 1967. Yep's chapter further refines the analysis by bringing in the tension between British diplomats in Beijing and the colonial administration. The mandate to maintain a 'foot in the door' in China and vulnerability in the face of violence prompted the diplomats in the British Mission in Beijing to propose a more accommodating approach in handling the disturbance in Hong Kong, whereas David Trench firmly believed in using a more confrontational style for preserving British interests. As Bickers and Yep suggest, British officials were convinced that this was the approach which would best bypass the slippery road to a 'Macao-style' scenario. London acted as the final arbitrator of the contrasting views during this period. While the colony's analysis might have prevailed during the most turbulent months of violent confrontation, the concern of diplomats in preserving Sino-British relationship resumed primacy once signs of Communist China's desire for normalcy were on the horizon.

Conclusion

This volume is not a definitive account of the 1967 events. There are clearly lacunae in our analysis. Firstly, given our reiteration of the importance of contextualizing Hong Kong developments in the frame of Cold War politics, an evaluation of the role of the United States in the unfolding of events in 1967 is imperative. London's decision to withdraw from 'East of Suez' and its subsequent reduction of the British military presence in the Far East further enhanced the relevance of the American factor in the strategic thinking of the British government towards Hong Kong. For the communists, the response of the Americans — the leading imperialist power and a 'special friend' of the British Empire — towards the crisis in Hong Kong was certainly a factor to be considered as well. The Taiwan factor should also be further explored. Secondly, the role of Beijing in the disturbances in Hong Kong warrants more in-depth analysis. Interviews with left-wing leaders conducted by Wong and others have provided some valuable access to their partisan views of the origin of the event, yet more archival research is essential. The selective opening up of the 1950s and 1960s archives of the Chinese Foreign Ministry may herald a possibility for further research. In addition, Red Guard activities in Guangdong also warrant a re-examination given that party activities in the colony came under the jurisdiction of the provincial party organization. A deeper knowledge of the PLA activity in the province would also be valuable. Thirdly, the general mood of the local population before the riots remains unexplored. Cathryn Clayton's current work, which is based on the oral testimony of events in Macao and Hong Kong in 1966–67, will provide new insights here. The official conclusion that the events of 1967 were simply a political provocation by the communists might overlook domestic causes of these social disturbances. It was, claimed William Heaton, 'a good place to start a revolution', owing to its social disequilibrium.[46] As Smart and Lui have further pointed out in this volume, the colony had gone through a series of confrontations in the post-war years and these should make us ponder the general frustration with the colonial regime on the eve of the 1967 riots. While our focus here is on urban Hong Kong, we trust that more research in future will be carried out to explore the course and impact of the events on the New Territories. The border territories were indeed the site of a number of important events and it is our hope that Benton's work exploring the impact of the events in London's Chinatown can be further developed to help us better understand how overseas Hong Kong people responded to the crisis in the colony.[47]

We have grouped the chapters into three sections. The first section explores the actions of the main actors in the unfolding events: the Hong Kong leftists, the Hong Kong government, the Foreign and Commonwealth Office (FCO) and Beijing. These chapters discuss such issues as the evolving strategies adopted, the debates and disagreements about those strategies, and the decisions that needed to be made. The chapters also locate the angry days of 1967 in the longer-term history of Hong Kong and Sino-British relations, and more widely, British late colonial history. The second section analyses specific policies that were carried out both before and during 1967. The essays here explore the legacy of the events in social policy, housing, and labour policy. In the third section, we have included transcribed testimonies of a number of 'witnesses' to the events. They had personally experienced the confrontation as adults, or as children, and reflected on the events for us at the 2007 conference. They joined our public forum and shared with the audience their accounts of the events after forty years. Their input provides us with an important supplement for our analysis — testimony to the emotion unleashed by this turbulent period in the 1960s. A systematic study of the state of mind of the local population is, however, required for a more refined understanding of the impact of the events and the ways in which they have shaped Hong Kong society and politics since. In retirement, British administrators such as Trench or Arthur Maddocks (Trench's political advisor from 1968) argued for the 'storm in a teacup' view, and claimed that it was 'a rather curious sequence of events' (Maddocks), a 'fleabite' (Trench), one which really ought to embarrass those concerned and really should not be taken seriously. 'They wanted to riot,' said Trench, 'and we didn't want them to.'[48]

We hope that this book has instead demonstrated that the May days of 1967 and their impact on the 1960s should be taken more seriously. The events have not been explored widely in the last forty years, and we hope that in this book we have provided new questions and a new research agenda for the study of colonial rule in Hong Kong.

Acknowledgements

Most of the chapters included here were presented at a workshop on the 1967 riots held at City University of Hong Kong on 26 May 2007. The project and production of this book were generously funded by the Governance in Asia Research Centre (GARC) and the Department of Public and Social Administration, City University of Hong Kong. In addition to the contributors to this volume, we are also grateful to the participants of the two-day events for sharing their comments and insights with us, in particular, Laurence Ho, Ma Ngok, Lu Yan, Lam Wai Man, Liu Shih Diing, Camoes Tam, Josephine Smart and Gary Cheung. We are grateful to Tim Ko, John Carroll and Georgina Sinclair for providing the photographs for the cover. We are also grateful to Colin Day and Clara Ho at Hong Kong University Press and the anonymous reviewers for their constructive comments.

Section I
Strategy and History

2
The 1967 riots in Hong Kong:
The domestic and diplomatic fronts of the governor*

Ray Yep

The crisis sparked by the anti-colonial riots in 1967 is arguably the most important historic episode of the colonial history of Hong Kong in the post-war era. Triggered by an industrial dispute in May 1967, the colony was soon swamped by violence, demonstrations, strikes, bomb explosions and even military confrontation at the border. Many commentators regard the event as the turning point of the colonial governance in Hong Kong, as post-riot Hong Kong witnessed fundamental changes in socioeconomic policies of the colonial administration. Nonetheless, the significances of this episode extend beyond the revelation of the self-reforming capacity of the colonial state; the riot also gives us a window to explore the nature of colonial governance. More specifically, it provides us an opening to look into the dynamics of interaction between the Crown's agent, the governor, and the sovereign state. Sir David Trench, the Hong Kong governor during the riot period, appeared to play a key role in defining the strategy towards local disturbance. His proposal of a containment policy towards the local communists served as the basis of the colony's responses during this turbulent period. However, many of his critics, including senior officials in the British administration, regarded the provocative stances suicidal given the rampant Red Guards radicalism in 1967 and the vulnerability of the colony to possible military incursion by the PLA across the border. With the survival of Hong Kong hinging ultimately on the self-restraint of Peking, how could he justify his provocative line? More importantly, how could he win the endorsement of London?

Based mainly on newly released archives at the National Archives in London, this chapter tries to uncover the dynamics behind the formulation of Hong Kong policy during the turbulent period. More specifically, this chapter focuses on the debates on the adoption of two of Trench's most provocative measures in combating

---

* This article was originally published in *China Quarterly*, No. 193 (March 2008), pp. 122–139. The author is most grateful to Cambridge University Press for their permission to reprint the article in this volume.

communist initiatives: the closure of communist newspapers and schools. It argues that the governor's strategy was premised on the assumption of the passive role played by Peking (Beijing 北京) in the local disturbances. Accordingly, the best chance for Hong Kong's survival was to prevent the local crisis from unfolding into a full-scale confrontation, a scenario that left Peking no option but to fully support the local initiative. And for Trench, central to the game plan was to stay offensive. The debates among the British diplomats in Peking, Foreign and Commonwealth Offices officials and the colonial administration, provide important clues to the policy-making process of Hong Kong during the riot. In the process, both the British mission and the Hong Kong government tried to assert their respective authority on the interpretation of events and the validity of the proposed strategy. This chapter argues that David Trench's 'victory' lies in his political shrewdness in exploiting London's uncertainty over the future of China and its lack of viable options in defending British interests. Throughout the whole debate, the governor demonstrated his acumen in deciphering the changing configuration of the Sino-British relationship and the consequent fluctuation in assessment among officials in London. His skilful presentation of his policy proposal and success in staging a facade of local support for his stance further reinforced his case. However, the policy debates must be contextualized in the larger strategic thinking of Britain at that time. The prevailing political and military parameters defined the notion of British interests and determined Whitehall's receptivity to different policy options.

Different diagnosis of the nature of the riots

The disturbances started in an artificial flower factory in Kowloon when an industrial dispute turned into a riot. The communist-dominated Federation of Trade Unions immediately intervened on behalf of the workers. Four demands were made:

(1) immediate release of the workers arrested,
(2) punishment of the evil-doers and compensation,
(3) guarantee of the workers' personal safety, and
(4) no interference henceforth by the police in labour disputes.

The turning point was the intervention of the Chinese Ministry of Foreign Affairs (MFA) (Waijiaobu 外交部) on 15 May 1967. A protest statement was passed to the British chargé d'affaires in Peking, followed by anti-British demonstrations in Peking and Guangzhou (廣州) and sympathetic editorials in the *People's Daily* (*Renmin Ribao* 人民日報).[1] For many local radicals, these were clear signs of approval for action in Hong Kong. The formation of the All Circles Anti-Persecution Struggle Committee (*Xianggang Gejie Tongbao Fanying Kangbao Douzheng Weiyuanhui* 香港各界同胞反英抗暴鬥爭委員會) in Hong Kong heralded the full-scale mobilization of local communists into the territory-wide anti-colonial campaign. The labour dispute was quickly subsumed by demonstrations, strikes, marches and bomb explosions, and the original concern for industrial relations was replaced by highly politicized slogans of anti-imperialism. British soldiers were also mobilized during the turbulent period. Normal life was also affected by the interruption of public services. Although attempts of full-scale and sustained strike remained futile, public transport and utilities companies appeared to be major constituencies for the communists.

Sir David Trench's diagnosis of the situation is a major factor shaping the general strategy towards the disturbances. From the very beginning, he was convinced of the 'spontaneous' character of the event, i.e. it was not a premeditated act by Peking. 'There is every indication that this (original industrial dispute in Kowloon) was a spontaneous incident,'[2] and the latest wave of militant unionism was 'a reflection of the increased freedom allowed to the "masses" as a result of local propaganda based on the Cultural Revolution in China,'[3] he argued. Trench's theory was that the later escalation of events was largely a result of the Hong Kong communist leaders' survival instinct. They needed to win a victory for Mao Zedong thought in Hong Kong, 'mainly to save their own neck', argued Trench.[4] The sense of vulnerability among communist leaders in the capitalist enclave of Hong Kong was vividly reflected in a self-reflection made by Liang Wailin (梁威林), the Xinhua News Agency (Xinhua Tongxunshe 新華通訊社) Hong Kong Director, the de facto Party boss in the colony during a meeting in late 1966:

> I have been indulging in a solemn and painful reflection. Who am I? What will happen to me? Am I a capitalist roader, or is it still possible for me to be a leftist?[5]

For Liang, the colonial administration may appear to be a convenient alternative to the local communist leaders themselves for revolutionary struggle.

The theory was further reinforced by a number of factors. First, Trench probably found some comfort in Peking's policy of 'long term planning, full utilization' (*changqi dasuan chongfen liyong* 長期打算 充份利用) towards Hong Kong. For Peking, despite her denial of the legality of the colony status of Hong Kong, the status quo of the territory was seen as in the best interest of the motherland. Hong Kong was regarded as a window to the outside world; this was particularly evident during the period of heightened tension with the United States in the 1950s and 1960s.[6] Empirically, 40 percent of China's total annual foreign exchange income came from exports to Hong Kong.[7] Second, there are hints of moderation from the China side as well: most notably, the self-restraint observed by the People's Liberation Army (PLA). With the exception of the armed conflict in Sha Tau Kok (Shatoujiao 沙頭角) in July 1967, the PLA seemed inclined to keep the conflict between the Chinese personnel and Hong Kong border guards under control.[8]

Trench's reasoning was, however, more than naive optimism over the moderation of Peking. He identified two worst case scenarios for Hong Kong. The first one was complete anarchy in the Mainland, and by then, Peking could no longer exercise any control over the local hotheads in Hong Kong. For Trench, the political development in mainland China was probably most decisive, but unfortunately there was not much Hong Kong could do about this. But he also perceived another possible scenario under which all-out confrontation with local communists was unavoidable even though the central leadership could still maintain power. There was a danger of Peking being hijacked by the extreme actions of radicals in Hong Kong and in this case Peking was simply 'pushed' to support the Hong Kong communists. Under this logic, Peking could be spared from this undesirable eventuality if Hong Kong managed to contain the disturbances before they grew completely out of hand.

Nevertheless, British diplomats at Peking did not fully subscribe to the governor's view. For the diplomats, their self-perceived mission was to preserve and promote the British relationship with communist China, though security issues of the colony were to be reckoned with. So what was the state of Sino-British relationship by the mid-1960s? Despite the communist takeover in 1949, engagement was still regarded as the best option to preserve the British economic empire in China. Nevertheless, the policy of keeping a foot in the door was hardly a success.[9] Britain's voting policy on the decision format for Chinese representation in the United Nations also alienated China.[10] However, the twenty two-year long effort by Britain in establishing full diplomatic relations with China and her vote for China's admission into the United Nations in 1961 speak volumes of Britain's incessant interest in nurturing a relationship with the People's Republic of China. Such an argument is probably reinforced by Britain's desire to avoid war in Asia and her conception of positive engagement as the best means of restraining China.[11] The British mission also had more immediate concerns during the riot period. In retaliation against the suppression of local communists by the Hong Kong government, a dozen of British citizens, including Anthony Grey, a Reuters correspondent in China, were detained by the Chinese authority from the early days of the disturbance. The well-being of these hostages was a key variable affecting the position of the diplomats in China. In fact, the personal safety of the staff of the British mission was at stake too. Their first-hand encounter with radicalism in the Mainland certainly led to a different assessment of China's inclination towards violence from their colonial counterparts.

These concerns explain the critical stance of Donald Hopson, the British chargé d'affaires in Peking, towards Trench's policy in Hong Kong throughout the event. Hopson did not challenge Trench's conclusion of the passive role of Peking in the original dispute. In fact, he agreed that the long gestation between the first confrontation on 6 May and the MFA response on 15 May was proof that Peking was taken by surprise by the escalation of the Hong Kong disputes.[12] However, this is where the agreement ends. He argued the influence of 'revolutionary rebels' was on the rise, and he was not sure whether the moderates in the MFA, Minister Chen Yi (陳毅) in particular, were still in power. For Hopson, it was evident that there were 'grave temptations to those responsible for making decisions to show themselves as real revolutionaries, by acquiescing in adventurist policies over Hong Kong'.[13] Thus, he believed that the danger did not only come from the success of the extremists in Hong Kong in forcing Peking to support them as suggested by the governor, but there was also a possibility that under the current political atmosphere, the leadership in Peking might feel the need for a real victory in Hong Kong. And as the Chinese government was now putting 'politics in command', she may have decided to accept any necessary economic damage.[14] If so, the chance of a physical intervention in the colony cannot be taken lightly.[15] He also challenged the governor's faith in the continuation of Peking's Hong Kong policy when the Pandora's box was now opened. Hopson argued,

> There has been no sign that the Chinese leadership has yet decided that the time has come to try to end British rule in Hong Kong. Nevertheless the problem of Hong Kong and its future has been brought to the surface with a bang, that we can no longer be sure that the Chinese will feel able to accept the continuation of the present status of Hong Kong almost indefinitely, as we might have imagined until recently . . . China today is in a very difficult and explosive mood. One cannot be sure that policy decisions will be taken on accord with the logic of the situation.[16]

In short, Hopson's prescription was to observe self-restraint in handling the local communists so as to avoid provocation.

Limited options for London

What matters here is that London appeared to be more convinced of the governor's diagnosis. As a colonial governor, David Trench saw his primary role in defending the British interest in the colony. The 'Hong Kong: Long Term Study' report produced by the Cabinet Ministerial Committee on Hong Kong in 1969 identified a list of British interests in Hong Kong. Politically, Hong Kong was a 'Free World enclave on the mainland China',[17] thus helped score a moral victory over the communist order across the border. Economically, the colony also brought substantial economic benefits to the sovereign. The annual volume of British-Hong Kong trade was in the region of 150 million pounds in 1967, and there was also a similar level of British investment in the territory. More importantly, Hong Kong was a member of the sterling area and its sterling balance was 'very large of the order of 350 million pounds'. Britain was also obliged to maintain order in the colony due to the fact that there were 46,000 British subjects and Commonwealth citizens of non-Chinese race residing in the territory during the riot period. Their safety was certainly the responsibility of the British government.[18] With these interests at stake, Trench argued that a containment approach was probably the best option for preserving the authority of the colonial government — the main leverage for protecting British interests in Hong Kong. The persuasiveness of Trench's argument was further enhanced by the lesson of Macao (澳門). Macao witnessed a similar communist confrontation in late 1966. The accommodating approach of the Portuguese eventually ended in total surrender. Humiliating demands including a public apology, compensation, the dismissal of officials and even the handover of Guomindang (國民黨) agents to the Chinese authority were accepted. London was neither prepared to swallow similar humiliation, nor did she see much merit in an appeasement policy in this case.

The assessment of the military played a key role in swaying London to Hong Kong's call for a firm position. Despite reinforcement by one unit and the possible back-up from Singapore in case of emergency, the 7,000-strong force in the colony could hardly survive a determined military intervention from China. The difficulty in defending Hong Kong also needs to be contextualized within Britain's global strategic planning. Although the Second World War had left Britain economically exhausted and rendered her traditional imperialist outlook obsolete, Britain's extensive overseas commitments continued. Such military overstretch, however, constituted a severe drainage on the British economy. Consequently, the search for a balance between Britain's global commitment and a sustainable military budget had become a key concern of the British government since the 1950s. The 1966 Defence Review represented the final verdict of the decade-long evaluation of the appropriate balance between Britain's role in world politics and fiscal sustainability. The central message of the document is clear: Britain decided to withdraw from East of Suez and Europe would become its main concern. Specifically, Britain was scheduled to leave Singapore, Malaysia and the Persian Gulf by the mid-1970s and would only maintain a small maritime force in the region. The decision to withdraw from the area may certainly have affected the calculation of London in assessing the military option for defending Hong Kong.[19]

Britain's military calculation involves the assessment of the American response as well. The colony served several strategic interests of the United States in the post-war order. Its proximity to the Mainland and the acquiescence of the friendly colonial administration enabled the Americans to establish an elaborated network of intelligence, covert action and propaganda in the territory.[20] The strategic value of Hong Kong was further illustrated during the Korean War. Hong Kong was utilized as a leverage of economic warfare against China, as the colony was included in the American grand scheme of export control against China in order to deprive the latter its supply of strategic materials. During the Vietnam War, the territory also served as a key service port for American soldiers and battleships. Notwithstanding these utilities, for the US decision-makers the importance attached to Hong Kong was certainly not only a result of its own intrinsic value; it was more related to the larger policy objective of strengthening Anglo-American cooperation in Asia.[21] In order to nurture the 'special relationship', the United States had to show considerable sympathy for Britain's concern for Hong Kong. According to Harold Macmillan, the United States 'had agreed to regard Hong Kong as a joint defence problem and discuss ways and means with us'.[22] The American commitment to Hong Kong should not, however, be overestimated. During the trying time in the mid-1960s, the United States did make several gestures of support for the colony. For example, on the initiative of the American Consulate General, the American Chamber of Commerce was founded in Hong Kong in 1968 as proof of American confidence in the territory.[23] The governor also calculated that a more evident American presence, including visit of major US warships, might help deter the communist aggression as well.[24] Military support for Hong Kong was, however, never an option for the Americans. In a telegram sent to the American Consulate General in Hong Kong in May 1967, Dean Rusk, the US secretary of state, made it clear that the 'United States would not expect to defend Hong Kong for British' interests, and the consul general 'should not intimate in any way readiness to discuss joint military planning'.[25]

Even worse for the British, the option of full-scale evacuation was also deemed impossible. London first raised the issue of evacuation in May 1967. The governor and the commander of British forces in the colony, however, responded with vehement opposition. Logistically, the transport facilities were hardly adequate to transfer 150,000 to 200,000 people who were identified as eligible for the retreat within a short time, and the British force predicted that they could defend against Chinese hostility for not more than forty-eight hours. Yet, it was the political risk that counted most. It was argued that while forced evacuation was impossible for logistic and military reasons, negotiated retreat was politically suicidal. Rumours of a British intention to withdraw would quickly lead to the collapse of the local society, and would probably be perceived as a sign of surrender by the Chinese side. Leaving millions of locals in the hand of communists might also bring severe repercussions for Britain in the international community. In an internal Whitehall communication in May 1967, an official reached the following fatalistic conclusion:

> if Peking decided to make an all out effort to bring us to our knees in Hong Kong, the chances of our then being able to negotiate our withdrawal from the Colony with any semblance of orderliness or dignity would be virtually nil; we should rather have to face a humiliating capitulation.[26]

Such assessment was officially endorsed by the Cabinet Ministerial Committee on Hong Kong in September 1967.[27] As previous attempts to settle the disputes with the Chinese side both in Hong Kong and Peking had failed or been bluntly rejected, and there was nothing the British could do to affect the course of political development in Mao's China, London's options for handling the Hong Kong crisis were, in fact, very limited. In reality, what really matters is not whether London was fully convinced of the governor's analysis of Peking's non-committal to local rebels or not. As reflected in London's contemplation of evacuation at the very early stage of the disturbances, the British government did not appear to be fully converted by Trench's optimism. In fact, in early 1967, Foreign Office officials had also warned against the possibility that 'the Chinese might react more strongly than normally and take up a position from which they could not retreat' under the current political atmosphere and called for caution to avoid friction with China. This was apparently very much in line with the spirit of Hopson's view.[28] The hard truth was that, for London, all other strategies — appeasement, withdrawal, negotiation, or military confrontation — were either too costly or not viable. Trench's suggestion of firm action against rebels, though risky, was certainly preferable to supplication for the mercy of the Red Guards. Restrained and calculated offensives at least provided London with some leverage to intervene and maintain considerable initiative in the political crisis of the colony.

The facade of local support garnered by Trench may have also helped sway the opinion of British officials. In addition to his closest advisory body, the Executive Council, which stood firmly behind him throughout the riot period, Trench also managed to enlist support from local elites for his hard-lined approach. More than 600 social organizations, including students' unions, business organizations, neighbourhood bodies and social organizations, pledged their public support to the governor during the early weeks of the riot.[29] Ruttonjee, the senior unofficial of the Legislative Council of the time, provided his assessment of the public mood on behalf of the whole Council,

> At the moment of crisis the people of Hong Kong stood foursquare behind you and it was then the true spirit of Hong Kong emerged. By their words and by their deeds, the public has given you, Sir, and will continue to give you, a vote of confidence of a kind and unanimity which is the stronger for not being counted in upraised hands and nodding heads. In fact one may say that the situation we faced wrought a miracle — an unanimity of spirit and purpose which never before existed.[30]

Even critics of the government expressed their solidarity with the colonial administration during this turbulent time. Bernacchi, an urban councillor and a lawyer renowned for his concern for the underprivileged, showed his endorsement for governor's determination to maintain law and order:

> For the first time we have had to choose. For the first time we have all had to choose where our allegiance lies in such an emergency, and the vast majority of the people of Hong Kong have demonstrated that it lies in support of the conception of Hong Kong as a unit with a Government that does not support disturbances from either right or from left that are engineered from without. Basically, they have chosen to support law and order of the present Government of Hong Kong.[31]

Some even went further than the governor in the advocacy of a non-compromising approach. Sir Y. K. Kan (簡悅強), a legislative councillor, had been a strong advocate of the death penalty for offenders of crime involving bombs. 'I doubt . . . that the punishment prescribed by the existing law is sufficient to deter . . .

those who perpetuate them without regard for human life must be made to realize that if they are caught they may have to pay the extreme penalty that the law can impose,' he argued.[32]

Social support was also reflected in the popular attitude towards the local police force, which had been instrumental in combating local subversion. Public endorsement of the police handling of the rioters was reflected in the general enthusiasm for the private initiative of launching the Police Education Fund designed to support children of police officers. More than 3.7 million was raised within a short time. Edward Eates, the police commissioner at that time, also appreciated the government's support for affirmative action against rioters. He recalled that the morale of his officers improved significantly after the government had decided to intensify its efforts against the communists in July 1967.[33] Praise for the police came from different corners. The Federation of Hong Kong Industries (Xianggang Gongye Zonghui 香港工業總會) opined,

> At no time was the situation out of control and for this the community owes an unrepayable debt of gratitude to the Hong Kong Police for their steadfastness and restraint in the face of extreme provocation, and for their exemplary devotion to duty.[34]

Ming Pao (明報), an influential Chinese-language newspaper, also raised its support for the Police. In response to the concern over police violence in handling the confrontation, the paper argued,

> [A]lthough it is unavoidable to see isolated extreme measure, or imprudent decision made by individual police officers in handing the situation, we understand that these actions are not the intention of decision makers of security policy; the individuals concerned should be solely responsible for these mistakes, and these incidents should not affect the general reputation of the police force.[35]

Banning communist newspapers

Propaganda warfare was a key battlefield between communists and the colonial administration during the confrontation, and the governor believed that this was where firm action must be taken if Hong Kong was to weather the storm. For the left-wing activists, the nine pro-Peking newspapers in Hong Kong provided moral support and encouragement, ammunition against imperialism, clues for action and major leverage for mobilization and propaganda. These newspapers, with daily circulations totaling more than 400,000 copies, constituted about a quarter of the total circulation in Hong Kong.[36] The governor was particularly concerned with its impact on the morale of Hong Kong police. Chinese members of the police force were targeted by the communist press in a constant propaganda barrage. Intimidating messages warning Chinese officers not to be the 'running dogs' (*zougou* 走狗) of the British were regular items in the communist press.

Therefore, Trench argued that action must be taken to stop the press campaign. It was suggested prompt legal action should be made against the newspapers which published subversive materials, 'not only to restrict their capability for doing damage but also because they stand openly in defiance of authority and may symbolize in the minds of many, including Government servants, a lack of will on the part of the Government to act against the left-wing.'[37] Consequently, in the governor's proposed action plan for London's consideration in May 1967, 'action against the principal communist newspaper, *Wen Wei Po* (文匯報) for either sedition or inciting police to disaffection' was suggested. The Commonwealth Office, however, was not convinced. Some officials still hoped that a settlement could be achieved either by secret negotiation with local communists or through a de-politicized approach of treating the event as a case of industrial dispute.[38] London called for restraint on the part of Hong Kong and rejected the plea on the technical grounds that 'sedition' was usually difficult to prove and the move may simply provide a propaganda opportunity for the communists.[39]

Trench, however, was undeterred by London's indifference. The governor contended that leniency towards the communist press would

> leave the initiatives entirely to them, and they will be free to wear us out trying, with waning public support, to cover their manoeuvres; until they eventually lead us — still trying to avoid provocation when provocation became irrelevant from one humiliating position after another into a Macao type compromise satisfactory to them.[40]

The governor tried to add weight to his argument by enlisting public support. He stressed that the Executive Council was unanimously in support of his analysis that the maintenance of public confidence was largely dependent on Her Majesty Government's determination to uphold law and order. Hopson, however, called for caution and recommended that no action should be taken against the communist papers until the intention of Peking was ascertained and all hope of compromise was exhausted.[41] Hopson's caution was, however, soon overtaken by events. Trench's offer of an olive branch to local communists was refused, as his proposed meeting between the governor's special assistant Jack Cater and Ho Yin (何賢) did not materialize. The rapid politicization of events also rendered London's industrial management approach a non-starter. By late May, the disturbances were going unabated and violence soon spread to the whole colony. It was evident that a protracted crisis was in store. On 25 May, the Commonwealth Office eventually agreed in principle that communist presses could be closed down if they continued or stepped up the campaign of sedition and intimidation. It was emphasized, however, that the Commonwealth Office must be consulted before any action was actually taken.[42]

Local communists did intensify their mobilization in the next two months. Calls for a territory-wide strike were made and violence escalated. Bombs were used to intimidate the colony. The escalation of violence, however, helped win more allies to the case for firm action. An Area Officer for the Far East Command of the British Military made the following observation after his visit to Hong Kong:

> While the situation in the Kwangtung province, adjacent to Hong Kong, was not known for certain, it was apparent that the local Chinese felt that if they took vigorous action against Hong Kong the Peking Government would support them. A situation therefore existed in which rapid erosion could take place unless the Government of the Colony took a much harder line against the Communist trouble-makers than at present.[43]

By late July 1967, the colonial administration believed that the time was right to move against the local communist newspapers. While approval in principle was already obtained from London in May, one issue remained unsolved: whom to strike first. Voices in the Foreign Office now appeared to be more in favour of more drastic action. Their argument was that the key communist papers had to be dealt with sooner or later. Jack Cater, the acting colonial secretary at the time, however, argued that 'action against lesser papers might provide the bigger ones with an acceptable excuse for moderating their tone if the alternative were likely to be suppression'.[44] Hong Kong also tried to win over the acquiescence of British diplomats in Peking, by supporting the latter's demand for the imposition of restrictions on Xinhua personnel in London in retaliation against Peking's action against the British mission in Shanghai.[45] Eventually, London conceded and on 9 August 1967, five editors and publishers of three pro-communist newspapers, *Tin Fung Yat Po* (田豐日報), *Hong Kong Evening News* (香港夜報) and *Afternoon News* (正午報), were arrested. The three papers were eventually suspended for six months and three of the prosecuted were sentenced to three years' imprisonment.[46]

Trench was no bull in a china shop and always showed restraint and political shrewdness despite his call for firm action. He decided not to follow up with an all-out attack on local communist papers. The furious response of Peking was an effective deterrent. Peking was expectedly incensed by the closure of three leftist newspapers in August and issued a strongly-worded ultimatum demanding the Hong Kong government to rescind its legal action. What happened next was, however, shocking to both the British and the moderates in Peking. The office of the British chargé d'affaires was attacked on 22 August and was set on fire. The scene was extremely ugly and horrifying.[47] Trench probably reasoned that the repercussions of an all-out attack on all papers would definitely be greater than a move against one or two of them. Strong action could be expected from China and this might provoke her to lend more active support to local communists. More importantly, Trench probably believed that even as he pushed for further action, the chance of getting support from London looked bleak. In October 1967, negotiation between Chinese authority and Hong Kong administration over the return of several Hong Kong police officers and border issues was in progress. Local communist presses also showed a change in editorial approach with more restraint exhibited in their reporting of local events. For example, coverage on confrontation and bomb attacks had evidently been reduced by late 1967.[48] The decision to hold the Canton (Guangzhou 廣州) Trade Fair — one of the few opportunities for foreign merchants to engage with China — as usual was also seen as a sign of Peking's moderation.[49] 'It would seem unwise to suggest this action (of further suppression of local communist newspapers) when the Foreign Office is attempting to improve relations with China,'[50] concluded an internal document prepared by the Colonial Secretariat.

Tackling the communist schools

Like the pro-Peking press, the colonial administration had always found the active communist involvement in local education irritating even before the outbreak of the riot. The administration viewed these institutions with suspicion and regarded them as potential source of political subversion.[51] The fear re-emerged during the confrontation in 1967. An internal report of the colonial government in late 1967 reiterated that 'there is evidence of sustained and intense communist and subversive indoctrination'[52] within communist-controlled schools. And the report suggested,

> there is little doubt that unless further restraint is applied to prevent pupils from subversive indoctrination', there would be a 'cumulatively erosive effect on the public's morale, and confidence in the Government's willingness to be firm, as well as the operations of the security forces.[53]

The government waited patiently for a chance to take firm action against these schools. An accident in Chung Wah Middle School (Zhonghua Zhongxue 中華中學) in November 1967 provided the long-awaited excuse for suppression. In the evening of 27 November, an explosion was heard from Chung Wah Middle School. An injured teenaged student was found with one hand and three fingers lost. The police found explosive powder and chemicals suitable for making explosives and evidence of explosions in the premise. Consequently, six persons were arrested and the director of education closed the school under section 51(1)(B) of the Education Ordinance and the closure would last until 15 August 1968.[54] Other communist schools were raided and searched in the following weeks and more than a hundred students and teachers were detained and arrested.[55]

In December 1967 the Executive Council advised the governor that the school should be de-registered, i.e. permanently closed, but leaving the time for action at the governor's discretion. The governor, however, chose not to take any immediate action and preferred to have more time to ponder over the latest political developments. As mentioned above, there were signs that Peking had resumed her control over local communists since late 1967. The eventual expiry of the closure order in August 1968, however, rendered further delay impossible. This time he concurred with the council's advice and recommended de-registration. This took Hopson of the British mission in Peking by surprise. For Hopson, the worst days for Hong Kong were over. He believed that excessive violence and large-scale demonstrations were now basically vanished from the public scene, though rhetorical attack against colonial rule went unabated and tension between left-wing organizations and the colonial administration lingered. Diplomats in Peking were probably also affected by the political developments in the Mainland. The Cultural Revolution appeared to be in a new stage of development and excessive violence between different factions evident in the summer of 1967 was at least temporarily suppressed. Hopson thus saw no logic in provoking Peking at this point.

The governor retorted by reiterating the imperative of maintaining public confidence and emphasized that what was at stake was not merely the ability of the government to de-register the Chung Wah Middle School, but the cumulative effect of concessions on public confidence. He believed that the majority view was still in favour of firm action against local communists, despite the relative tranquility at the time. In his rebuttal to Hopson's view, Trench made no secret of his determination to stop the spread of communist influence in local education. He argued,

> We cannot object to reasonably well conducted schools just because they are communist. But there are none such here, and I do object very strongly to the uncontrolled spread of a communist school system which is merely a deliberate breeding ground for hate and violence . . . And I shall be most gravely hampered if I am unable to take what steps I can, without too dangerous a communist reaction elsewhere, both to curb the more objectionable practices of existing ones and to restrict their expansion.[56]

In response, Hopson tried to win the support of London by escalating the level of debate to the general interest of Britain. 'Do we wish to end confrontation?'[57] Hopson put it bluntly in one of his appeals to the Foreign Office. He argued that the dangers of Trench's position of continuing confrontation against local communists might first provoke renewed violence in the colony, but more importantly, would worsen the general Sino-British relationship. He argued that

> the underlying safeguard for Hong Kong is not our strength in the colony, which will always be minute in relation to Chinese forces arrayed against it, but the Chinese Government's current unwillingness, mainly for economic reasons, to push matters to extremes. But this agreement to live and let live requires two to make it work.[58]

In other words, Hopson believed that Trench was in fact advocating 'an altogether different and tougher policy with serious implications'[59] that contradicted the overarching concern of Britain in maintaining normal relations with China and thus must be stopped. The altercations renewed the old debate over the validity of the appeasement policy. Trench retorted that Hong Kong had always been flexible towards communist encroachment and deliberate and unnecessary provocation had always been avoided. In addition, Trench argued that,

> we have always held that to be over-pliant in such circumstances was only likely to lead to additional pressures; but that opposition, when necessary and to whatever degree was possible in the current situation, even in the face of some risk, was more likely to lead to a modification of communist attitudes.[60]

And for Trench, public confidence in the government's determination to resist was the main bulwark against communists in Hong Kong, not unprincipled concession.

As a seasoned politician, Trench understood too well that he could not win his case simply by persuasion; as a general strategy, he never hesitated to offer compromise, or at least appeared flexible and accommodating. Several moves were particularly noteworthy. First, he tried to soften Hopson's opposition by accommodating the latter's private concern. Hopson's exit visa was expected in mid-August 1968, and he was understandably concerned with the possibility that Peking might refuse to issue the document as a retaliation against the de-registration of Chung Wah School in Hong Kong. Trench offered to release several confrontation prisoners arrested during the riot as sign of good-will to Peking. Second, Trench provided an option for the communists to open a new school with new staff in the premises of the de-registered Chung Wah Middle School, though the offer was never taken up. Lastly, the proposal of de-registration was followed by comprehensive recommendations for tough action against communist schools. Although it is hard to confirm whether this was a deliberate act of politicking, the contextualization of the de-registration plan into a even more radical package certainly made the former look moderate and thus more acceptable.

London, again, sided with Trench on the de-registration proposal and agreed that to back down from the Executive Council's decision of de-registration 'would be hailed as a very significant victory by the local communists in a sector which is of great importance to them and would demonstrate that a policy of blackmail over visas (of Hopson) yields result'.[61] A public announcement of the de-registration of Chung Wah Middle School was made a few hours after Donald Hopson's safe arrival in Hong Kong. London probably did not object to making concession to Peking and certainly was not prepared to jeopardize the long-term relationship with China, provided that the latter was ready to return to normalcy. It was true that the campaign of violence was over but London's confidence in Peking remained low. The signs of moderation in late 1967 appeared to be a false dawn. London's insistence on the contingency planning for Hong Kong was illustrative of her mood. Hong Kong was urged by London to consider amending the Requisitioning of Ships Order (1955) in late 1968. The purpose of the amendment was to empower the Hong Kong government to enlist any British ships in the territory for emergency evacuation.[62] Officials in Whitehall also appeared to be disillusioned with the failure to entice a reciprocal response from Peking to their concessions since late 1967. An assistant under-secretary of the Commonwealth Office complained specifically about the humiliation suffered from their concessions made during the negotiation over the release of several Hong Kong police officers,

> the recent negotiations on the border confirm our original suspicion that these were only undertaken to suit the Communists. I think they have scored a major propaganda victory in having been able to announce publicly that we have had to pay 'compensation' to the landlords for the loss of crops and that we have opened up the Man Kam To Bridge and agreed to remove the barbed wire . . . I do not think that we shall get anywhere with the Chinese by taking a soft line in Hong Kong.[63]

Conclusion

To what extent did Trench's approach of resistance contribute to the survival of the colony during the turbulence in 1967? One can hardly establish a causal relationship between the firm resistance of the colonial administration and the restraint observed by Peking. The difficulty lies in the obscurity of the Chinese side of the story. One thing is evident, however. The subsiding of violence in the colony coincided with a new twist in the factional struggle in Peking in August 1967. In the summer of 1967, China was on the edge of civil war[64] and the escalation of violence and uncertainty over the reaction of the military prompted Mao to reconsider his revolutionary tactics. Consequently, the power balance was at least temporarily tilted in favour of the moderate faction. The relative tranquility in Hong Kong since late 1967 apparently coincided with these developments.

London's uncertainty over future development in China and her confusion over the communist leaders' sincerity in resuming diplomatic normalcy are the major reasons behind her support for Governor Trench. In many ways, London's endorsement of Hong Kong's approach in handling the local disturbances was a big gamble. But given the non-existence of an alternative in the political and military reality of 1967, the choice seems justified. In addition, an insurance policy was inherent in this approach. The 'confrontation' approach deployed by Governor Trench was under the watchful eyes of London and the British diplomats in Peking and that implies its implementation was always under critical scrutiny. Trench's discipline in adhering to the final decisions of London certainly helped win more sympathetic voices back home. Such loyalty reinforced London's faith in the risky but manageable approach. It is too simple to categorize Trench as a hawk in the debate. In many instances, he demonstrated flexibility and a willingness to concede when necessary. Sometimes, such concession was prompted by the need to win allies. But very often, it was the result of his shrewd observation of the sentiment of London. His decision not to launch an all-out attack on all communist newspapers in late 1967 was probably a result of his awareness of the possible change in the mood of London. Friendly gestures from Peking in late 1967 may have prompted second thoughts on the validity of the appeasement approach, Trench pondered.

Nevertheless, the single most important determinant in shaping the outcome of the triangular debates among the colonial administration, British diplomats in Peking and the officials in London was certainly the prevailing definition of British interest. Both Hopson and Trench were assigned to defend different aspects of British concerns and it is the officials in Whitehall who acted as the final arbitrators. This implies that the validity of their respective analysis would fluctuate with the possible redefinition of British interests in the future. The developments since the late 1960s confirm this conjecture. Trench's fortune took a sharp turn when Britain was fully convinced of China's determination to resume normalcy. A decision to redeploy ambassadors overseas was made at the 9th Congress of the Chinese Communist Party held in April 1969, and in February 1971, the official residence of the British mission was rebuilt. The Sino-British diplomatic relationship was finally upgraded to ambassadorial level in 1972. The Hong Kong issue, particularly the matter of confrontation prisoners convicted during the riot, however, appeared to be a stumbling block in the process. Space does not permit a detailed discussion here, but Hong Kong was under immense pressure from London to release the remaining dozens of prisoners arrested during the riot in order to placate Peking. Trench stood firm in resistance but London was equally determined to get this issue out of the way. His firmness was now seen as a nuisance to Whitehall. Incidentally, the issue was settled with the arrival of a new governor, Murray MacLehose, who appeared to be more pragmatic and agreed to release the few remaining prisoners shortly after his arrival. The opening for assertiveness in the colony appeared to have vanished with the sovereign state's refined vision of her interests and strategy. After all, it is the fundamental duty of the colony to promote the sovereign's interest.

3
The 1967 riots:
A legitimacy crisis?

Lawrence Cheuk-yin Wong

The 1967 riots represented a landmark in the history of Hong Kong. The riots were initially triggered by an industrial dispute that escalated into violent clashes between the workers and the police. Subsequently the local leftists used the opportunity to challenge the Hong Kong government. There are two major arguments on the riots. On the one hand, local leftists saw the internal social contradictions and discontent among the Hong Kong people as the roots of the confrontations. On the other hand, the British Hong Kong government regarded the riots as an offshoot of the Cultural Revolution on the Mainland, and believed that the leftists had very little local support.

This chapter intends to fill the gap of these two arguments by studying the logic, trajectory and the internal dynamics of the riots. Specifically, the chapter tries to address the following questions:
(1) How did the Cultural Revolution in China affect the Hong Kong government in its dealing with the riots?
(2) How did the Hong Kong government perceive and respond to the actions of the leftists?

By focusing on these questions this chapter hopes to contribute to a renewed understanding of the riots, which relatively still lack in-depth analysis. This chapter characterizes the riots into three phases.[1] Phase One (May–June 1967) witnessed political demonstrations and strikes by local leftists. Phase Two (July–August 1967) was fuelled with bomb terrorism instigated by the leftists and the discussion in this section will outline how the three groups of actors reacted to it. Phase Three (from September 1967 onwards) was marked by the decline in political power of the radicals in China and the section here will show how this impacted the political actors in Hong Kong. The last section of the chapter will critically revisit the arguments by Ian Scott, who argued that the 1967 riots represented a crisis of legitimacy for the Hong Kong government. Indeed, this essay contends that the concept of legitimacy crisis does not seem appropriate for explaining the 1967 riots.

Phase One (May–June 1967): From violent demonstrations to general strikes

In a personal interview with Sir Jack Cater,[2] the author was told that intelligence operations under the Police Special Branch had already noticed the infiltration of leftists into union organizations from the mid-1960s. Although intelligence from Macao had foreseen possible problems in Hong Kong, 'there was no special preparation against a possible expansion of the Cultural Revolution into the territory even after the Macao incidents in 1966'. Separate and minor labour clashes in the spring of 1967 were not initially viewed with alarm. As he later said, 'There was nothing happening in Hong Kong in early 1967.'

The establishment of the 'Special Group'

The first hint of possible complications in Hong Kong came in April 1967 when the leftists created trouble on the streets in Kowloon. The Hong Kong government was quick to tackle this activity. Jack Cater left his position as secretary of defence but formed a 'Special Group' to handle the situation.[3] This was chaired by Cater himself, and the members included Denis Bray, Robert Locking, and David Ford.[4] It also included representatives from the Police Special Branch and Radio Hong Kong (now Radio Television Hong Kong), and a specially delegated assistant secretary for Chinese affairs. The group met every morning during the summer of 1967 to inform Governor David Trench of what happened the day before and received advice from him.[5] Although the work of the Special Group was never publicized during the period and no reports were produced for the public, the Legislative Council regarded it as engaging heavily in informing and influencing public opinion against the leftist campaign of anti-government propaganda.[6] Specific actions were then taken by regular agencies to satisfy public desires. For instance, the Transport Department reported frequently on the impact of the disturbances on vital transport operations. Radio Hong Kong increased special interest broadcasts, and Government Information Service issued a daily information bulletin to explain the government's purposes. These worked to help explain government responses to the struggle campaign.[7]

Despite this determined action to quell the riots, there was some initial hesitation about dealing with the leftists. Jack Cater acknowledged that it was not an easy task to develop a policy.[8] The Hong Kong government at that time shared the confusion of the London administration in identifying China's intention on Hong Kong and interpreting China's 'verbal support' for the local leftists.[9] In an interview Denis Bray recalled that the government was at the beginning worried about intervention from Beijing.[10] In fact, the government had planned for water rationing if China did not supply water as it had originally contracted to do so on 1 October. Arrangements were made to hire tankers and draw water from Japan and other places in Asia. There were also preparations for food rationing if China closed the border and blocked the supply of meat and vegetables to Hong Kong.[11]

After a few weeks of hesitation, however, the government became increasingly convinced that the violence originated largely from local grievances, and that China was unlikely to intervene directly. According to Cater,

> I had contacted Beijing, and it was quite obvious that Beijing, especially Zhou Enlai, did not like the trouble made by the leftists in Hong Kong.[12]

It was therefore commonly agreed in the government that Beijing appeared uninterested in toppling or fettering Hong Kong at that time, and that the struggle campaign was a distinctly local phenomenon.[13]

Maintaining law and order

In early May 1967, some leftists held their little red books and demonstrated in front of the Government House. The government tolerated them so long as they observed the law. However, violent demonstrations on 22 May directly affected the strengthening of government efforts in maintaining law and order. As Denis Bray argued,

> We tried to emphasize that we were not suppressing any political movements. But we simply were concerned about law, order, and public security.[14]

When it was obvious that law and order were undermined, the only answer was to use batons and to make arrests and even to impose a curfew.[15] But the government's summary dismissal of 1,651 strikers in government agencies (about 2.35 percent of the civil servants) did force the individual followers of the struggle campaign to rethink seriously before taking any further steps that could jeopardize their own future livelihood.[16]

The government was also trying to clamp down on any possibilities for further disturbances. The Guomindang branch in Hong Kong apparently offered to bring their own supporters onto the streets to attack the leftist rioters but this was forestalled by the government; for fear that it might provoke intervention from China on a massive scale.[17] According to Jack Cater, the government 'was trying in every possible way not to give any excuses for escalation, and to make sure not to create any incidents. However, the police needed to do something when they [the leftists] were breaking the law.'[18] Indeed, the efforts of the Hong Kong police to maintain law and order were widely approved of.

Phase Two (July–August 1967): Sha Tau Kok incidents and the burning of the British Embassy in Beijing

On 8 July 1967, Chinese soldiers crossed the border and five Hong Kong policemen were killed at Sha Tau Kok. The incident was 'surprising' in the eyes of the Hong Kong government.[19] Although there were 5,000 British soldiers based in the New Territories, including a full battalion within the vicinity of Sha Tau Kok, they could not be immediately involved after the clashes, for two reasons. First, they had not undertaken a direct military role before. Second, their role at the frontier could possibly lead to direct confrontation and result in a major Sino-British conflict.[20] Consequently, the request for military assistance could not be fulfilled straightaway.

Jack Cater, head of the Special Group, agreed that the only way in which the policemen in Sha Tau Kok could be rescued was to use the troops. Eventually, he decided to send the Gurkhas to the border.[21] Troops were immediately deployed alongside the police. They met no resistance and finally arrived at the police post which was then under fire. With the presence of the Gurkhas, the area quieted down.

At the beginning, the Hong Kong government had been somewhat cautious about the clashes in Sha Tau Kok for fear of possible intervention from China.[22] Later, when Jack Cater contacted the central leadership in China it was quite clear that Zhou Enlai had not approved of the incidents in Sha Tau Kok. According to Cater,

> Beijing told us to 'hold on' and that they would help. But then they were also in chaos. There were also riots and most of the provinces in China had serious problems. They could not do anything for us at that time.[23]

Zhou had said in a meeting that 'as the struggle continued to escalate, it is really difficult to stop and we are already "riding the tiger"'.[24] This confirmed Cater's remarks. Therefore, the Hong Kong government could conclude that the Sha Tau Kok incidents, though serious, were not an attempt at armed invasion of the colony as no regular units of the PLA were involved. All these suggested that the incident was purely organized and executed locally by the Guangdong villagers in the immediate vicinity.

Burning of the British Embassy

The arrest of the editors-in-chief of three communists' newspapers in mid-August in Hong Kong and the banning of their publication gave the Yao Dengshan–Wang Li group[25] in Beijing an excuse to escalate the case into a Sino-British diplomatic confrontation. On 20 August, Donald Hopson, the British chargé d'affaires in

Beijing, was delivered an 'ultimatum' by the Ministry of Foreign Affairs to lift the ban on all publications within forty-eight hours; otherwise the British were to be answerable for the consequences.

To the British, it amounted to a demand for total surrender. Compliance or even partial compliance was out of the question. As Denis Bray said, 'Even though they [Beijing] fired our embassy, we said no to them. We were very brave.'[26] Two days later, the Red Guards burnt down the British Embassy completely.[27] British staff were beaten when they rushed out of the building.[28]

The maltreatment of Hopson, and his consul in Shanghai, Peter Hewitt, would normally have become sufficient grounds for any foreign power to break diplomatic ties with China. But the British government did not take that logical step for several reasons. Most obviously, without any diplomatic relations, Hong Kong would have been placed in total jeopardy. Secondly, a break in relations might also result in leaving the staff in Beijing in Chinese hands, essentially depriving them of the remaining shreds of diplomatic protection. Most importantly, the British considered the burning of the embassy merely a result of the Red Guards taking over the Ministry of Foreign Affairs, and that the storm would probably pass, as it did soon. It was clear that the burning was triggered by extremists of the Red Guards such as Yao Dengshan and Wang Li, and not the central leaders like Zhou and Mao.

Terrorism in Hong Kong

Local leftists began to launch bomb attacks in Hong Kong and confront the government in the summer of 1967. From the perspective of the government, the continued bomb terrorism was not only anti-government but it also endangered the lives of innocent bystanders.[29] Because of this, the government began to adopt a more vigorous anti-riot policy after 12 July — to eliminate the leftists' bases before any more violence or bombings could occur. It was done mainly by police raids empowered by emergency legislation.

Two factors, both external and internal, explained why the government was determined to adopt the offensive policy at that time. Externally, the Hong Kong government was quick to discern the weakness of the leftists, who were anticipating direct popular support and intervention from China which apparently did not materialize.[30] The stationing of the PLA near the Hong Kong border to restrain popular demonstrations after the Sha Tau Kok incidents and the continued trans-border commercial and administrative contacts during the period basically confirmed this.[31]

Moreover, as seen by the British, there was a great discrepancy between supportive statements issued in China on behalf of the Hong Kong struggle and the actual concrete aid or intervention from the Chinese side.[32] As an official in the British Foreign and Colonial Office argued,

> Zhou Enlai has recently called for moderation of Communist tactics in the colony. It does seem likely that he, and others whose main concern is with the administration and economy of China, realize that the present extremist policies can only harm China and therefore try whenever possible to moderate their effects. If this is so, we must be particularly careful in our policy, both in Hong Kong and towards China itself, to act so as to encourage such moderating influences as exist and to provide the minimum amount of opportunities for the extremists to take the lead.[33]

All these hinted that the struggle would eventually recede. It thus provided a basis for the Hong Kong government to implement offensive anti-riot measures from mid-July onwards. Internally, the police in Hong Kong had acted with great restraint in the early phase of the riots. Various attacks by the rioters had been contained and they gained no ground in their struggle. It was argued that the strategies used by the police had earned them respect and endeared them to the general public. As attempts to control local leftists were met by violence, the public and the government both agreed that sterner measures were necessary if the rioters were to be kept in check. It became obvious that only deliberate action by the police could achieve the desired results. The activation of the emergency powers, followed by the 'crack down' or 'offensive' policy to maintain peace and order, therefore constituted the main tactic of the anti-riot policy of the government.

Consequently, Michael Gass, the colonial secretary, announced in the Legislative Council that from 12 July onwards the government was determined to 'grasp and maintain the initiative'. He said,

> We are convinced and determined now that the time has come to grasp and retain the initiative in this contest . . . and we have no doubt of the final outcome. Meanwhile it is time to be alert and resolute and steadfast.[34]

Emergency provisions were enacted under the long-standing Emergency Regulations Ordinance which allowed the government to deal with what was described as 'a threat to the stability of the colony in the special circumstances prevailing'.[35] Denis Bray argued,

> We know there are plenty of weapons, including guns and bombs, in their [the leftists'] hands. They were very easily imported from China. We determined to go into their premises to look for the bombs.[36]

Subsequently, strong parties of police, backed up by military units, raided the principal leftist strongholds, including union premises and schools. They seized stocks of homemade weapons and explosives as well as provocative posters and literature, and they took into custody a number of people suspected of subversive activities.[37]

The implementation of emergency powers gave the government and the police the authority to halt the riots and to arrest or detain rioters. The local leftists bore the brunt of this clean-up activity. These raids were met with charges in the leftwing press that the government, unable to control the growing strength of the struggle, 'merely used pretexts of misconduct to stage thinly-veiled physical attacks on fixtures and political decorations in leftist establishments'.[38] In response to this, Denis Bray said,

> It was very difficult to say that we only maintained the law and order since most people we caught were leftists. For example, the arrest of the publishers and the banning of the three newspapers, the *Tin Fung Yat Po*, the *Hong Kong Evening News* and the *Afternoon News* were not simply because they were leftwing press, but because they told people to plant bombs in the streets. They were creating the violence, and were much more extreme.[39]

In a highly congested urban environment, the police sought to discourage violent outbursts in the guise of conducting sanitary campaigns to confiscate offensive materials and to disrupt and isolate groups of possible anti-British political mobilization.[40] This finally led to the largest raid in the first few days of August, which was spectacular both in execution and in results. Over 1,000 members of the Hong Kong Police Force, assisted by army and military helicopters, were dispatched to North Point where a large stock of weapons and other suspicious materials were found in three different buildings. Some extraordinary discoveries were made. For instance, in a flat at Kiu Koon Mansion, an electrical circuit was wired to provide currents to a wire-meshed floor mat at the entrance to prevent the authorities from entering. A fully stocked clinic was brought to light and it was reported that a man carrying a booklet entitled *How to Make a Bomb* was detained.[41] Weapons uncovered in these raids alarmed the government and also prompted renewed public demands for government actions against violence.

Phase Three (from September 1967): Back to normal

In the autumn of 1967, the Hong Kong government, becoming aware of the relative dominance of moderate communists in Beijing, adopted a more hard-line attitude towards local leftists, including the Xinhua News Agency. For example, Governor Trench wrote in a telegram to the Foreign Office:

> We knew earlier that the local Communists' campaign had been haphazard and misdirected; and there was a good deal of evidence that they had been dissatisfied with the amount of assistance they received from across the border. It was clear that they steadily lost support. Now, their 'struggle' has little effects on the daily life of the Colony.[42]

In the spring of 1968, Xinhua News Agency made a request to Governor Trench and Sir Jack Cater to discuss issues of the 'struggle' and to restore the stability of Hong Kong,⁴³ but the governor gave it the cold-shoulder,

> Do we really need to talk? Is there anything we need to discuss? I do not think so.⁴⁴

Towards the end of 1967, with the governor's blessing a stern policy towards the local leftists was implemented to restore normal conditions.⁴⁵ Given the gradual resumption of political order, the government began to turn its eyes to the economy. Governor Trench said,

> At present the principal threat to the Colony appears to be the risk of long-term economic stagnation caused by reluctance to invest. If the policy of reviving trade with Hong Kong is pursued, it will become more difficult subsequently for the Communists to revert to the aim of making the Colony an 'economic desert', and to encourage terrorist activities that might have the same effect.⁴⁶

The government thus appeared to slide back into its customary complacency since the decline of demonstrations no longer made social reforms so critical.⁴⁷ However, in the wider society, both the masses and the elites began to advocate reforms.

Popular support for the government hinged on the people's belief that they had a lot to lose if the leftists were to win. It was therefore crucial for the masses to feel that they were getting their fair share of the fruits of economic growth and that the government was taking adequate measures to meet their aspirations for better living conditions and wider educational opportunities for their children. After the riots were over, it was commonly agreed that the government should launch a social programme that could change the image of the Hong Kong government and to improve its governance in the long term.

For instance, at the end of 1967, the United Nations Association in Hong Kong asked the Hong Kong government 'to produce a happy and law abiding population, amenable to reason, self-respecting, and self disciplined'.⁴⁸ It demanded the government to institute the following programme forthwith:

1. Compulsory free education
2. Civil rights for residents of Hong Kong be equal to those enjoyed by the residents of the United Kingdom, in particular freedom of assembly and peaceful demonstration
3. Protection against uncompensated rises in the cost of living
4. More and better social welfare provisions
5. More and better medical care
6. More and better housing
7. Equal facilities to travel and enter neighbouring and other countries
8. Protection against governmental, commercial and industrial exploitation⁴⁹

A letter to the *China Mail* in 1968 also raised serious doubts about the government. Writing under the pseudonym 'Awake', the correspondent questioned if the government really knew what the vast majority of the people in Hong Kong were thinking, and queried if the governor got full, proper, and genuine information from his advisors. It further criticized the government for not investigating the feelings of the general population: 'It is useless asking what the populace wants the government to do. Someone in Choi Hung Estate who has a very sick wife would want more hospitals. Another who has five children but only one attends school because he could not afford the fees for the others would want help in that regard.'[50] In effect, most Hong Kong people did not believe that the government could share their feelings, and that it did not know what the majority of the people needed.

The elites also joined the masses in criticizing the colonial government for not doing enough. Brook Bernacchi, Urban Councillor and chairman of the Reform Club, warned:

> More riots 'a repeat performance of 1967' will happen as a result of the government's broken promises. But the people will not rally round next time. In 1967 a whole lot of people elected to back the government because they had come to Hong Kong on their feet. But the Hong Kong-born younger generation living in an atmosphere of frustration will be in the saddle by the time of the next crisis. They will not back the government.[51]

Bernacchi therefore suggested that the government spend more than just 1 percent of its total budget on the Social Welfare Department, provide free compulsory education for pupils up to fourteen years of age, and develop new towns with complete communal facilities. The principal welfare officer in charge of the youth welfare section of the Social Welfare Department also agreed that more should be spent on youth,

> Youngsters are an integral part of our society. We must help them towards a greater awareness of their role. We must assist them on the road to social maturity and the acceptance of their future responsibilities. The government this year [1967–68] gave $3.8 million to help pay for youth services. We are fully conscious of the pressures on the younger generation.[52]

On the other hand, Elsie Elliot, another Urban Councillor, called for reform in the area of labour, since, as she said, the undesirable industrial conditions which motivated the riots still existed.[53] But despite the fact that the elites also made strong demands on reforms, they were not perceived as sharing the same line with the masses. In fact, the masses even criticized what the elites had done during the riots. A letter to *Tin Tin Daily News* asked:

> Have the Urban Councillors forgotten who they are or have they undertaken to act as defense counsels for the riots? During the riots, the elected Councillors seldom spoke on behalf and in the interests of the public. Whenever they came to problems pertaining to the present situation, the Councillors just advocated something impractical and irrelevant with the situation. . . . Such elected Councillors were very disappointing indeed because they had failed in their mission entrusted them by the electors.[54]

Elected councillors were therefore seen as hypocrites. This abhorrence of the elites was echoed by 'Awake', who accused the government of focusing only on the interests of the elites. He asked,

> Which Hong Kong was the government talking about? The one bounded by Causeway Bay, Tai Hang Road, Conduit Road and Victoria Street in the south to Jordan Road, Gascoigne Road, Chatham Road and Hung Hom reclamation in the north? Or do they mean Shamsuipo, Shekkipmei, Wongtaisin, Choi Hung and Kuntong [Kwun Tong] where nearly half the colony's population is located?[55]

In short, during the final stage of the riots both the masses and the elites demanded social reforms in the areas of labour conditions, youth, and education policies. But the masses perceived the government as having bias in favour of the elites. In order to pre-empt potential social and political disturbance, the colonial administration had to take prompt action to strengthen its governance in the long run.

Revisiting the arguments of Ian Scott: Myth of 'the Legitimacy Crisis'

Arguably, the 1967 riots were attributable to a legitimacy question rather than a legitimacy crisis. Ian Scott argued that 'a crisis of legitimacy occurs when a significant proportion of the governed or powerful political groups necessary to the maintenance of the system withdraw their consent or acquiescence to government actions and/or when the government loses its relative autonomy from these groups or from other governments.'[56] He pointed out that the 1967 riots were essentially concerned with questions of consent or acquiescence to government actions while there was a relatively little loss of governmental autonomy.[57] While Scott did not define crisis, he argued that for 'a crisis of legitimacy in a government, there should be, at least, situations [in which] the government may face potential difficulties in making and implementing authoritative decisions'.[58] In short, Scott argued that a legitimacy crisis must entail demands for transformations and implementation of reforms. If we define crisis in this way, it seems that the concept of legitimacy crisis is not very meaningful for us to explain the 1967 riots, which was not a crisis to the government of Hong Kong, but just a 'test' or a 'question' of legitimacy at that time.[59]

Problematic assumptions

There are several problematic assumptions made by Scott. First, he assumed:

> Colonial regimes have particular problems with legitimacy by their nature. They find it difficult to claim a popular mandate and they normally accept change only when there is a challenge to government practice or intentions of such proportions that the authoritative basis of decisions is threatened. Threats of this kind may take three forms . . . riots are the most obvious manifestations of a loss of legitimacy.[60]

Following the argument of Scott, one can conclude that there are problems of legitimacy in the colony at the very beginning. Then, these legitimacy problems may take place in the form of riots. However, Scott also argues that riots represent a crisis of legitimacy. In short, he presents a circular logic or argument as shown in Figure 3.1.

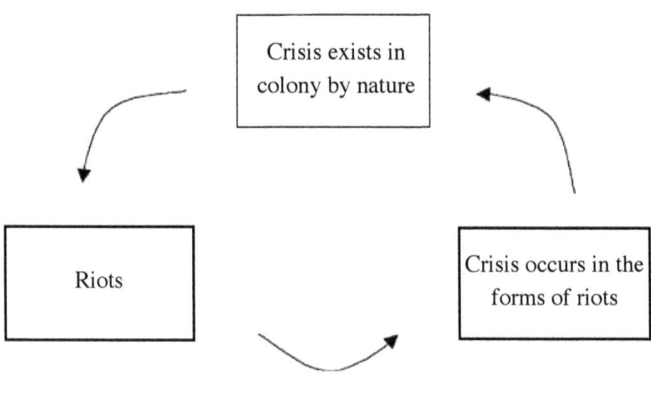

Source: Scott (1989, 36–37)

Figure 3.1 Scott's circular argument

As we all know, the result cannot explain the reason by itself. Therefore, what actually is the factor(s) explaining the 1967 riots? Scott's circular reasoning cannot really contribute to our better understanding of the dynamics of the 1967 riots.

Secondly, it seems that Scott's perspective on the concept of legitimacy was premised on 'the procedure and moral basis'.[61] Samuel Huntington has divided the concept of legitimacy mainly into two types: performance and procedural legitimacy. 'Legitimacy based on performance' means that the government legitimacy usually depends on the extent to which it meets the expectations of the masses such as economic growth,[62] that is, on their performance. However, what Scott focuses on

Hong Kong is another type of legitimacy: 'procedure legitimacy', which according to Huntington is based on the ability of voters to choose their rulers through elections.[63] As Scott argued, '[l]egitimacy is not solely about capacity. It is also about the moral basis of authority.'[64] However, the legitimacy of the colonial administration cannot be justified on procedure or moralistic terms. In the early period of the colonial era, the legitimacy of the Hong Kong government was arguably nothing but one of coercion. The successions of governors were mainly military brass supported by contingents of armed forces. But later, the colonial government needed to perform well in order to win the hearts and minds of the Hong Kong people. In short, as one 'benign authoritarian' rule, the British officials exactly shared the perspective of Huntington's 'legitimacy by performance'. It was easy to see the people of Hong Kong generally accepting the colonial administration without great difficulties.

Thirdly, Scott seemed to assume that reforms after the riots were mainly preventive, and aimed at avoiding another future riots. However, reform after the riots was not simply preventive but also proactive and aggressive in the sense that they would improve the colonial governance. Scott argued that most of the proposals had been put forward as remedies for discontent after the 1967 riots,[65] implying that the reforms were simply used to reduce the effects of the legitimacy crisis. However, the reforms after the riots were more than remedies for discontent; they were also measures to improve governance. As Hase argued:

> Before the riots, there was a trust gap which could not be bridged. What the government do is only to think what is the best for Hong Kong. But after the riots, it showed that masses in Hong Kong also trusted the government. So we are going to expand and improve the communications between the masses and the government.[66]

He continued to explain that:

> The riots would only occur if the government ignored the public opinion even when it knew what people think. Therefore, I could only agree that the purpose of the CDO was to prevent the riots in the sense that, by getting information from society, it would then make sure what the people think. However, the CDO was not like the Special Branch. The CDO would not actively find out the potential area for the riots. We did not act and do anything to prevent the riots.[67]

Similarly, Cater asserted that 'we have already planted trees, what I did after the riot is planting more trees.'[68] In short, Scott oversimplified reforms after the riots as remedies to prevent another riot. However, reforms could be seen as not only preempting the communists-inspired riots, but also a genuine desire to improve colonial governance.

Last but not least, Alan Liu argued that Scott applied the concept of legitimacy crisis to Hong Kong primarily due to his 'personal preferences of seeing Hong Kong remain politically separate from China in the colonial period'.[69] In addition, Scott regarded China as a homogeneous factor. However, Norman Miners has suggested that the Beijing factor is heterogeneous. He wrote, '[e]veryone agrees that China was in chaos at that time. There were the Red Guards, the gang of four, Lin Biao, Zhou Enlai, the army and Chairman Mao to affect their decision-making in China. The local leftists in Hong Kong also split between extreme leftists and those following the capitalist road.'[70] In short, Scott seems to have a monolithic view of the PRC factor.

The 1967 riots: A legitimacy question rather than a crisis

Scott's definition of crisis contradicts his acknowledgement that most Hong Kong people supported the colonial government at that time. For Scott, the riots in 1967 represented a crisis of legitimacy in the sense that a significant proportion of the governed withdrew their consent to government action.[71] If the 'significant proportion of the governed' can be represented by the masses in Hong Kong, it is crystal clear that most of them supported the government rather than the rioters or Beijing. As Norman Miners argued:

> The 1967 confrontation was largely a spillover from the excesses of the Great Proletarian Cultural revolution in China; it ended as soon as stable conditions had been restored in Canton and Beijing and while it was in progress the Communist instigators received little spontaneous support from most of the population.[72]

Scott himself echoed this argument. He mentioned that 'faced with a choice between communism of the Cultural Revolution variety and the unreformed colonial capitalist state, most people chose to side with the devil they knew'.[73] Though he did not state clearly who was the devil chosen by the masses, he implicitly admitted that most Hong Kong people supported the government in the riots even though its usual performance was not very satisfactory. Therefore, how can Scott argue that the 1967 riots were crises defined as 'a significant proportion of the governed withdraw their consent to government' on the one hand while admitting that a large portion of people supported the government on the other?

Moreover, there is no evidence to prove Scott's claim that the élites in Hong Kong at that time 'withdrew their consent to the government'. To Scott, another condition of a legitimacy crisis is that 'powerful political groups necessary to the maintenance of the system withdraw their consent to the government'.[74] If the groups Scott referred to were the élites in Hong Kong, the 1967 riot was by no means a crisis. Most, if not all, of the Hong Kong élites at that time, even the members of the Reform Club, chose to side with the government.

In addition, there was no evidence given by Scott to prove his claim that the Hong Kong government had 'govern-ability problems'. According to Scott, 'if crisis of legitimacy occurs, the government may face potential difficulties in making and implementing authoritative decisions.'⁷⁵ That is, governability problems occur if there is a crisis. However, the Hong Kong government was a strong authority at that time as it received strong support from the British government, the masses and the élites. The PRC government also told Jack Cater that there was no direct intervention from Beijing.⁷⁶ In short, as there were little difficulties for the Hong Kong government in making and implementing authoritative decisions, it is farfetched to argue that the 1967 riots represented a 'crisis of legitimacy' in Hong Kong.

In the final analysis, arguably the term 'crisis' was not a perception of the British officials in Hong Kong and some Chinese police constables at that time. David Akers-Jones argued that the term 'crisis' was unsuitable for us to describe the 1967 riots:

> A crisis is only a word used by the social scientist. It is not a very accurate description for the actual situation in 1967. I don't think we had a legitimacy crisis at that time.⁷⁷

Echoing Akers-Jones, Cater argued that 'Scott was just talking nonsense about the crisis of legitimacy'.⁷⁸ Moreover, a Chinese police constable I interviewed also argued:

> If you felt the living condition in Hong Kong was poor in 1960s, then most countries in East Asia, except Japan, were very very poor. As I knew, the employment rate in Hong Kong was very high at that time, especially in the manufacturing sector. We [Hong Kong people] were all happily living in this British colony. I ensured that the Hong Kong government was not an 'absolute king'. There was no need for the Hong Kong people to 'overthrow' the government. Therefore, I do not think the riot was a crisis.⁷⁹

In fact, the 1967 riots represented a 'test' or a 'question' of legitimacy, rather than a crisis to the Hong Kong government. Test can be defined as 'examination or trial' (OED) of the legitimacy and govern-ability of the Hong Kong government. Another definition is 'action that the government must do in order to indicate how well they are able to rule (Collins) [in Hong Kong]'. Question can be defined as a 'raising of doubt or uncertainty on the legitimacy of the government at that time' (Collins). These definitions of 'test' and 'question' fit the mentality of the British officials in Hong Kong at that time. As Bray argued:

> I don't think there is a crisis of legitimacy in the 1967 riots. Instead, the riots just represent a question or a test to us [Hong Kong government]. And most importantly, the answer we find from the Hong Kong people is they chose our side rather than the Cultural Revolution in China.⁸⁰

Conclusion

This chapter contributes to our understanding of the 1967 riots by combining a historical perspective with the internal dynamics of the Hong Kong government and the leftists. The 1967 riots could be divided into three phases: (1) political mobilization from May to June; (2) radical dominance in the PRC and terrorism in Hong Kong from July to August; and (3) back to normal from September 1967 onwards. Different phases in the period witnessed different orientations of the political actors.

Then, the chapter further argued that the 1967 riots were attributable to a legitimacy question rather than a legitimacy crisis. In this sense, the Hong Kong government passed the 'test' or answered the 'question' of their legitimacy. The 1967 riots confirmed that the Hong Kong government was legitimate as perceived by most, if not all, of the Hong Kong people. As Scott also pointed out, 'the end result of the disturbance was to increase the support for, and the legitimacy of, the existing order'.[81] If so, it is clear that the riots cannot be regarded as a 'crisis' as claimed by Scott.

4
On not being Macao(ed) in Hong Kong: British official minds and actions in 1967[1]

Robert Bickers

The question was: What was to be done with the flag? Inspired by events in Aden, and the removal to safety there in the face of the British withdrawal of the statue of Queen Victoria, Emrys Davies, assistant political advisor in the Hong Kong government, and Hugh Davies (later head of the Foreign and Commonwealth Office's Far Eastern Department, and British senior representative [ambassador] on the Sino-British Joint Liaison Group), but then an FCO language student in Hong Kong, decided to act. Despite the quiet scuttle of British officials from Macao on 25 May 1967, the Union flag had continued to fly over the abandoned Consulate on Avenida de República through the long, humid summer, forlornly competing with the slogan-bedecked building in a battle of signs. Most of it had rotted away, but a third still hung limply from the flagstaff, a 'tattered disgrace' and a nice focus for photographs.[2]

For some reason, the spare flags were eventually discovered secreted in the Amah's bedroom. Discretion had meant that Davies and Davies were working in the dead of night, and a developing typhoon also meant that they struggled in 'high wind and driving rain' to lower the remnant flag and run up a new one. The pulley was broken, however, so they had to give up, and then instead of a secret and symbolic final lowering of the standard they had to uproot the entire flagpole. Ragged flag in hand, and with suitcases containing some remnant 'secret and confidential material of some antiquity', which they discovered in the Consulate strongroom, they made their way to the very early morning ferry back to Hong Kong, and its sullen leftist crew.[3]

For a historian of Sino-British relations before the 1950s, the 1967 Macao side-show contains very familiar ingredients. It has the flag, the consular stiff upper lip, the nationalist crowd, the cravenly weak local authority and, lurking in the background, it even has nuns, ever the bane of a China consul's life.[4] After a two-week confrontation with communist demonstrators, the consul, Norman Ions, and his deputy, had snuck out of the colony on the morning of 25 May on a nine o'clock ferry to Hong Kong. The Consulate was never reopened. The lengthy despatch outlining the events seems never to have been completed or circulated.⁵ The episode will be recounted here for its interest as a side-show to the main confrontation in Hong Kong, but also because the events in Macao in May, building on lessons drawn from the Portuguese debacle in December 1966/January 1967, known as the 12.3 or 123 incident — were very much in the minds of British officials and commentators. The political advisor had briefed senior staff about the course of events in the Portuguese colony and their implications on 25 January, and other analyses of the lessons for Hong Kong had been circulated within the administration.⁶ 'Some local people,' reported the correspondent of the *Times* on 18 April, 'have begun to wonder whether Hongkong may be in for a dose of the "Macao treatment".'⁷ 'Their aim is to Macau us,' Trench told one reporter on 29 June.⁸ 'The Hong Kong governor must learn from Nobre de Carvalho' (the Portuguese governor of Macao) was one of the slogans used in Macao in May. Trench certainly did learn from his neighbour's experience, but not in the manner demanded.⁹

This chapter explores the ways in which both before and during the 1967 events, Macao was routinely used in the presentation of an alternative colonial model, one which in fact built on much longer-term representations of Macao, which British colonialism had no wish to emulate. Although it had a romantic place in British imaginings of China coast history overall, not least through the work of Austin Coates, Macao — Charles Boxer's 'curious colony' — had never had particularly positive connotations for contemporary British observers, either those who visited or those who fed on the imagined Macao of salacious reportage. It had always stood for unwelcome compromise and cohabitation: with Catholicism, with Portugal and Portuguese power, with China, and with Chinese, and had long been associated with vice.¹⁰ From W. H. Auden to Hendrik De Leeuw it was, on the whole, not a place taken seriously.¹¹ Looked at over the longer term, Macao was always a source of British colonial anxiety, but it nonetheless provided the model initially on which the entire British China coast presence was based. The first British embassy to the Qing, led by Lord Macartney in 1792, was instructed to request a 'depot' for the British China trade. Up to that point, and indeed until 1841, the British had to operate from the shelter of the Portuguese colony. Restrictions on residence and trade at Canton itself were compounded by some of the religious and other practical inconveniences of accepting Portuguese hospitality in Macao. The Portuguese bridgehead was the chosen model for the British China enterprise — it was offshore (up to a point, in Macao's case, but preferably literally so), and thereby provided a safe zone which would minimize the potential for Sino-British conflict and provide for British traders an attractive respite from the inconveniences and the dangers of China (of Chinese legal jurisdiction for instance). It was another fifty years before Britain secured that objective. While the British did secure it, and there were other likely candidates for the location of the British bastion, notably Zhoushan Island near Ningbo, it was Hong Kong that became — at least until the 1860s — the headquarters for the British trade.

As Hong Kong developed, and as communities of Britons developed in the steadily increasing open ports — in the British concessions, international settlements and other zones of foreign residence in China — Macao continued to hold a place in the British imagination. It also served a related practical function: Macanese (the Sino-Lusitanian Eurasian community) worked across the Chinese treaty ports, as Portuguese or as British-protected subjects. They passed as Europeans — in dress and through language — and thereby secured access to employment in ancillary occupations throughout the open cities. They were the clerks and the shop assistants who serviced the foreign communities. They worked in the outdoor staff of the Chinese Maritime Customs, and in the printing shops of the treaty port newspaper world. We presently know very little about the history of these communities in China outside the colony.[12] They were clearly visible in the treaty port world, but they also loomed large in its imaginings.

So we need to remember that Macao had long been a synonym in British minds and writings for unwelcome compromise, and unwelcome 'compromise' was the most positive gloss that British observers and officials could put on the 29 January 1967 resolution of the 12.3 episode in Macao. Understandings of the situation in Macao during and after the December/January events were very much in British minds; indeed Macao became shorthand for understanding events in Hong Kong, and for one possible resolution. There were of course critical differences, which will also be outlined here. But the central point remains: British perceptions of the situation on the ground in Hong Kong, and its possible outcomes, were strongly influenced by, if not at times hampered by, the question of Macao, where serious things did happen in 1966 and 1967.

Retreat from Macao

'British consulate in Macao invaded', shouted the banner headline of *The Times* on 13 May 1967, 'Envoy besieged in office by Chinese demonstrators'. This was Norman Ions, born in 1919, who had spent nineteen years in the Foreign Office (FO) since joining after the Second World War and had been appointed consul in Macao in 1965. It cannot be said that his was, in normal times, a busy post. With his vice-consul, John Kemble, and a small local staff, the flag was flown and business transacted as it had been since a consulate was first established. Between November 1965 and October 1966 it issued 14 British passports, 3,059 visas (refusing another 5,300 applications), and 63,000 permits for travel to Hong Kong. There were four births registered, and one death. There were 101 pensioners. Amongst the three hundred British subjects and Commonwealth citizens, there were those eight Canadian nuns. The Permit Office aside, it was not a busy station.[13] Nonetheless, Ions was, suggested Hong Kong Governor Sir David Trench, 'a very prominent member of society' in the small Portuguese territory, and it must have been an affable change for a career consul who had spent time in the European anonymity of Sofia, Amsterdam and Hamburg, as well as in London.[14] However, the disastrous turn of events in the colony in December 1966 had raised the temperature and put the team on guard for rough times to come.

'12.3': The Macao events, 1966

On 2 and 3 December left-wing demonstrators, as part of a series of protests against the government's handling of a planning controversy involving a communist school in Taipa on 15 November, invaded the precincts of Government House.[15] Events on 3 December spiralled out of control as the police attempted to eject them. By the end of the day crowds had driven the police from the streets, sacked the Municipal Council building, and destroyed symbols of Portuguese control, such as the statue of Coronel Mesquita.[16] Rioting that followed over the next few days led to eight deaths as Portuguese troops, who patrolled the curfewed streets in armoured vehicles, fired on the crowds. Although the colonial administration acceded swiftly to some of the demands of the organized demonstrators, and the authorities of Guangdong Province which weighed in — senior police and military officials were replaced for example — the events were not formally resolved until 29 January. The Portuguese government took a harder line than the governor, which slowed down the proceedings. As negotiations continued, mindful of the guns of the Chinese warships which sailed into the harbour to concentrate Portuguese minds (and in fact to repel Red Guard assaults on the colony), and in the face of the paralysis of the colonial administration and a boycott, the Portuguese asked the Hong Kong government on 14 January 1967 whether it would be able to assist in the event of any evacuation. The following day the ambassador in London reinforced the request, in the face of a possible 'violent measure on the part of China'.[17] An informal evacuation was already underway — over 700 Portuguese arrived in Hong Kong on 16–17 January alone (a tenth of the number it expected to have to evacuate in an emergency).[18] This set off the Commonwealth Office to instruct the governor in Hong Kong to plan for the evacuation of the British community.[19] Given that there were few suitable landing grounds, and given that to get to Macao involved crossing what the PRC claimed were its territorial waters, this was hardly going to be easy.

The Macao crisis raised all sorts of concerns for the British. They wanted a quick settlement there which would avoid a formal Chinese take-over, so as to avoid any 'emotional pressures in China for a similar take-over of Hong Kong'.[20] However, when the resolution came, it still had 'substantial' implications for the colony, in Trench's later view:

> It appeared that the CPG still considered that the advantage[s] of having Macao and hence Hong Kong under alien administration were too important to sacrifice and that they had deliberately avoided taking back Macao, but had used the opportunity provided by the dispute to secure

more limited aims; the elimination of KMT activities and influence in the province and the imposition of the maximum degree of humiliation on the Portuguese authorities.

'There were obvious lessons for us here in Hong Kong,' he concluded.[21]

The agreements of 29 January saw an official apology issued by the Portuguese governor, Nobre de Carvalho. The Portuguese renounced the use of force, and agreed the payment of compensation to families of the dead and injured, and the dismissal of senior officials. The activities of Guomindang agencies in the colony were to be banned, and seven Guomindang agents serving jail sentences for arms offences were handed over to the Guangdong authorities. While the Portuguese interpreted both the actions of the PLA in particular — which clearly protected the colony from an external Red Guards assault — and the tenor of the agreements, as serving to confirm their control, British observers felt that the Portuguese had effectively surrendered to the exercise of Chinese power in the colony. In fact, the administration lost control of a great deal of the ordinary business and organization of governance, policing in particular. The administration remained in name, but lacked much of the substance of rule.[22]

Hong Kong spills over: Macao, May 1967

As far as the British were concerned Macao was then quiet again, but a clandestine radio link was set up with the Consulate, in case of any future emergency. As events began to unfold in Kowloon and Hong Kong in early May, leftists in Macao began to organize their own response. As well as solidarity with the struggle in the British colony, there was suspicion locally that the Consulate was spying on activities in Macao, and that the permit system operating under Ions' control was being used to keep politically suspect individuals out of Hong Kong. Moreover, the pro-Beijing Chinese business elite had long opposed the permit regime instituted in 1961 to control movement between the colonies.[23] On 11 May Consul Ions received a tip-off that something was planned for the following day. At eight o'clock on the following morning he found a group of activists steadily painting slogans on the wall of his garden. Forced by a gathering crowd to forgo his car and walk to work, and accompanied as he strolled by a personal slogan chanter, Ions soon found that another redecorating team had been set to work on the Consulate itself. 'Death to all running dogs' and 'Down with British Imperialism' were plastered on the walls. The teams also painted and bedecked Vice-Consul Kemble's car with posters. All that day Ions was followed by demonstrators who were shouting Maoist slogans and damning the fascist British for their persecution of Hong Kong compatriots, allowing the use of Hong Kong by US forces from Vietnam, and other iniquitous crimes. A crowd entered the Hong Kong Government Permit Office, run by the Consulate, 'painted everywhere possible, . . . besmirched the portrait of Her Majesty the Queen', and bombarded him with demands for answers about British policy.[24] Aside from moving out of his home and into the Hotel Estoril, Ions did his best to run the affairs of the Consulate and Permit Office as usual despite the crowds that surrounded the offices and came chanting and singing into the public areas. But after the Permit Office closed on 13 May, eleven of the fourteen local staff decamped to Hong Kong.

The Portuguese authorities expressed sympathy, but offered no practical support. Given the collapse of their ability to police the colony, this was hardly surprising. On the morning of 15 May Ions visited the governor and 'berated him in unequivocal terms' about the failure to provide assistance. The picketing and haranguing continued the following day, aided by new temporary bus routes set up to ferry demonstrators to the Consulate and Permit Office, although rumours that Ions and Kemble were to be seized and paraded in dunce caps proved unfounded. Ions strove to maintain business as usual to avoid any possible provocation: to close the office would be to suspend the issue of travel permits to Hong Kong, for example, and the barring of Chinese visits to Hong Kong from Macao was one of the issues he was being berated for from the start. He did make a brief trip to Hong Kong, however, offloading the Consulate ciphers, just in case. The Far Eastern Department in London agreed on 16 May that Ions should stay put. Closure and evacuation would 'be taken by extremists in Hong Kong and Macao as a sign of weakness and a demonstration of how seriously we view the situation'. As long as no personal danger was perceived, then London wanted him to stay.[25]

From 17 May, a new strategy was developed by the demonstrators. 'Deputations' started arriving at the Consulate to present protests about the situation in Hong Kong. The pattern became, Ions noted, 'familiar, well-organised, and relentless'. Megaphoned, Mao-badged, little red-booked, and carrying banners, the deputations would assemble, march up to the Consulate to the strains of 'The East Is Red', and then request that Ions leave the building to meet them:

> Each deputation would stand no longer than ten minutes, each session consisting first of singing, then quotations, a reading of the protest in Cantonese, an interpretation in English, receipt of the protest by me (both hands, otherwise not polite!) more quotations, final chorus, photographs and good-bye.[26]

This went on for four days. Ions was at least permitted by the demonstrators to have Kemble deputize for him and the pair took it in turns to receive the deputations. In the evening the remaining Chinese staff were required to participate in sessions aimed, it seemed, at soliciting criticisms of Ions, as well as raising their Cultural Revolution consciousness. Various letters of protest were sent on from the Consulate to Hong Kong and directly to London, and Ions was able to telephone Hong Kong. The radio link proved less than clandestine after all — the crowds surrounding the Consulate could follow his every move inside the office, and Ions decided not to use it.

Asked on Sunday, 21 May, to 'receive a protest on behalf of "all the Chinese people of Macau"', Ions found himself positioned in a circle chalked one foot in front of the Consulate gates while about 13,000 people marched past. Making what he could of his surreal but intensely public predicament, and still concerned to offer no slight that could cascade the situation into violence, Ions stood impassively to attention for the ninety minutes it took the slogan-chanting marchers to pass. He was also very concerned about photographs, counting fifteen photographers ready before the march when yet another petition was handed him, this by the chairman of the labour union. Ions was determined to offer no photographic hostages to anti-British propaganda (and he and the Hong Kong government were swift to deny a *Daily Mirror* story that he had actually been forced to read out quotations from the little red book — when there were many more pressing issues to communicate).[27] 'Not one photo has appeared,' he claimed later, 'which would have given the much sought-after look of humility which they wanted.'

Retreat

Things were slightly quieter on the following two days, setting aside the singing and the chanting, but rumours abounded that an 'intensification' of the campaign was planned. On Wednesday, 24 May, he was asked to receive more petitions, but this time it would not be from his, by now, usual spot, just outside the door of the Consulate. Instead, the demonstrators wished him to stand in the middle of the road, in a post already chalked out when he strolled down to inspect it. Standing on his consular dignity, Ions refused but was persuaded to compromise by standing exactly mid-way between his parade-reviewing position, and that now demanded. By his own account this was a much more difficult and aggressive day, with the delegations becoming much more physically aggressive, some demanding that Ions should bow his head when receiving the petitions, and thrusting their little red books in his face when he refused. They attempted to make him repeat such slogans as '"All British are filthy imperialists", "Hong Kong is Chinese Territory", "Macao is not Portuguese Territory"', which he refused. After another uncomfortable, hot day, eight hours of which Ions spent standing in the road (although they gave him a two-hour lunch break), parrying questions about British involvement in Vietnam, and about the Hong Kong confrontation, he retired to the Estoril Hotel. There he gave an interview to the *Daily Express*, outlining the secret behind his resilient fortitude: 'I am a Yorkshireman,' he noted.[28]

Even so, this Yorkshireman had had enough. That night Ions telephoned Hong Kong to say this, and was given permission in principle to leave. Trench had telegraphed London for advice earlier that afternoon, weighing up the pros and cons of a withdrawal and closure of the Consulate. The arguments in favour of closure were strong, aside from the fact that normal business was being disrupted, as the potential for an escalation of the situation into a physically violent one was real.

It was already placing a strain on Ions and Kemble, and their continued presence provided a focus for the demonstrators (and the media). Moreover, the Portuguese were already failing to offer any protection, and could hardly be expected to provide further help if more dangerous events threatened. On the other hand, aside from some disruption to consular and Permit Office activity, closure would be 'taken as a sign of weakness not only in Macao but also in Hong Kong and might suggest that H.M.G. was losing interest in the area'. Ions at that stage was still prepared to soldier on, noted Trench, and there was the potential threat of any withdrawal creating a near-hostage situation, with demonstrators preventing staff from leaving.[29]

Events seem to have moved too fast for the FCO to debate the situation, however. Ions reported that he had heard that the demonstrators were going to demand an all-day session, without breaks on 25 May. Hong Kong phoned back to give him permission to leave when he saw fit.[30] The next morning, following their usual routine, Ions and Kemble set off for the Consulate at 8.45, but then had their car diverted to the ferry terminal and caught the hydrofoil to Hong Kong. Their families were already there, as were all the Permit Office staff. Remaining consulate staff soon followed. The demonstrations that still took place that day did so without their centrepiece attractions, and the British were not minded to send them back, fearing the development of a hostage situation. There were documents and personal possessions to retrieve, however, as Ions and Kemble had abandoned everything. Their haste has been thought unseemly in retrospect — even as a dereliction of duty — but they clearly had permission to leave when they saw fit, although they certainly used it with alacrity at the earliest opportunity. It was not until 17 August that Emrys Davies took two FCO language students — George Walden, later a conservative MP and higher education minister, and David Laughton — over from Hong Kong in a dead of night, torch-lit mission to rescue the Consulate's documents from its strongroom. It being Macao, they apparently decided that a casino visit would provide appropriate cover until midnight. Davies returned with Hugh Davies on the night of 5/6 September under similar cover to recover that 'tattered disgrace' of a flag, and anything else that could be carried. They sent the flag to Ions.[31] Meanwhile, the FCO and Hong Kong government had decided not to reopen the Consulate. Its business could be done from Hong Kong, they concluded, with little extra burden on the Hong Kong government. As the Hong Kong confrontation continued, it seemed pointless to reopen a second front for leftist activism, especially as British confidence in the Macao government remained low. The local staff were generously paid off (so that no disputes might arise for the leftists to seize upon), and the Portuguese ambassador in London was berated privately and publicly — through unofficial press briefings — for his government's lack of support during the crisis.

The decision to close down the office was a permanent one. While it was thought that 'there is no doubt that the British Consul was something of a traditional landmark in Macao', and that 'the "British connection" there would suffer by his removal', the prominence the Consul had now been accorded was hardly that which

Sir David Trench was thinking of when he discussed Ions' position in January 1967. Closure would demonstrate a lack of confidence in the Portuguese administration as well. Yet, whatever its symbolic value, it was now deemed appropriate to call time on this British outpost. The trade commissioner in Hong Kong could take on the office of Macao consul, but remaining based in Hong Kong. That office could still fly the flag, and might organize the usual event on the Queen's birthday, but otherwise the Macao establishment was recommended for closure. There was 'some face-saving value' in the proposal for the British, and it also softened 'the blow to Portuguese prestige'.[32] So, symbolism and ritual were still British considerations: they were in Ions's mind as he argued with the leftists about where precisely he would or would not stand in Avenida de República, and in how he presented himself for the assembled press, and they were present in discussions about the future of the Consulate after his withdrawal. The individual consul's sense of his own dignity, and the dignity of his office, and the FCO and Hong Kong government's sense of the symbolism of withdrawal and of not appearing to show weakness in the midst of the confrontation meshed smoothly in the discussions that developed over the Macao crisis. But as will now be discussed, both the Portuguese debacle in Macao and the leftist attack on Ions and his establishment were part of a wider set of reflections on the crisis in Hong Kong and its possible ramifications. The British did not wish to be Macao-ed, and that was partly how they understood the events that unfolded in Hong Kong itself.

'They are trying to Macao us'

This Macao miniature exhibited in its manoeuvres and potential scenarios many of the characteristics of the crisis facing Hong Kong, and both it and the wider Macao settlement were very much in official minds in the spring and summer of 1967. There was, for example, humiliation, the (ultimate) impotence of the British in the face of Chinese might (in this case popular, but military was also factored in), the need to go out of the way to avoid undue escalation, evacuation of personnel, and the danger of offering hostages. In British eyes, the situation had only managed to get so out of hand because of what they and many others saw as a Portuguese surrender to the communists. The Consulate crisis was one of the pieces of evidence offered to the cabinet underpinning an analysis that although 'the administration of the Colony remains nominally in the hands of the Portuguese, it is clear that their authority to impose their will, at any rate on the local communists, has almost entirely disappeared'. Authority had vanished because of the acceptance by the Portuguese in January of the 'humiliating demands' put forward by their opponents: dismissal of the chief of police and the military commander, payment of compensation, release of arrested demonstrators, and an official apology from the governor, 'for his "crimes"'.[33]

Learning from Macao

When Sir David Trench met officials in London on 27 June, he made it clear that he felt that the aim of the leftists in Hong Kong 'was to try to enforce a Macao-type situation in Hong Kong'. Indeed, he felt that 'fear of escalation' of the crisis had already 'inhibited' the freedom of action of the Hong Kong government to move against the press or leading activists, and that in a sense a 'Macao-type' situation was already developing.[34] In the colonial administration's first draft of an official history, its 1967 report, the Cultural Revolution more widely, and the Macao events which 'had shown that a colonial government could be made to accept the communist demands', were highlighted as showing that Hong Kong might have seemed 'ripe' for confrontation.[35] This was a routine analysis, and the Macao settlement was clearly a factor in encouraging the leftist upsurge in the first place. Special Branch claimed on 15 May that the Hong Kong leftists had made 'a close and detailed study of the "Macau campaign"', including the range of tactics used (*dazibao* [big-character posters], use of school children in protests, tax strikes).[36] The China and Korea section in the FCO's Joint Research Department produced a report on 18 May 1967, systematically exploring comparisons and contrasts with the 'recent Macao troubles'.[37] Trench had been discussing possible events and resolutions in relation to Macao since the crisis began to unfold.[38] 'Of course, Peking,' reasoned Sir Arthur Galsworthy's report on 31 May, 'would like to put us in the same position as the Portuguese in Macau, which is one of complete subservience to her wishes.' It would also fulfil the desire of 'Peking' to 'humiliate Britain in order to repay us for the humiliations we are held to have inflicted on China in the past when we were the dominant power'.[39]

At its 25 May 1967 meeting, the cabinet's Defence and Overseas Policy Committee (OPD) concluded that '[w]e could not resist a determined attempt to force us out altogether, nor could we tolerate a situation similar to that in Macao'.[40] The committee asked for two studies to be undertaken, one focusing on the consequences of a sudden withdrawal, and the other assessing long-term Hong Kong policy and possible 'adaptations' in policy. Assessment usually began with the assumption that 'we could not in any circumstance accept a Macau-type compromise', and that contingency planning for withdrawal therefore needed to be set in motion.[41] But this was also followed by the conclusion that the British were trapped.

Macao, then, provided a running theme for officials at all levels in Hong Kong and in London, and also for the press, including the British left-wing press. 'The success in Macao apparently shamed Peking's sympathisers in Hong Kong,' ventured Roderick MacFarquhar in the *New Statesman* in July. 'We were right to take stern measures to maintain order in Hong Kong,' editorialized the magazine in September, 'and thus avoid the miserable fate of Macao.'[42] 'The Macao crisis showed that if local left-wing elements get the bit between their teeth,' noted the

Times correspondent on 12 May, 'the authorities across the border feel obliged to give them at least moral support.'[43] Even so, noted David Bonavia on 15 May, 'The left wing may be finding Hongkong a tougher nut to crack than Macao.'[44] The *Economist* ran with the comparison in various pieces, most pithily heralding the fact on 3 June, prematurely perhaps given that the crisis had months yet to run, that Hong Kong was 'unmacaoed'.[45]

This should hardly surprise us, considering that it was clear that those leading the confrontation had taken inspiration from the Macao success. However, to some extent, Macao may have distorted British analyses of the underlying issues in Hong Kong and coloured reactions to the events. The Macao template offered what seemed to be a glimpse of the leftists' programme, and therefore a way for the British to understand the unfolding events in Hong Kong. Again and again the line taken by British officials was that the local left and 'Peking' were aiming for a Macao-style solution. As a result, other explanations of the support base for the movement and it socio-economic context — at least in its initial phases — were played down, and it may also have misled observers trying to identify the depth of CPG support for the movement.[46]

Not Macao

It is also worth emphasizing — as analysts and observers did not at the time — that there were important differences between the two confrontations that went well beyond perceptions of the commitment to exercise authority properly and effectively. The social basis of the events in Macao was far wider than that in Hong Kong: it was a genuinely mass movement amongst the Chinese population, and it had the support of (and was eventually tightly led by) the business elite. Secondly, the regional Chinese authorities took a much more interventionist line, both to ratchet up pressure on the colonial administration and the Portuguese government, and at the same time preventing a potential complete collapse through the naval security cordon. A further important factor was that, unlike Britain, Portugal had no formal bilateral relations with China (these were not established until 8 February 1979). Hong Kong was one issue in a wider British diplomatic relationship with China, and while its importance varied over time, it had to take its place and governors and their officials sometimes needed to be reminded that they were not the most important issue in bilateral relations, if indeed they were ever in the front rank of bilateral concerns, at least in British eyes.

Moreover, although the Commonwealth secretary urged Trench to use contacts with the left to try to convince them that Hong Kong would provide no 'Macao-type compromise', such a compromise was also in fact actually discussed in London. The worst-case scenario needed contemplation, even if it was routinely dismissed as unacceptable.[47] After all, the British were clearly caught in a Hong Kong trap: 'we do not now have a real option to withdraw from the Colony; we are in fact trapped there, and have no alternative but to sweat it out,' minuted Galsworthy on 31 May.[48] Their analysis quickly showed them that, all allowance being made for politics being in command in the PRC, the economic and other benefits China derived from Hong Kong were so great that it had no pressing need to accelerate any formal extension of control. The expiry of the leases in 1997 was a fact, and the colony would need to adapt and plan for that fact, and this also relaxed any 'emotional' or other pressure on the Chinese government to demand formal retrocession. It was also apparent to the British that while they might contemplate a unilateral withdrawal, there could be no guarantee, given prior experience of the tactics of the CPG, that it would be recognized and accepted.[49]

At its first meeting on 26 June the Defence Review Working Party set up by the cabinet's OPD to discuss the Hong Kong situation and policy outlined a proposed interim report.[50] Henry Jenkyns from the Department of Economic Affairs was probably the source from the start of some counter-intuitive thinking. While the majority of the group assumed that a permanent Macao-type settlement would be unacceptable ('in that it would leave us with the responsibility for governing without the means of discharging it'), might there not be, he proposed, 'advantage in some form of Anglo-Chinese dual control which might preserve our commercial and financial interests in Hong Kong?'[51] Jenkyns returned to these points at the second meeting on 17 July, when the majority view was again that any such settlement was 'totally unacceptable'. A different type of settlement might be negotiated, and Jenkyns argued that the British did at least have some negotiating assets, notably the sterling holdings of the Hong Kong and Shanghai Bank and the important role Hong Kong played in China's trade. There might be 'some tactical considerations in favour of acceptance of the Macao situation for a limited period', Rogers concluded as he summed up the feeling of the meeting, but the general view of the group was that this 'was not a tolerable course'. It would entail relinquishing 'control of the police and civil administration and leaving hostages with the Chinese Communists, who could force us to take any action they wished locally contrary to our interests, with no prospect of a termination of this state of affairs.'

It was also, he concluded, 'contrary to our material interests'.[52] Jenkyns argued that on the contrary, it was in Britain's material interests. As others had argued before him, when facing challenges to Britain's positions in China earlier in the twentieth century, it was important to keep a British foot in the China door, and an Anglo-Chinese settlement would possibly ensure some continuity of the commercial functions and facilities afforded by the colony. It would allow the British to 'make the best (admittedly a very poor best) of a very bad job by doing our utmost in most unpalatable circumstances to salvage what we could of lives, trade, relations with China over a generation or two'.[53]

Hostage colonialism

Jenkyns had played devil's advocate, but while the interim report on the possibility of an immediate withdrawal considered by ministers on 24 July conceded that a 'Macao-type situation' might limit 'immediate bloodshed and conceivably might make it easier eventually to surrender the Colony in an orderly fashion', it warned against this option. It might make disengagement more difficult, and would 'involve us in a humiliation as great as that involved in withdrawal, but longer lasting'. It was 'quite unacceptable'.[54] Ministers agreed.[55] Civil servants were ordered to continue developing an evacuation plan, despite the seemingly insurmountable practical difficulties posed by Hong Kong's geography, China's overwhelming strength, and the size of Hong Kong's population. At the barest minimum the authorities worked on assessing ways in which they might remove mostly Chinese officials — Special Branch staff were singled out — who would almost certainly suffer from falling under CPG control.

The report on the feasibility of developing an evacuation plan was presented to ministers on 20 September 1967. It makes for lurid reading, worthy of an end of empire thriller:

> Communist mobs, smelling victory and swelled by recruits to the winning side, would be out in pursuit of a number of the people who were to be evacuated . . . Any congregation of evacuees would be vulnerable; they would at once attract a crowd whose attitude might well be hostile. . . . bombardment, sabotage or even human obstruction might put Kai Tak airport out of commission

While a 'fighting withdrawal on the lines of Dunkirk, when all else had been over-run, could not be entirely excluded . . . it seems most improbable'. The most that the working party could conceive of doing in planning terms was concentrating on the estimated two thousand people who would be in immediate grave danger.[56] The Ministerial Committee agreed and asked that the Hong Kong government explain what local evacuation plans were in existence for vulnerable personnel. However, these turned out to be 'incomplete and out-of-date', and it would prove impossible to update them without revealing that contingency planning was in hand.[57]

Catherine Schenk has argued persuasively that sterling devaluation on 19 November 1967 was a blow which fell heavily on Hong Kong, and which threw into sharp relief the colony's colonial status.[58] Coming as it did while the confrontation was still unresolved, it seemed a betrayal of the six-month long opposition of the colony's administration and the majority of its population to the leftist challenge. It must also have fed very swiftly into the still incomplete contingency planning for evacuation. In early December the Commonwealth secretary recommended to cabinet colleagues that a halt be called to the planning. Any effective planning would have to involve so many Hong Kong officials that the news would surely leak, with 'the most grave effects' on popular confidence, and on financial and economic stability. There could be no evacuation. His colleagues and officials concurred.[59] As the long-term study eventually drafted by OPD also pointed out, Hong Kong was 'entirely self-supporting', aside from the military commitments, but 'it could become a major liability if a crisis of confidence' damaged the economy or panicked investors.[60] So sensitive was the issue of withdrawal or evacuation considered that many documents opened to researchers under the former thirty-year rule initially even had sections dealing with the issue withheld. So British options, as officials had argued from the start, were in fact clearly limited, and like it or not, while they were not 'puppets' or 'pawns' of an Anglo-PRC dominion over the Crown Colony, they were not colonial masters of Hong Kong's destiny. Shades of degree, rather than sharp contrast, ultimately signalled the Hong Kong-Macao colonial difference.

Conclusion

Norman Ions had negotiated his place in the Avenida de República, on occasion acceding to the demand that he stand in the marked chalk circle, on other occasions refusing to do so, instead standing on his personal and official dignity at a compromise position. He had acted to protect his local staff — and himself — and to give no cause for any escalation. But when the time came he was able to leave, hopping on to one of the regular ferries to Hong Kong. Thereafter, with a touch of farce or two for good measure, the administration in Hong Kong was able to lower the flag and formally wrap up the exit from the Macao Consulate establishment. Before summer was underway, Ions was at his new post in Hamburg. However, an early departure was not an option for the British in Hong Kong. They were clearly trapped, although it was clearly also in the country's material interests to stay on. They had felt certain as the confrontation commenced, and as they analysed it in Hong Kong, London and in Beijing, that a Macao-style compromise was either the premeditated aim of the leftists, or else it was the model for a resolution which was adopted by those struggling to co-opt and to prolong a spontaneous manifestation, or those in China who scented a possibility of success, and thereby a 'cheap victory on the Macao pattern'.[61] Concerned to develop strategies to maintain public support in Hong Kong, and to counter the evolving tactics of the leftists without giving any cause for any major escalation of the crisis that would drag the CPG in, formally or informally, the colonial establishment seems to have established a working analysis of the leftist programme based on an understanding of the Macao model.

As the movement began to subside late in the year, and as the battle for popular opinion was clearly won, Macao slipped out of the discourse and conversations. The British increased and prolonged their military commitment in Hong Kong, Trench instituted various educational and labour reforms, and a series of major infrastructure projects were launched, such as the first harbour tunnel.[62] After the devaluation debacle, a new arrangement was agreed to apportion the costs of the military presence. The construction projects in particular were enmeshed in official thinking about how to maintain confidence in the colony, that confidence on which it seemed it all hinged and, effectively, how to make the most of the hostage situation the British found themselves trapped in.

5
A historical perspective:
The 1967 riots and the strike-boycott of 1925–26[1]

John M. Carroll

The 1967 riots have generally been considered in terms of effect: as one of the main reasons for the colonial government's attempt to 'close the gap' between state and society, as a powerful example of how the Cultural Revolution across the border could shape events in Hong Kong, and as a significant step in the formation of a distinctive Hong Kong identity. Rarely, however, have the riots been placed in their wider historical context. Alan Smart's chapter in this volume considers some of the connections with earlier events in the 1950s and 1960s, but an important historical comparison has for the most part eluded scholars: the great strike-boycott of 1925–26. As Gary Catron, one of the few scholars to have compared the two disturbances, noted in 1971, they differed in several ways. Although one part of the leftists' repertoire in 1967, a general strike, was inspired by the 1925–26 strike-boycott — the aim being to target government services and big European firms, thereby harming only British interests — they lacked the co-ordination and the mass of their predecessors. Leftist unions struck at different times over the course of June rather than all at once, and for the most part only 10,000 to 15,000 workers went on strike, mainly from the two major transport companies, China Motor Bus and Kowloon Motor Bus. There was also less outside support in 1967 than in 1925 and 1926, as the PRC government sometimes urged moderation and caution. This caused 'wavering and hesitation' among some leftist workers who lacked the patience for a long-term strike. Most significantly, the 1967 leftists were unable to force the colonial government to accept their demands.[2]

More striking than the differences between 1967 and 1925–26, however, are the similarities. The most obvious parallel is how events in neighbouring China could affect this relatively stable colony, whose history was forged from the outset by its dynamic yet sometimes uneasy relationship with the Mainland, but the similarities extend much further. Both cases show how relations with mainland China often exacerbated tensions between British diplomats and the Hong Kong government. Although both disturbances were influenced by events on the Mainland, they had distinctive local elements and were preceded by smaller-scale but nonetheless significant incidents, revealing serious social tensions that the respective colonial administrations were simply not prepared for, or else tried to downplay. In both cases, governors — still an understudied element of Hong Kong's colonial history — played an active role in maintaining order and received help at many levels from different parts of a local population that was alienated by the intimidation and violent tactics of the rioters and strikers. Perhaps most notably, although the two episodes forced the colonial government to make long overdue changes, in both cases these changes were not nearly as dramatic as they have often been made out to be.

The China factor

The events of 1967 and 1925–26 both reflected local social, economic, and political conditions, but they could not have occurred — let alone continued — without extensive support from within China. Governor David Trench was convinced that Beijing was not behind the 1967 riots, yet there was considerable enthusiasm in the PRC for the Hong Kong leftists. At least in the early stages, the Anti-British Struggle Committee enjoyed strong support in China, both from the central government and from the population at large. Like the leftists in Hong Kong, the Chinese government insisted that the struggle in this British colony was part of the worldwide fight against imperialism. (Note also that during this period China's relations deteriorated with almost every nation, not only with the so-called imperialists.) In mid-May Luo Guibo, the PRC's vice-minister for foreign affairs, presented Donald Hopson, British chargé d'affaires in Beijing, with a formal protest and list of demands: accept all of the workers' demands, free all arrested people, end all 'fascist measures', apologize to victims and compensate them, and guarantee that there would be no more similar incidents. Luo condemned the British 'atrocities' and 'sanguinary oppression' as part of the British government's 'collusion with American imperialism against China' and accused the British of letting the United States use Hong Kong as 'a base for aggression against Vietnam'. Crowds marched outside Hopson's office, shouting slogans, waving flags and placards, and burning effigies of Prime Minister Harold Wilson. On 17 May one million protesters marched past the British office in Beijing armed with posters demanding that the British leave Hong Kong and vowing to 'Hang Wilson'. The PRC state radio condemned the British atrocities in Hong Kong as a carefully orchestrated part of Britain's collusion with the United States against China. A mass rally on 18 May at the sports stadium in Beijing drew 100,000 people, including Premier Zhou Enlai. In Shanghai protesters broke into and destroyed the home of Peter Hewitt, the British diplomatic representative. 'The main event', wrote Catron, 'was between the British and Communists in Hong Kong, not between Peking and London.'[3] Still, London was understandably never quite convinced by Trench's optimism about Beijing.

It is also worth remembering that one of the most sensational and violent episodes of the 1967 riots was launched not from within Hong Kong but from across the border. On the morning of 8 July, villagers and local militia from the Chinese part of Sha Tau Kok, a border village divided into Chinese and British sectors, attacked a police post with stones, bottles, bombs, and, finally, automatic weapons. A violent clash had already occurred in the same village on 24 June; five policemen were killed in this second attack. With more than eighty of their policemen holed up in the police post but desperate not to provoke China, Hong Kong authorities had to await approval from London before sending in the military. This assault at Sha Tau Kok, along with reports of several thousand people in uniform moving towards the Man Kam To bridge, a major border-crossing point, sent the colony into panic. Followed by violent clashes from 9 July to 11 July between rioters and policemen throughout Hong Kong Island, which left another policeman dead and prompted the government to impose curfews in Hong Kong and Kowloon on 12 July, the Sha Tau Kok incident made the police take a much less restrained approach to dealing with the leftists, raiding suspected centres of leftist activities and seizing weapons, bombs, and Communist literature. Although there is no evidence that regular units from the People's Liberation Army were involved in the killing of the five policemen, the leftists — as well as many other people in Hong Kong — understandably took the assault as evidence of support from the PRC.

Like the 1967 riots, the strike-boycott of 1925–26 showed how radical movements in revolutionary China, divided during this period by factionalist warlord politics and by various inter-party and provincial rivalries, could affect Hong Kong. In June 1925, after the Shamian Massacre in the French and British concession in Guangzhou, where more than 50 protesters were killed and almost 120 more were wounded, labour and union leaders in Guangzhou — which in the 1920s was not only ruled by several successive regimes but also became a centre for Chinese Communism — called for a general strike in southern China, especially in the most blatant example of British imperialism, Hong Kong. Anti-British pamphlets and placards in Hong Kong beckoned Chinese to rise up and drive out the British colonialists and their Chinese 'hunting dogs'. Strike leaders in Guangzhou called on all Chinese to leave Hong Kong, spreading rumours that the colonial government planned to poison the colony's water supplies and offering free passage to Guangzhou by train or steamer. In less than two weeks after the massacre at Shamian, more than 50,000 people left Hong Kong in protest; by the end of July some 200,000 more had left for Guangzhou. Hong Kong's economy nearly came to a halt. Though the worst was over by early 1926, the strike lasted for more than a year, and the British government had to provide a trade loan of three million pounds to prevent the colony's economy from collapsing. Even after the strike ended, the accompanying boycott against British goods, which helped make the strike so devastating, went on for several more months.

Whereas David Trench insisted that the PRC government was not behind the 1967 riots, Reginald Stubbs and Cecil Clementi were adamant that the 1925–26 strike-boycott was directed by 'Bolshevik' agitators in Guangzhou and their Soviet advisors and had nothing to do with economic or political conditions in their colony. Stubbs in particular has often been criticized for not understanding the political situation in China and for failing to differentiate between Chinese nationalism and Communism, but he was not exaggerating the extent of the influences from Guangzhou. Even before the strike, left-wing intellectuals and union organizers had tried to encourage nationalist sympathies in Hong Kong by distributing handbills urging workers to strike. Although some funds came from overseas Chinese, Russian workers, and an anonymous British trade union, the bulk of the strike committee's financial support came from the revolutionary Guomindang government in Guangzhou.

Extensive propaganda campaigns in both cases also revealed tremendous support from the Mainland. The 1967 leftists had a powerful propaganda machine: almost ten left-wing newspapers; the Xinhua News Agency, which directed the propaganda campaign and sent exaggerated reports of local support to newspapers in China; loudspeakers placed outside buildings such as the Bank of China; posters demanding 'Blood for Blood', 'Stew the White-Skinned Pig', 'Fry the Yellow Running Dogs', 'Down with British Imperialism', and 'Hang David Trench'; and effigies of the governor and other local British and Chinese leaders, often decorated with real or simulated bombs to discourage the police from removing them. Since the 1950s, Beijing had been sending 'proven mainland cadres' to fill important posts in Hong Kong, such as in the Xinhua News Agency and the *Wen Wei Po* enabling the Chinese Communist Party (CCP) to maintain a degree of communication and control.[4] According to the Hong Kong government's Special Branch, on the eve of the 1967 riots the left-wing newspapers had a total daily circulation of almost 350,000 — around 25 percent of Hong Kong's Chinese population. Although Gary Catron observed that the most successful leftist newspapers were generally the least political ones, and that most readers chose the left-wing papers less for their political content or the reliability of their news, and more for their short stories and racing reports, the massive amount of leftist propaganda in both Chinese and English during this period is a testament to the strength of the pro-Communist press and its support from the Mainland.[5]

The strikers of 1925–26 also benefited greatly from a well-orchestrated propaganda campaign supported, if not directed, from across the border. As Robert Kotewall, the Eurasian businessman and unofficial member of the Legislative Council who, along with fellow Legislative Council member Chow Shouson and prominent Chinese merchants, helped the government combat the strike, explained, the mastermind behind all of the unrest had been the propaganda machine of the Guangzhou government and the strike committee. Subsidized newspapers, such as the *Chung Kwok San Man Po* (China News), had 'preached Bolshevism, while from time to time attacks, most veiled, were made on the merchants and ruling classes'.

The paper eventually 'over-stepped the utmost limits of toleration by ridiculing' King George 'on the eve of his birthday'. Only weeks earlier the same paper had published a 'scurrilous article' referring to His Majesty as the 'Big Devil' and to Governor Stubbs as the 'Little Devil'. Soon even members of the Chinese middle class, especially women and children, were in a 'veritable stampede' to board steamers and trains for Guangzhou and Macao 'as a result of the wild and lying rumours spread by our enemy'.[6]

The potency of the China factor is perhaps even more evident in how the governments there could end disturbances in Hong Kong when they chose to do so. Especially given the chaos that engulfed China in the mid-1960s and the widespread support there for the Hong Kong leftists, the PRC policy towards Hong Kong — as Lawrence Wong's chapter demonstrates — was rather cautious and often ambiguous. Chinese leaders resisted calls from the Red Guards to overthrow Hong Kong's capitalist and colonial systems, and ultimately helped keep the movement from becoming too powerful by rerouting supplies after the Red Guards disrupted supplies to Hong Kong. Ships from China also broke the Hong Kong Seamen's Union boycott in September. Having monitored events closely from the outset, the central government became increasingly critical of the leftists' tactics. The PRC government also became upset when it realized that the leftists were exaggerating local support and sending inflated or even fabricated accounts of police atrocities. Though the water supply from China had been reduced during the height of the disturbances, on 1 October the PRC followed its annual tradition of honouring its agreement to provide water to Hong Kong twenty-four hours a day.

Similarly, while efforts by the colonial government and various parts of the local population helped to prevent the 1925–26 strike from becoming even more widespread, it was ultimately forces in China that brought the strike to an end, in this case the Guangzhou government. Although Stubbs had attempted a variety of methods to help end the strike, including trying to use public and private funds to assist anti-revolutionary forces in Guangzhou and hoping to persuade the Foreign Office to bribe the Beijing government into wiping out the revolutionary government in Guangzhou, none of these was successful. After various attempts at negotiations by Clementi, as well as threats of military force, and after a series of negotiations and political swings, in October 1926 the Guangzhou government finally ended the strike. This, along with the important role that Guangzhou had played as a sanctuary for strikers, demonstrated to the colonial government that Chinese nationalism could not be taken lightly. Clementi paid a visit to Guangzhou in 1927, 'symbolically inaugurating an era of rapprochement between China and the British colony'.[7] Realizing that the strike had shown the power and the reach of Chinese nationalism, Clementi and subsequent governors made sure to stay on good terms with the Guangzhou government.

Diplomats versus colonial officials

As Ray Yep's chapter shows, the 1967 struggle was not only between the leftists and the colonial government or between the leftists and other parts of Hong Kong society, but also between the Chinese and British governments and between the Hong Kong and British governments. Thus, the policy debates among Trench, London, and British officials in Beijing must be contextualized in British strategic thinking of the time. As in 1967, the events of 1925–26 revealed and exacerbated the existing tensions between British diplomats and the Hong Kong government. In both cases, Hong Kong officials disagreed with the diplomats on how to deal with local events. Correspondence in 1967 between the Hong Kong government and the British embassy in Beijing reveals diplomats' concerns about how the Hong Kong government's annual report might implicate Beijing, thereby harming Sino-British relations.[8] (The official Hong Kong report for 1967 began by noting that the year had 'been a testing time for the people of Hong Kong', but carefully avoided blaming Beijing for the riots: 'The origins of confrontation stem directly from the cultural revolution in China, which has inculcated among its adherents a fervent patriotism and an intense adulation of Chairman Mao Tse Tung and his teachings.')[9] Documents declassified in recent years by the National Archives reveal that the British government decided after the 1967 riots that Hong Kong would eventually have to be returned to China.[10]

Like in 1967, the strike-boycott of 1925–26 showed how Chinese nationalism could provoke enough of a crisis in Hong Kong to affect British policy towards China. The strike-boycott hurt Hong Kong's economy enough to reconvince the Foreign Office, soon under tremendous pressure from Chiang Kai-shek's revolutionary Northern Expedition, of the need to make concessions to China, which it was to do by surrendering Zhenjiang and Weihaiwei (peacefully, after negotiations) and the British concessions at Hankou and Jiujiang (which had been seized during attacks orchestrated by the revolutionary forces). While the Foreign Office became more convinced that working with Chiang's Guomindang was the best way to protect British interests in China, this strained relations among the British consul general at Guangzhou, the British legation in Beijing, and the Hong Kong government, which feared that the others might sacrifice Hong Kong to improve Britain's political and commercial position in China. On several occasions during the interwar period, British officials suggested surrendering Hong Kong as a gesture of British goodwill in the face of rising Chinese nationalism, arguing that Britain no longer needed a colony to maintain its trading interests in China. Exacerbating these tensions was the fact that although the Hong Kong government logically had to deal directly with Guangzhou, the British diplomatic corps was in Beijing and insisted on being the sole diplomatic channel for dealing with China. The Foreign Office often criticized Hong Kong governors for trying to interfere in Guangdong politics, dismissing them as being out of touch with broader British goals in China.

Local factors and earlier disturbances

Although they were influenced and fuelled by radical movements in China, both disturbances were preceded by smaller yet significant incidents that revealed pre-existing social tensions. They also had distinctive local components which the respective colonial administrations generally downplayed in official reports. Below the glossy veneer of Hong Kong's legendary post-war 'economic miracle', when the colony's economy shifted from the entrepôt trade to light manufacturing, lay tensions and anxieties, some of which are discussed in Smart and Lui's chapter. Far from ending in the 1950s, these pressures increased. Since 1960, Hong Kong's population had risen from around four million to almost five million, mostly during the catastrophic and inappropriately named Great Leap Forward and the subsequent three years of famine. By 1964 almost 500,000 people, mostly recent refugees, were living in hillside shacks or rooftop huts. Given such poor housing and working conditions, extreme gaps in wealth, and rampant government corruption, the Star Ferry riots of April 1966 should not have come as a surprise. Within days after the young So Sau-chung protested an increase in Star Ferry fares by declaring a hunger strike in front of the Star Ferry pier, one rioter had been killed and more than 1,400 youths had been arrested. The colonial government insisted that the riots had not been caused by economic, political, or social conditions and tried to blame the riots on Elsie Elliot, the advocate and activist who had tried to expose police corruption and solicited public opinion on the fare increases, but the official inquiry commission nevertheless conceded that overcrowding, the struggle to maintain a living, and 'the underlying insecurity of life in the Colony, resulting from international political and economic conditions, create tensions which elsewhere would be more than sufficient cause for frequent disturbances'.[11]

To be sure, Hong Kong had never experienced anything like what colonial officials called the 'confrontation' of 1967. As Cheung Ka-wai has demonstrated, local left-wing groups generally stayed neutral during the Star Ferry riots.[12] Nevertheless, the 1967 riots revealed many of the conditions in Hong Kong that provided a favourable environment for civil unrest. Half of the population was under the age of twenty-one, and only 13 percent of youths between fifteen and nineteen years old were in school; some of these students were enrolled in leftist schools, where they were inspired by the Cultural Revolution and by the anti-imperialist movements around the world. Lower labour costs in Taiwan and South Korea had stoked fears of unemployment and dislocation. John Cooper, a Briton living in Hong Kong who wrote one of the most thorough accounts of the disturbances, explained how San Po Kong, the neighbourhood where the riots began, had 'all the natural advantages' for civil unrest. 'Street upon street of tall dilapidated buildings vied with each other for the limited space available, hundreds upon hundreds of hostile citizens lived out their lives in human rabbit warrens, plenty of workers were available to start a riot, plenty of workers' organisations existed to support it and plenty of students would come along to give it political backing.'[13] In such an environment, by the morning of 11 May the strike in San Po Kong had turned political, with posters condemning the 'British authorities of Hong Kong' and workers waving Mao's 'Little Red Book', chanting revolutionary slogans, and singing revolutionary songs. When demonstrators started banging on the factory gates, the police were called in.

Just as the 1967 riots were preceded by disturbances that reflected local tensions, pressures, and anxieties, so too was the strike-boycott of 1925–26. Interwar Hong Kong is often characterized as a sleepy colonial backwater, particularly when compared with cosmopolitan Shanghai, but this quaint image overlooks how in the 1920s Hong Kong became more tightly woven into Chinese, British imperial, and world history. Though the Hong Kong dollar had depreciated by 50 percent since the outbreak of the First World War and prices had risen significantly, most workers' wages were no higher than before the war. Exports of rice to Europe in 1919 to relieve food shortages there had caused such severe shortages and price increases in Hong Kong that the government had to impose price limits. Inspired by struggles for political unity and accompanied by increasing vocal calls for abolishing extraterritoriality and foreign concessions, the revolutionary nationalism in China launched an era of strikes and boycotts, both in China and in Hong Kong. In Hong Kong this decade is best characterized by strikes and boycotts, influenced by the rise of Chinese nationalism and by workers' movements in China and around the globe. These sentiments made the 1920s more volatile and politically charged than any other time in Hong Kong's history until 1967.

The 1925–26 strike-boycott is the best-known event of this period, but it was preceded by two smaller but nonetheless important strikes, the mechanics' strike of 1920 and the seamen's strike of 1922. The first strike in Hong Kong to be organized by a labour union, the Chinese Mechanics Institute, which demanded a 40 percent increase in wages, the mechanics' strike lasted for more than three weeks in the spring of 1920 and had important ramifications beyond the economic realm. A victory for organized labour, the strike showed how workers had learned the importance of organizing and how to use strikes for collective bargaining. Organized by the Chinese Seamen's Union, the seamen's strike of January–March 1922 began with about 1,500 workers demanding wage increases to match the rises in the cost of living. By the end of January more than 10,000 seamen had left for Guangzhou, where they were welcomed by the mayor, Sun Fo, son of Sun Yat-sen. After extensive negotiations, the workers won a settlement close to what they had demanded. Lasting more than fifty days, writes Ming Chan, 'the seamen's strike was the first real demonstration in Hong Kong of the strength of the Chinese worker'. The end of the strike on 7 March resulted 'in a total victory for the Chinese seamen but complete capitulation of the British establishment, with its dignity and prestige in shambles'.[14] Moreover, the impact of the strike expanded well beyond Hong Kong and Guangzhou. As Robert Bickers has shown, British authorities in China became concerned about the potential threats posed by the changing nature of industrial and political conflict. In March 1922, for example, the deputy commissioner of the Shanghai Municipal Police, drawing lessons from the strike in Hong Kong, not only revised emergency plans in case of similar incidents in Shanghai but also urged business leaders there to take labour demands seriously.[15] Both cases also revealed the colonial government's worries about schools becoming breeding grounds for revolutionary and anti-colonial nationalism, as well as how education might be used to combat the growth of nationalism.[16] Trench had always been concerned about the existence of the pro-communist 'patriotic schools' and was eager to clamp down on them. Indeed, two of his most provocative measures in 1967 were closing communist schools and newspapers. In the wake of the 1925–26 strike-boycott, the colonial government used education to curb the growth of radical nationalism in Hong Kong. Cecil Clementi tried to provide a cultural, moral, and political alternative to the revolutionary nationalism that had inspired the strikers. In 1927 he encouraged some of the most distinguished Chinese scholars in Hong Kong, most of whom had left China after the 1911 revolution or during the iconoclastic May Fourth Movement, to promote traditional Chinese culture and morality in Hong Kong, promising to provide government support for a Chinese department at the University of Hong Kong to train teachers for local schools.

Governors in action

In both 1967 and 1925–26, colonial governors played an active, sometimes heavy-handed, role in maintaining order and trying to end the disturbances. Overshadowed by his successor, Murray MacLehose, David Trench is not generally known as an especially proactive governor, but Yep has shown otherwise. As he argues, what really matters is not whether London was fully convinced of Trench's view about Beijing's support for the leftists. Rather, what matters is that Trench was able to do what he wanted to do. Trench's government responded with its own extensive counter-propaganda campaign, whose organizer, Jimmy McGregor, received frequent death threats and was condemned by the leftists as a 'vagabond and a criminal', the 'governor's jackal', and a 'wolf whining in the night'. Under the Emergency Regulations Ordinance, the police were allowed to detain suspected activists without a trial. In mid-May, Trench's government banned loudspeaker broadcasts such as those coming from the Bank of China. Trench appeared on television and encouraged the public to stand tall during the disturbances. On 1 June the government prohibited inflammatory posters and specified punishments for anyone who produced, distributed, or displayed such posters. The PRC government and the local branch of the Xinhua News Agency condemned the ban as a 'political provocation' and 'fascist decree'. When Trench requested the British Admiralty to dispatch the HMS *Bulwark* from Singapore as a show of force, Xinhua rightly accused the British of using this commando carrier, supposedly in Hong Kong on a routine training exercise, for intimidation. Trench went on leave in the last week of June. His leave prompted local criticism, but it enabled him to explain things in person when he was in London, which may have helped to sway the British government.

While Trench has not traditionally been known for playing an active role in local affairs, Stubbs has gone down in Hong Kong history as a bully, and for failing to understand the political scene in China and for aggravating local tensions. In 1922, for example, he mismanaged the seamen's strike by overreacting and insisting that it was political and led by agitators in Guangzhou. When the seamen's union posted armed pickets along the coast and seized food from trains on the Canton-Kowloon Railway, Stubbs banned the union as 'an unlawful society'. After colonial police arrested some of the union leaders and closed down the union headquarters, the union responded by beckoning all workers in Hong Kong to strike and leave for Guangzhou. More than 100,000 additional workers heeded the call, including the entire staff at Government House. As Ming Chan argues, the colonial government's counter-strike measures helped to transform the strike 'from an economic strike into an all-out political confrontation between British colonial might and Chinese patriotic pride and national interests'.[17]

Although Stubbs inflamed local tensions in 1925 by overreacting rather than trying to understand the cause of the strike, the emergency measures that he passed may have prevented the strike from expanding — declaring a state of emergency, prohibiting the export of foodstuffs and money, imposing a moratorium on Chinese banks, limiting the amount of currency that could be taken out of the colony, dispatching policemen to guard water supplies, sending troops to operate the Star Ferry and patrol the streets, closing schools early for summer vacation, imposing a curfew, and censoring Chinese mail, telegrams, and newspapers.

Cecil Clementi, Stubbs's successor, is generally better known for his interest in Chinese culture (especially Cantonese love songs) than for his efforts to end disorder in Hong Kong. Convinced that the strike was an attempt by the Guangzhou government to ruin the colony, Clementi insisted that his government would deal only with the Guangzhou government, not the strike committee, and that the Guangzhou government should be responsible for ending the strike because the boycott was a violation of Britain's treaty rights and would mainly harm Chinese commerce. Still, he actively promoted a variety of approaches to ending the strike. In late December 1925 he suggested that the Hong Kong government and local merchants offer 'compensation' to the strikers in the form of a trade loan to Guangzhou, instructing representatives of the local Chinese business community to elect delegates to present the payment plan to Guangzhou. Although Clementi turned down the idea of formal negotiations with the Guangzhou strike committee, which included former workers from Hong Kong whom he did not want back in the colony, he was open to trying to persuade the Guangzhou government to accept British rather than Russian assistance. Rejecting the possibility of a British military attack, which would harm British trade with the rest of China, Clementi nevertheless suggested helping the Chinese navy defeat Guangzhou or putting pressure on Moscow to end the boycott.

Local support

In both episodes, the colonial administrations appear to have initially been taken off guard by the local backing for the riots and strikes. Considerably more noticeable, however, is how many members of the population supported the colonial government in both cases. It is not hard to see why in 1967 the leftists never found widespread local support for their cause, especially among a population that included so many people who had fled the Communist government in China and who viewed the Cultural Revolution with horror and revulsion. Though some young people participated because of the way they had been treated by the police in the 1966 Riots, the leftists failed to obtain widespread support from students. The Federation of Students called for an end to the violence, and the University of Hong Kong Students' Union sent the government a message of support. Many community organizations, professional associations, and schools expressed their support, while scores of local people joined the Hong Kong Auxiliary Police Force. While the left-wing Chinese press supported the disturbances as the natural, heroic, patriotic reactions of an oppressed people, other Chinese newspapers called for people to stay out of the disturbances. Letters to the editor in both Chinese and English newspapers often called for the government to take stronger measures but also appealed for an end to the disturbances and suggested ways of conciliation.

In 1925–26, the leaders of the Chinese and foreign communities actively assisted the government. Volunteers worked at hospitals and drove the trams. Members of the Tung Wah Hospital Committee operated food stalls and sold food at low prices, while many Chinese and Eurasians joined the Volunteers, the Special Police Reserve, and the St. John's Ambulance Service. Other 'loyal Chinese', as colonial officials described them, helped the government censor cables, mail, and newspapers. Many joined the volunteer fire brigade and formed street committees and street guards to patrol their neighbourhoods. The District Watch Force helped maintain order, mediate, and prevent intimidation. Although they received anonymous letters threatening violence and murder, and although rewards for their heads were posted in Guangzhou, Chow Shouson and Robert Kotewall orchestrated an intensive propaganda campaign to fight the strike. The two formed the Counter-Propaganda Bureau, which plastered posters and distributed leaflets encouraging the population to resist the strikers, and established a counter-propaganda newspaper, the *Kung Sheung Yat Po* (Industrial and Commercial Daily Press), which was circulated widely in Hong Kong and among overseas Chinese in the United States and Australia. Chow and Kotewall also recommended that the governor order routine military marches and demonstrations as a show of strength. They also formed the Labour Protection Bureau, a counter-propaganda organization run by General Liang Weichen, a former pirate who had previously served as a general in Chen Jiongming's Guangdong Army. The organization, membership, and operation of the Labour Protection Bureau were kept secret, while the bureau itself was shrouded in mystery. Although it consisted of more than 150 men, the bureau was never mentioned in newspapers or government publications, and although the public never knew who or how many people were in the bureau, everyone knew of its existence. Officials in London expressed doubt about the bureau's 'staff' members and their previous experience, but Chow and Kotewall were unconcerned. As Kotewall argued, 'they should not be required to furnish proof of having worn kid gloves from their youth up'.[18]

In both cases, the government was worried about the morale and loyalty of the police force, though in both cases such concerns were generally unwarranted. Jack Cater, who in 1967 was deputy colonial secretary and special assistant to Governor Trench, recalled: 'throughout the whole of this period the Hong Kong police acted most bravely, I would say magnificently . . . The police held their tempers and behaved with great restraint, even when the occasional teenage brat went up to them and poked fingers in their eyes, and otherwise taunted them.'[19] For its loyal service, in 1969 Queen Elizabeth renamed the police force the Royal Hong Kong Police Force — even though, as Sinclair's chapter shows, the spectre of corruption continued to threaten the force's 'distinguished record'. In 1925 many government employees resisted the call to strike, and the colonial government hardly had reason to worry about mutiny or subversion among its Chinese employees. In September 1925, Captain Superintendent of Police P. P. J. Wodehouse praised the strong performance and loyalty of the Chinese members of the police force. Of the 105 Chinese clerks, telephone operators, and interpreters, only one had left his post; out of 335 policemen, only 7 had deserted. Wodehouse reported similar performances among the Water Police and the Chinese detectives stationed along the border in the New Territories.[20]

Identity, violence and terror

This support for the colonial government during both disturbances certainly reflected concerns to preserve order and, especially in the case of the business and professional elites, class interests. However, it also reflected a growing sense of local identity. For the majority of Hong Kong people, the 1967 disturbances gave the government new popularity and legitimacy. The disturbances, and the events on the Mainland that influenced them, seemed to be proof that life in Hong Kong was better than on the Mainland and that people in Hong Kong had little to gain from any sort of anti-British campaign. Forced to choose between the PRC and Hong Kong, most people in Hong Kong identified with the colonial regime as their government. At the same time, they increasingly saw themselves as members of a special community, separate from both the colonial government and their compatriots on the Mainland. As John Young put it, 'the people of Hong Kong saw themselves as a community, separate from their British-Hong Kong government, but also separate from their Chinese motherland'.[21] Similarly, contrasting the stability of Hong Kong with the turbulence in China during the 1920s led many local Chinese, especially wealthier residents whose fortunes depended on Hong Kong's colonial status, to identify increasingly with Hong Kong, witnessed by the way in which they collaborated with the colonial government to end the strikes of the 1920s. This sense of belonging deepened as the colonial government became more willing to incorporate Chinese opinion, especially after the general strike of 1925–26. To sociologist Henry Lethbridge, the strike-boycott represented an important coming of age for the colony: 'it was no longer simply a congeries of various groups, composed of acquisitive, rootless, transient individuals, but was beginning to coalesce into a community and, if all racial divisions are included, into a plural society, its members bound together, as it were, in a network of contractual arrangements. It had begun to acquire an identity'.[22]

This sense of local identity emerged as people in Hong Kong compared living conditions there with those on the Mainland and had been a defining theme of Hong Kong society since the late 1800s, as China entered an era of turbulence and confusion. But in both 1967 and 1925–26 this identity must also be contextualized within the violence and terror that characterized the two periods. In both cases, violence and terror seem to have alienated a populace for the most part unused to such tactics. Several incidents in 1967 appear to have been particularly shocking. One was the assault at Sha Tau Kok in June. Another took place in August when two children in North Point were killed by a bomb planted in a ball. On 24 August the leftists attacked the car of Lam Bun, a popular radio commentator who had criticized their activities. After setting Lam's car on fire, they poured gasoline on Lam and his cousin and set them on fire. The 'Headquarters of the Underground Attack Corps for Weeding Out Traitors' claimed credit for killing Lam. The leftists, who had already been sending threatening letters to Chinese business and community leaders, now issued lists of other so-called traitors to be executed. David Faure, who was then a student at the University of Hong Kong, writes that 'the riots of 1967 were the first taste of open action directed against an established government, but for many, the demonstration, the bombs, and the occasional riot, confirmed what they were learning in the press of the excesses of the Cultural Revolution'.[23]

We lack a systematic study of the sustained violence during 1967, especially how the populace dealt with such prolonged anxiety and uncertainty. On 9 July the leftists began their campaign of 'guerilla warfare, shock tactics, and sparrow warfare'. This campaign began as armed struggles with the police, usually at union headquarters and leftist-owned stores, but soon escalated to planted bombs and guerilla-style attacks on the police that lasted until the end of the year. The 'New Territories Action Group' tried to blow up a police helicopter. By late July, the targets of the bombings expanded to theatres, parks, markets, and other public places. Buses and taxis were set on fire, and bombs (real or fake) were planted nearly everywhere. On 20 July the government put into effect nine emergency regulations enacted in 1949, giving the police wider powers of search and arrest. The editors, publishers, and printers of three leftist newspapers were charged and convicted of false reporting. When in August the leftists shifted from riots to attacking people who opposed them and planting bombs, the police stepped up their crackdowns. After the most dramatic police raid, on 4 August, when more than one thousand policemen and soldiers, supported by three helicopters from HMS *Hermes*, launched an attack from the ground and the air on three leftist-held buildings, one of which was booby-trapped and contained bomb-making equipment, the leftists turned to planting bombs where children could easily find them. In one incident, a bomber's children (whom the bomber had taken with him while planting bombs) were killed when the bombs exploded prematurely. Not surprisingly, such violence pushed many people to support the colonial government and made the police look like heroes, even when they attacked rioters with tear gas and clubs and when they arrested and imprisoned teenagers.

In 1925 and 1926, violence and terror also played an important role — not only in encouraging local residents to support the strike-boycott but also in drumming up support for the colonial government's anti-strike campaign. Robert Kotewall insisted that the reason workers in Hong Kong had left both their jobs and the colony so spontaneously was due neither to 'patriotic indignation' nor to 'unbearable living conditions'. Rather, it had been 'an exhibition of pure terror, of panic fear, in all but a very few cases. One would imagine that only desperate danger could induce such extreme fright, but in point of fact, the very slightest causes — an unsigned scrawl on a slip of paper, a mere warning word or look, or a telephone message from an unknown person — were sufficient to send them hurrying and scurrying out of their jobs'.[24] Those who later tried to return were prevented from doing so by pickets hired by the strike committee; others were flogged or forcibly exposed in the sun for hours. Escaping sampans were burned. One woman was shot while trying to cross the border at Shenzhen; several others drowned in the river.[25] In early February 1926, Clementi reported that the strike pickets had intensified their aggression against Hong Kong. They were shooting at Indian troops on the Hong Kong side of the border and at police launches in the Shenzhen River, blocking trains to and from China, and preventing villagers from crossing the border back into Hong Kong. Throughout the strike-boycott, prominent Chinese and Eurasian businessmen received death threats for supporting the colonial government as 'hunting dogs' and 'running dogs'. Even after the strike-boycott had ended, a sense of fear persisted. In late March 1927, Cecil Clementi reported that four gunmen from Guangzhou had been sent to assassinate him and the secretary for Chinese affairs as well as Chow Shouson, Robert Kotewall, and other 'loyal Chinese', and to blow up the Labour Maintenance Bureau.

Reform and its limits

What conclusions can be drawn from this brief comparison of the 1967 and 1925–26 strike-riots? One is that the history of Hong Kong cannot be viewed, as it so often has been, simply in terms of stability. Both disturbances were influenced mightily by the revolutionary events in mainland China, but they both revealed deep-seated local tensions that have yet to be fully explored. The significance of 1967, as Ray Yep argues, extends beyond the colonial state's ability to reform itself. Here too the strike-boycott of 1925–26 offers a helpful comparative perspective. Although 1967 and 1925–26 have often been described as watersheds in Hong Kong history, these events must be viewed in terms of both change and continuity. The events of 1967 and 1925–26 forced the government to make some political and social changes, although in both cases these changes were of uneven significance. The 1967 riots prompted demands locally and in London for the Hong Kong government to improve labour relations and communication between government and people, expand education, and foster a sense of belonging in what had become one of Britain's last colonies. The city district officer system appointed district officers to mediate between government and people, assigned to 'assist those suffering from a sense of grievance to present their cases coherently and, when necessary, to act as their advocate'. Public relations within government departments were improved and various advisory committees expanded, while unofficial members of the Legislative and Executive Councils were given larger roles. The secretary for Chinese affairs was renamed the secretary for home affairs. Although many of these reforms would not be implemented until the early 1970s under Trench's successor, Murray MacLehose, the 1967 riots 'marked a crucial turning point in the development of the colonial regime's irreversible awareness of and irrevocable commitment to a more conscientious and responsive social policy with greater care and concern for the grass-roots community'.[26] Jack Cater later recalled that 'it is an ill wind which blows nobody any good, and, in the case of the 1967 disturbances, the opportunity was offered and seized with alacrity'.[27] Had the 1967 riots not occurred, Cater explained in an interview in 1999, 'I don't think there would have been any reform at all.'[28]

Not only must we move beyond viewing 1967 through the lens of the self-reforming colonial state, we might also consider it through continuities and parallels rather than through change and reform. Trench's attempts to 'close the gap' should not be exaggerated. Although proposals were offered for an ombudsman who would investigate complaints against maladministration, such a post would not fully materialize until 1989. When the government introduced legislation making Chinese an official language in 1974, it did so mainly in response to demands from local activists. Government policy papers and internal documents continued to be written entirely in English for another twenty years, while laws were not issued in Chinese until 1989. Stephen Waldron concluded from interviews with colonial officials that 'there appeared to be little indication in 1971 that Hong Kong's officials (or the general public, for that matter) were much interested in the social conditions that had been protested or recognized as sources of unrest in 1967'.[29] As David Clayton's chapter argues, the longstanding ideology of growth before equity was not destroyed by the events of 1967. Consider also the problem of corruption, which had plagued Hong Kong since its earliest days but became more rampant and widespread in the post-war era. The 1966 Riots had raised concerns about corruption in the police force and other parts of government, but the police force's performance in the 1967 riots had improved its reputation. Leo Goodstadt has argued that this made the public ready to 'overlook conduct that would have been unacceptable in less troubled times'.[30] Serious attempts at tackling corruption would not be made until the Peter Godber scandal of 1973. Most important for Hong Kong's already retarded political development, the 1967 disturbances effectively shelved Trench's plans for constitutional reforms. The British government announced that because of Hong Kong's unique geographic and political status, an elected council would be out of the question, especially given the turbulent conditions in China and the tense Sino-British relations during the Cultural Revolution. The buzzword now was 'consultation'. Justifying Hong Kong's lack of democracy, Trench argued in 1969 that 'there is no one brand of politics, or one line of policies, which is right for all places at all stages of development'.[31]

Moving back four decades, there is no doubt that the 1925–26 strike-boycott also prompted some significant changes. The colonial government realized that it could no longer take workers for granted and that it needed to work more closely with leaders of the Chinese community. In May 1926, Cecil Clementi appointed Chow Shouson as the first Chinese member of the Executive Council. Chow's appointment was no doubt a strategic move designed to show strikers in Hong Kong and Guangzhou that the government was willing to compromise, but it also represented a major shift in local colonial policy. Although the Colonial Office had advised some fifty years earlier that 'it would be invidious to and inequitable to lay down that Chinese subjects of the Queen shall be debarred from appointment to the Executive Council, and therefore the possibility of the appointment being hereafter filled by a Chinese gentleman must be reckoned with', most Hong Kong governors had tried to resist any such reforms.[32] In August 1895, for example, Governor William Robinson explained to Secretary of State Joseph Chamberlain that 'it would be extremely difficult, if not impossible to find a Chinese gentleman fit to sit in the Executive Council. A Chinaman pure and simple would not and could not be an independent member, and I do not think he would be an acquisition.'[33] Although Chamberlain ordered that Robinson add two unofficial members, with 'no reference to the particular class or race to which the persons chosen belong', a Chinese was not appointed to the Executive Council until 1926.[34]

Finally, this important change in local colonial policy should not obscure some of the repressive measures taken by the government to control its subjects. Although mainland Chinese historiography of the strike-boycott of 1925–26 has usually treated these events as a 'watershed' for the development of labour and anti-imperialist movements in China, the colonial government took measures that inhibited the growth of labour unionism in Hong Kong. The government banned all unions that had been involved in the strike and all politically motivated strikes. Union funds could not be used for political purposes outside of Hong Kong, and no branch of any union in China could be formed in Hong Kong. The Illegal Strike and Lockout Ordinance of 1927 made strikes illegal if they tried to coerce the government or had any objective beyond a dispute within a certain industry. The government also made it harder to express provocative or anti-government views. Well after the strike-boycott had ended, groups involved in anti-imperialist movements were forbidden to place advertisements in local newspapers, while news stories from abroad that deal with imperialism, communism, or socialism were edited or even censored. Newspapers were required to pay a security fee. In 1927 the Printers and Publishers Ordinance was revamped to prevent attacks against the colonial administration. As with 1967, in some respects 1925–26 was not such a watershed after all.

Section II

Policies and Legacies

6
'Hong Kong headaches':
Policing the 1967 disturbances

*Georgina Sinclair**

In 1967, during some of the most serious incidents of civil disorder in Hong Kong, David Bonavia noted in the *Times* that '[t]he Hong Kong police have emerged from the recent disturbances as one of the world's most formidable paramilitary forces. Denounced as fascists by the Chinese communists their prestige both here and abroad is riding high on their victory over Maoist revolutionary tactics last month.'[1] Certainly by the 1960s, the Hong Kong Police (HKP) had acquired a reputation amongst police forces worldwide as a 'Class A' constabulary. Following the 1956 disturbances, it had improved its public and riot control tactics to deal effectively with the events of 1966 and 1967.

The HKP was set up in the mould of a British 'colonial' police force as distinct from its 'English' counterparts: the Metropolitan Police and the county constabularies. Both models of policing have over time contributed to the notion of a *British* policing system, the starting point originating in the 1780–1850 period. By the mid-nineteenth century, police forces, as understood in the modern sense, were widespread, and public order responsibility had been transferred from the army to the police. Sir Robert Peel who was both chief secretary for Ireland (1812–18) and home secretary in Britain (1822–27 and 1828–30) developed two new operational models. In Ireland, where the maintenance of order was considered a priority, Peel created a police force along military lines. The Irish Constabulary that was subsequently established in 1836 had greater similarities with the 'continental' models found in Western Europe than with Peel's other creation, the 'new' and theoretically unarmed Metropolitan Police that had emerged in London in 1829.

In essence, the colonial style of policing which developed throughout the nineteenth century was more akin to a gendarmerie: armed police officers who lived in barracks, separated from the local community, whose policing procedures relied upon discipline and drill, coercion rather more than consent. The structure

---

* I am indebted to Ted Eates for his helpful comments and general guidance during the preparation of this chapter.

of each police force within a colonial territory was divided between the gazetted ranks, or 'European' officer corps,[2] and the rank-and-file recruited from the local population. While these colonial police forces varied enormously from one colony to another, they *all* provided two essential functions. First and foremost, they were perceived as a key line of defence within a colony, and secondly, they upheld the traditionally held notion of law and order. Policing colonial peoples was facilitated by the widespread use of force to establish and maintain colonial rule. However, the British government made repeated claims in the post-Second World War period that the colonial police 'tradition' would over time allow for the 'conversion of these semi-military constabularies into civilian police forces, following in most essentials the British pattern of police organization, but still retaining certain continuing supplementary functions of a military character'.[3] This was reinforced by attempts to standardize colonial police forces during the early part of the twentieth century in terms of their organizational structure and police policy and procedures, resulting in the creation of the Colonial Police Service in 1936. Despite attempts to regulate and subsequently reform colonial police forces in line with Colonial Office views, they retained their own individual ethos and traditions, which were sharpened further during the turbulent post-war era of decolonization.

The HKP, however, projected an image that was unique amongst British 'colonial' police forces: a hybrid of the metropolitan/civil and colonial/paramilitary in terms of its policing policy and procedures. This stemmed from the geographical and historic situation of Hong Kong that theoretically necessitated civil policing, within Kowloon and Hong Kong Island, while within the area of the New Territories, the police had a greater 'paramilitary' role, supported by a large British garrison. When it came to policing the 1967 disturbances, the HKP relied partly on the back-up of the army and a longstanding police/military relationship. In theory, the police held primacy for law and order throughout Hong Kong. In practice, during this period, the army provided support for specific duties within the urban centres. Within the rural areas of the New Territories, and specifically along the border with China, the HKP were forced to concede primacy on occasion. This chapter considers the role of the HKP during the Double Tenth riots in 1956 and explores how it evolved before and during the 1967 disturbances within the police/military framework. In line with the traditions of colonial policing through the British Empire, the HKP converted to colonial rather than civil police practices at times of crises.

Hong Kong police traditions

The HKP was formed on 30 April 1841, becoming official on 1 May 1844.[4] At this point the Royal Navy was relieved of its policing duties and a Water Police (later to become known as the Marine Police: the 'China Squadron') was set up as a permanent Hong Kong-based branch of the Navy. By 1869 a Water Police distinct from the HKP (or land police) was set up to patrol the islands and harbours and control piracy.[5]

Charles May became the first captain superintendent of police and it is clear that he intended to model the HKP along the lines of the Metropolitan Police.[6] While May failed to establish a police force along civil lines, owing to the disturbances taking place within the colony during the mid-nineteenth century, there began a tradition of close ties between the Metropolitan Police and the HKP, a contributing factor towards the emergence of a hybrid policing model. This continued until 1997, except for the war years when Hong Kong was occupied by the Japanese and its police force incarcerated.[7]

Yet, the HKP upheld the traditional colonial structure with an officer corps (made up essentially of European officers until the process of localization took place) and a rank-and-file recruited locally and from outside. This reflected a HKP tradition of using outsiders for certain specific duties: riot control, traffic, and the Royal Irish Constabulary concept of 'policing by strangers', whereby officers did not police their hometowns. Recruits were drawn initially from India and later from Weihaiwei, a British enclave on China's north coast. It seemed that the colonial government did not fully trust locally recruited officers to maintain security.[8] By the 1950s, the rank and file was split between the Hong Kong Chinese and a small contingency of around 1,000 Asian officers and recruits from Northern China. Both the Asian and Shandong Weihaiwei officers spoke little or no Punti, the local Cantonese dialect.[9] A tradition for recruiting outsiders was retained for some time with Pakistanis and Indians highly favoured by the European cohort. 'They were extremely good at dealing with drunken expatriate soldiers, for instance,' commented Ivan Scott, who served in the HKP as a gazetted officer from 1955–1987, 'because generally they were bigger than your average Chinese officer, tougher and stood their ground.'[10] Essentially though, this was more about retaining the colonial traditions of policing with an emphasis upon maintaining control of the local population until the later stages of colonial rule when policing by consent could potentially take place. This, of course, questions the type of police force that emerged in Hong Kong.

The earliest British historiography has pointed to two distinct models of policing: Peel's civil/metropolitan model that emerged in the guise of the New Police in 1829, and his slightly earlier paramilitary/Irish model. Yet, there has always been a considerable amount of overlapping between the two models both within Britain and throughout the Empire. The British government was theoretically more comfortable with a civil style of policing, seeking to export a 'British ethos' to the colonies, particularly as the era of decolonization took hold in the post-war years. However, the notion of transforming colonial style outfits into their civilian counterparts was fraught with difficulties at this time. In practice, colonial governments resorted to the paramilitary practices they knew best.[11] Essentially, this revolved around coercing rather than co-operating with the local population. However, this does provide a complete picture when it comes to examining models and concepts of Britishness within policing. The HKP displayed elements of both *colonial* and *civil* models of policing within the police practices undertaken.

For example, theoretically within the urban centres of Hong Kong and Kowloon, there was a greater attempt at civil policing and co-operation with local communities,[12] while in the New Territories, particularly on the border with China, colonial police practices were more in evidence. Part of this was about maintaining the status quo in a small area that was heavily populated with, as former commissioner Ted Eates noted, a 'big police force in a small area'.[13] As a port, Hong Kong's particular feature was one of a continual movement of people. It was also an important centre for migration and the colony suffered from overcrowding and the subsequent need to maintain public order. This entailed, for example, the regular removal of squatters, restriction and control of unlicensed street hawkers and strict enforcement of traffic regulations. While this could easily distance the public from the police, the HKP were keen to display a 'hearts and minds' attitude wherever possible to keep the peace.[14] By extension, this reinforced police legitimacy in the eyes of the public. 'Pressure policing' was how one officer referred to this type of policing, which saw a high ratio of uniformed officers on the streets of Hong Kong and Kowloon. Pressure policing meant that the HKP were typically well financed and thus well equipped in terms of weaponry, general transport and police equipment as compared to other colonial police forces.[15] Moreover, the HKP could rely on the presence of a constant army garrison that could be called out in aid of the civil power. Prior to this time, the HKP were forced to reassess their crowd and riot control tactics when serious disturbances broke out in 1956.

The 'Double Tenth' riots

The Double Tenth riots in 1956 were a watershed for the HKP, forcing a reappraisal of their crowd and riot control tactics. The level of public disturbances which occurred indicated that neither the riot squads nor the regular police were sufficiently equipped or trained to prevent widespread problems without the assistance of the army. As a result, a number of reforms, in terms of riot control methods, were introduced to the HKP which would give them international recognition.[16]

The 1956 disturbances occurred as the Nationalists prepared to celebrate the 45th anniversary of the 1911 Revolution to mark their loyalty to Chiang Kai-shek. On 10 October, the Nationalists had organized a large number of rallies and meetings with their flag flying, provocatively it would seem, throughout Hong Kong, Kowloon and the New Territories. The disturbances were triggered initially within the crowded resettlement estates of Kowloon, home to thousands of Chinese refugees. In Block G of an estate, a resettlement office worker began removing nationalist posters prompting a disturbance between the residents and officials. Many police officers have claimed that the Triads were behind moves to pit the nationalist versus communist elements of the general population against each other.[17] As a result, the situation in Kowloon literally exploded, turning into three days of bloody rioting which resulted in sixty-two people being killed and hundreds wounded.[18]

From the onset, the HKP had extreme difficulty in containing the crowd disturbances, principally owing to a shortage of riot squads and manpower.[19] By the afternoon of the first day, three hundred mobilized police officers were facing crowds of well over two thousand. Anthony Annieson who was in charge of a riot squad that day explained: 'We each had a three-foot long riot truncheon and rattan riot shield. Mr Guatt [the other European officer present] the NCOs [non-commissioned officers] and I had Colt .38 revolvers and some spare ammunition. We also had four C-tear gas grenades. Not a lot for dealing with a howling mob in excess, it was estimated, of 3000 people but enough possibly for a disciplined group of men to have a go at it!' The riot squads were unable to quell the rioting and violent attacks upon the police: 'They tore at us with clubs, knives, metal bars, spikes, and bamboo spears, we responded with truncheons, the rough edge of our riot helmets . . . Triad members . . . could be seen redoubling their efforts in the crowd, whipping them up and encouraging them to attack us.'[20] 'Triad gangsters set up roadblocks in many streets and stopped all cars. Drivers who were not flying Guomindang flags on their vehicles were offered a chance to buy a 50 cent flag for a $10 fee. . . . Any vehicle with a European couple inside was stopped.'[21] The Swiss consul Fritz Ernst and his wife Ursula, who were in a taxi, were set on fire. Though both were rescued, the driver and Mrs Ernst died as a result of their injuries. After an emergency meeting that day, the army was called out in aid of the civil power.

However, as events in Kowloon were slowly brought under control, the rioting spread northwards to the industrial centre of Tsuen Wan. On 11 October, Tsuen Wan flared into bloody disturbances where the 'outnumbered police were unable to stop the massacres'. The army was quickly dispatched to the area but not before 'scores' of people had been killed. While the official figures put the number dead at only six, it was widely suspected that political factions and Triad leaders had secretly hidden as many bodies as possible to prevent future recriminations. As politicians attempted to find a solution, the army and police went ahead and arrested more than 6,000 riot suspects, as Peter Schouten commented (then police inspector), 'to allow the bad hats to be recognised'. Acting on intelligence, CID arrested top Triad leaders — some were senior members of the Green Pang gang of Shanghai, many of whose members had been executed by the communists after their victory in China.[22]

In the post-mortem following the Double Tenth riots, it became clear that the police had to become more efficient in terms of their crowd and riot control capabilities. The 64-man, 8-section platoons were seen as outmoded and useless in modern Hong Kong. As a result, the Police Training Contingent (PTC) was set up in an old army camp near Fan Ling in the New Territories.

Chief Superintendent John Leese was given the task of reorganizing the riot platoons and Les Guyatt was promoted to become chief instructor. Peter Godber, who gained international notoriety in the 1970s when he was prosecuted for corruption, became the school's commandant. Leese came up with a leaner and meaner version of original riot squads, which would be 'fast, compact, well armed, very flexible, and sensibly structured so that no one section could ever again be sent into the kind of situation that we had faced in 1956 without appropriate armament'.[23] The two-month courses at PTC saw the creation of the Police Tactical Units (PTU), moving the concept of riot squad training onto a more formal footing. These self-contained mobile strike forces had an establishment of roughly fifty men in each company.

Within each PTU were Snatch Squads, responsible for going into a crowd to make arrests while members of the Tactical Unit held the line. From the late 1950s, every uniformed constable was expected to go through PTU training just once and to be available for call up into the Emergency Units (EUs), fifty to sixty-strong per district. The riot control capabilities of the HKP were strengthened; transport and communications used were improved.[24] This would be put to the test when it came to the management of the Star Ferry riots in 1966 and the 1967 disturbances.

The Star Ferry riots

The Kowloon disturbances — referred to locally as the Star Ferry riots — were not directly linked to either the Communist or pro-KMT movement. The problem was sparked by the ferry company's decision to increase second-class cross-harbour ferry fares. The disturbances occurred following a protestor, So Sau-chung, staging a hunger strike at the Star Ferry pier on 5 April 1966. Eates later described the events that followed as a 'storm in a teacup'. With 3,600 police officers and 1,167 operating within the PTUs, affected areas were brought under control quickly, contributing to the notion that the HKP had evolved from their disastrous experiences of 1956.[25] Nonetheless, one person was killed as a result of police fire and sixteen people injured and treated in public hospital, though the figure was thought to be much higher. There were 1,465 people arrested and 907 charged with various offences — 790 with breach of curfew.[26] Ten police casualties were reported but none[27] were detained in hospital. As a result, a report on the disturbances highlighted perceived weaknesses within PTU practice and the police/military communication channels.

The report stated clearly that a public disorder situation had flared, with the crowds becoming rapidly violent. Throughout the two days of rioting, the PTUs were able to contain the disturbances and to prevent their spread into the densely populated resettlement areas in the north of Kowloon, and subsequently within areas around Nathan Road. (The HKP had failed to do so during the Double Tenth riots.) At the same time, a decision was taken at the police/military headquarters to use firearms if 'lawful and justified', and to call out the 'troops in aid of the civil power'.[28] Eates explained that this was about responding promptly and efficiently to the rioting, described in the government report as 'profoundly disturbing . . . and full of menace', with violent incidents having taken place.[29] Yet, it emerged that the police had readily resorted to arrests — even if some of the demonstrations had been peaceful — and had used physical violence.[30] Certainly any police force will be accused of violence and brutality in the aftermath of civil disturbances. The point here is that the HKP were keen to prevent another 1956 situation from occurring and wanted to make full use of the PTC companies within the overall emergency structure. The report highlighted two specific areas: the size of an individual PTU should be smaller to allow for more units and the possibility of dealing with numerous smaller incidents throughout Kowloon and Hong Kong Island, and communication between the police/military headquarters and company commanders should be improved — with wireless use — to ensure swift response to ongoing events, benefiting This benefit the overall 'police presence' throughout the colony.[31] This fine-tuning would benefit the HKP and the police/military structure when it came to dealing with the 1967 disturbances.

The May disturbances

China's Cultural Revolution impacted directly upon Hong Kong, culminating in the 1967 disturbances. In Trench's secret report dated 25 July 1967, he claimed that the 'lessons of Macau had been learnt by the Communists in Hong Kong'; the aftermath of the Hong Kong Seamen's Union and Royal Interocean Line management dispute in March, and subsequently by April 'pro-Communist workers in a number of other companies began to put pressure on their management and a new spirit of militancy amongst the rank and file became obvious'.[32] Eates,[33] in a confidential report, put the 1967 disturbances down to the 'effects of the cultural revolution, and in particular the intense patriotism and the devotion to Chairman Mao Tse Tung and his teaching [which] were bound to spill over into Hong Kong'.[34] While the government had professed that it 'was not engaged in a "war" with the communists', the global Cold War context remained a prevailing factor.

The spark that ignited the disturbances came during a labour dispute in San Po Kong where workers at an artificial flower factory were in dispute with management in early May. Picketing workers with legitimate grievances were augmented in strength by outside demonstrators showing their support for communist China. Additional support came from other factory workers within the local vicinity. Many were reported simply as being curious onlookers.[35] While the dispute at San Po Kong was contained, these disturbances spread to north Kowloon and then quickly on to other areas. With the first fatality — a 14-year-old boy with head wounds found dead in Wong Tai Sin — and twenty people arrested in connection with the troubles appearing in South Kowloon Court on 16 May, the disturbances escalated into serious rioting and tension throughout many areas. By 23 May, a series of token strikes began in all public transport and utility companies. Trench noted that 'the battle is now one, on our part, to preserve public confidence in our ability to maintain control here . . . and on their part to break this confidence down and persuade or terrorise sufficient numbers into compliance with their commands'. As such, the rule of law would be applied in all cases; police leave was cancelled and all police units placed on standby.[36]

Accounts describing the events of 1967 point to the 'thin khaki line' (the HKP) and how they retained control of urban areas despite mounting police casualties. Emphasis has been placed on how police morale remained high and indeed was bolstered by public confidence in the forces of law and order and the fact that the police showed remarkable restraint during the early stages of the disturbances.[37] Certainly, the police continued to maintain a high profile in urban areas arguably as a result of successfully reinventing the PTUs, which were used alongside the divisional riot companies. Moreover, there were sufficient lulls in the disturbances during the entire period to allow the police to regroup and rest. Yet, there is also evidence that the police became demoralized temporarily, following incidents like Sha Tau Kok and the onset of a bombing campaign.[38] It was at these times that the role of the army took on increased importance.

The maintenance of law and order — internal security — remained the Hong Kong government's overriding priority coupled with the need to shore up defence and ensure that tensions with China did not escalate.[39] Weekly confidential priority reports from the commander-in-chief of the Far Eastern Forces (CINCFE) to the Ministry of Defence (MOD) for the seven-month period spanning from May to November 1967 placed Hong Kong at the top of the agenda. The reports typically differentiated between the urban *and* border areas with details of bomb s occurrences, strikes and border incidents. Reading these reports gives the impression that the police dealt efficiently with the incidents taking place within urban areas, though often through the use of force. Attempts at maintaining control also included 'newer' methods of crowd control. By the end of May, police riot squads were issued cameras and telephoto lenses to photograph all those taking part in 'illegal' gatherings. Yet, by the same token during the early stages of the disturbances, reports from the Hong Kong government were keen to illustrate the public support for the government, reflected, for example, in the contributions to the education fund for children of junior police officers, which had reached $400,000.[40] It appeared from the frequent reports that once a situation deteriorated in police eyes, it would be contained often through the use of curfew, after which the police could rest and regroup. Attempts at serious disturbances, however, occurred routinely with incitements to violence made with continuous broadcasting from the Bank of China, including 'kill Trench' and 'police turn your weapons' (i.e. against your officers)' [sic].

Trench believed the situation could only be contained through the maintenance of public confidence and police morale 'otherwise a landslide could quickly follow'.[41] Police morale would improve with the arrival of the commando carrier, HMS *Bulwark,* with forty Royal Marines commandos. Her arrival ship, 'might be represented by Peking as saber-rattling' but that would be worth the risk in order to improve police morale.[42] This was in line with Plan Outlet Sea which had recommended that Hong Kong should be reinforced by either infantry or commando units.[43]

Overall, the constant shift in police morale seems to have been of greater concern to Trench than the police commissioner throughout this period. Trench was particularly affected by public opinion 'from the top down' and was always interested in the countless reports of the public coming out in support of the police by, for example, bringing food and provisions into the police stations to ensure that officers had food and drink. Essentially, it was felt that many people 'didn't want Hong Kong to fall and were frightened of the concept of Communist China'.[44] Clearly, the HKP reacted negatively to comments made in the leftist press about their handling of the riots, however close to the truth this may have been. Repeated demands were made by Beijing to the FCO about stopping the police attacks on Chinese citizens of 'armed troops, policemen and riot policemen attacking with clubs, riot guns and tear bombs . . .'[45] Indeed, police and riot squads were accused of carrying out 'extreme Fascist atrocities in persecuting our patriotic compatriots . . .'[46] Police work during the 1967 disturbances revolved around dealing with chargeable offences which included riot, unlawful assembly, breaking the curfew, assault, common assault and affray, and the most common during this period was 'riot' control. By mid-July, the HKP were said to have disrupted trade union activities to the point where they were no longer functioning effectively.[47]

When a police force maintains order in a manner perceived by the general public as legitimate (often because the legislation is in place for this to occur), police morale typically will stiffen. The question arises as to the manner in which order was maintained in 1967 and how this was perceived by the general public. Despite Trench's protestations that 'the Hong Kong police have shown great restraint in carrying out their responsibilities and have used the minimum force',[48] paramilitary policing was glossed over with a 'hearts and minds' approach and the added bonus of an army garrison in situ. Generally, the HKP could rely on the military's presence when dispersing crowd disturbances or operating a cordon, sweep and search. Combined police/military operations like the 'spectacular' raid on 4 August, when police and military launched search parties — airlifted onto 27-storey 'communist-owned' buildings by flights of Wessex helicopters from the British naval carrier HMS *Hermes* — did much to bolster police morale and to offer a guarantee that the Hong Kong government remained committed to containing the overall situation.[49]

Yet, the Beijing government repeatedly denounced police action as 'persecution and suppression and speaks of hostile measures against China in Hong Kong'.[50] This period saw the police's reputation taking a battering with rumours spreading of brutality.[51] There were the occasional reports of Chinese police officers being charged with offences including inflicting grievous bodily harm.[52] Police morale was further dampened when a more violent phase began with the Sha Tau Kok incident on 8 July. At this point, the disturbances shifted up a gear when the bombing campaign beginning in earnest on 10 July, the police becoming the principal targets. By the end of September 1967, the police/military headquarters had noted a total of 588 'genuine' bombs leaving 6 people dead and 168 injured.[53] There were also other numerous 'hoax' bombs that had to be investigated. At the time, the HKP had only two bomb disposal experts: Norman 'Bomber' Hill and Fred Ewins, and relied upon constant army backup.[54]

The Hong Kong police/military agenda

Britain's post-war era of decolonization provided the backdrop for police and military relations to develop into a cohesive command and operational structure. Theoretically, civil-military relations depended upon their being a balanced distribution of political power between the two, which could in practice shift according to a given situation. Both institutions operated within the legitimate authority of the state. Yet, this necessitated high levels of professionalism from both parties and a realization of the limits of their professional competences particularly when it came to the use of force.[55] By 1967, the British army had modified its counter-insurgency military tactics following a series of small colonial wars — starting in Ireland in 1919 and moving on throughout the long era of decolonization. The army had 'learnt' how to co-operate with the police and civil administrators within situations of unrest and operated reasonably comfortably within a joint command and operational framework. From their low point at Amritsar, the army was perfecting its doctrine of minimum force whereby the concept of civil unrest was disentangled from a 'war' situation. By minimum force, the army (and indeed the police) considered that the notion of restraint could be applied and force was used in a 'selective' manner. The principle of minimum force set limits within which the police and military had to work; this in turn exerted impact upon the management of violence.[56]

In Hong Kong, there had always been an historic precedent for a civil-police-military network. The army, theoretically, was in place to 'support the civil administration and the police in the maintenance of law and order within the colony and its frontiers'.[57] Historically, military forces had been garrisoned in the colony to assist the Hong Kong government in maintaining internal security and control of the frontier and importantly to identify 'aggressors'. In May 1967 there were approximately 4,000 British troops, 5,000 Gurkhas and 1,300 locally recruited soldiers garrisoned in Hong Kong, as well as a small naval and RAF contingent. It was clear that Hong Kong remained a valuable centre not only from a strategic perspective, but also in terms of its intelligence communications: Government Communications Headquarters (GCHQ) overseas station, the Secret Intelligence Service (MI6) intelligence base, police special branch and US intelligence staff.[58] During the 1967 disturbances, police primacy was on occasion called into question and the police/military boundaries became blurred. Yet, the military forces in Hong Kong (both regular and volunteer) were charged with an internal security role.

The basis of the working arrangement between the police and the military was set out in a joint directive on the command of security forces, and, in the

HKP Emergency Manual. Even by 1967, the structure was described by the former commissioner of police as 'fairly primitive'. Police/military headquarters (known as 'Colony' police/military) was stationed in Boundary Street, then the HKP Headquarters (HK) with three district centres: Hong Kong Island (Central Police Station); Kowloon (District Police Headquarters) and the New Territories (Yuen Long); each manned by a battalion commander (typically a lieutenant colonel) and an assistant police commissioner. Each centre reported to the joint security committee and to the colonial government. In theory, the principles upon which joint action was based and the steps to be taken when a threat to internal security was perceived were as follows: arrangements were made between police and military commanders for a joint police/military operations room to be set up and for the army to be in a state of readiness.[59] (This was based on a mutual arrangement between the police and military commanders and did not require higher authority.) The commissioner of police would then ask the governor to request that the army be called out in aid of the civil power. Once the armed forces had been called out, the governor, the police and military forces worked in liaison under a joint headquarters' command. Throughout the operation, the HKP remained *primarily* responsible for the maintenance of law and order *unless* a formal handover to the army was necessitated, for example, in the case of martial law being declared. At this point, the military commander of the British forces in Hong Kong (CBF) would assume overall command.[60] Traditionally, the CBF had to be 'readily available to advise on all questions bearing on the emergency . . .'[61] By 1966 discussions were even underway to formalize the notion of a unified command in Hong Kong, with Lt. General Sir John Worseley being appointed to the post in May 1967.[62]

Regarding longer-term security arrangements, a 'dormant commission' had initially been drawn up in 1947 and then reshaped in June 1951 amid the ongoing war in Korea. This accorded the CBF in Hong Kong with overall civil and military command in the case of an extreme emergency were the governor be forced to leave the colony. Importantly though, emphasis was placed on the 'civil police' having primacy with the army 'assisting as necessary'.[63] Yet, this was more about theoretical arrangements because, if the police failed to adequately contain a situation, the army would, practically speaking, assume 'primacy' at that moment in time. By May 1967, Special Branch reports were warning that Chinese militia activity on the border could 'preoccupy the attention' of the British military to the extent that they would be unable to support the HKP in the case of civil disturbances.[64]

In partial response to the previous year, the numbers of HKP officers rose by 387 to 11,383 in 1967. The Hong Kong Auxiliary Police Force (volunteers for emergency duty) had a total strength of 1,600.[65] Both the army and the police force had always been included in the plans for the security of the colony, despite concerns that the local volunteer police and army forces (auxiliary) might not perform well in internal security operations. Typically, the auxiliary Hong Kong regiment was needed for border duties and was dependent upon its ability to 'get there in time'. Yet, because of the severe limitations perceived, the auxiliary forces, even if they were augmented, were not capable of assuming the roles of the British forces in the security of the colony. For this reason, increasing the garrison strength with the regular British army was seen as key.[66] With the ongoing disturbances, military reinforcements were requested. These included an additional Gurkha battalion, a troop of Life Guards on secondment from Malaysia, members of the Army Information Team on a six-month tour from Aden and naval and air force backup.[67]

By September 1967, the Hong Kong garrison stood at '7 2/3' major units with consideration given as to whether another British battalion should be sent out. Prior to this period, the commander-in-chief of the Far Eastern Forces, Air Chief Marshal Grandy, had been convinced that a garrison of '6 2/3' was sufficient to meet any internal security threat in parallel with a naval presence and for an air force staging post and signal and radar station. Though linked to this was the view that disturbances could flare up within a very short space of time as the riots of '1958 [sic] and Easter 1966 had shown'.[68] This had been agreed in the 1966 Defence Review along with the colonial secretary suggestions of 'a few coastal minesweepers but no aircraft'. Prevailing thought reasoned that the Hong Kong government could meet a defence budget of approximately £5.5 million, a defence contribution to Britain of £1.5 million annually and defence works contribution of £6 million over six years beginning in 1966.[69] The shifting garrison strength was part of a much wider survey undertaken by the Hong Kong Committee to consider its future. Any earlier plans to reduce the garrison to '5 2/3' units by 31 March 1968 had been 'put into cold storage for the time being owing to the danger of a leak'.[70]

'Bilateral border incidents'

Security around the border screen had always been of primary importance in terms of police/military command. The year 1967 saw an escalation in tensions on both sides of the border with several serious incidents that necessitated the army coming to the aid of the civil power. Moreover, while the HKP traditionally held primacy, the British government's unofficial line was that 'primary responsibility in this sector [border area] for security rests with the army'.[71]

With an escalation of public disorder events, security on the frontier 'screen' was tightened. Reports from this period describe the extent to which the British were aware of militia activity on the Chinese side of the border. By June 1967, the police were being regularly asked to 'reason' with crowds on both sides of the border, with an emphasis on showing restraint.[72] With minor incidents, for example, stone throwing, the burning of police effigies and posters of the Queen, the decision was taken to send in additional companies of police, and Gurkhas. They were specifically requested to shore up the perimeter fence and gates, particularly at Lo Wu and Shenzhen, and to make their presence felt while at the same time avoiding provocation. The Chinese, the police felt, were 'unwilling to control their own people'.[73] Rumours abounded at the time that the 'there was military support for confrontation by the Chinese government', which had provoked widespread demonstrations on both sides of the perimeter fencing.[74] Typically, police posts in this area were manned by one army officer, four soldiers, one police inspector, and seven constables.[75] Police and army concerns were that a 'most dangerous situation' had been triggered by a rise in border incursions by the 'hooligan element'.[76] Indeed, following the notorious incident at Sha Tau Kok, on 8 July until 26 July, forty-two border incidents were reported necessitating a police/military presence.[77]

An official and confidential FCO report on the events of 8 July at Sha Tau Kok concluded that following a build-up of hostilities in the area, there was a serious attack on the police post which led the police to open fire. The Rural Committee Office and the police post then came 'under heavy sniping and machine gun fire from Chinese militia'. By the time a detachment from the 1/10 Gurkha Rifles had arrived to relieve the police companies, five police officers had been killed and eleven wounded.[78] Yet, police officers who were present at the scene have argued that they saw the Chinese militia crossing the border and opening fire. The Sha Tau Kok incident was witnessed by Pedro Ching, then a PTU instructor at Fan Ling whose riot company was called out to the village. 'We simply were not prepared for machine gun fire,' recalled Ching, 'several officers were killed straight away but we were all pinned down behind our vehicles and could not rescue them. The Gurkhas were immediately dispatched, arriving in armoured vehicles and contained the situation.'[79] Ching also witnessed a similar attack at the border post of Ta Ku Ling where local farmers had not been able to prevent Chinese militia from setting up Bren gun emplacements on their land. Once again, the situation proved impossible for the police to contain within the support of a detachment of Gurkhas. Indeed, the army's role in containing and cordoning areas along the border screen usefully allowed the HKP to search for arms and ammunition and do 'police work'.

Following the border incidents in July 1967, the Commonwealth secretary asked the Ministry of Defence to consider ways in which military action might be taken on the border 'screen' to 'deter the Chinese' in view of considerations that 'violent attacks' would continue, however isolated. The Beijing government, meanwhile, 'accused' both the army and police of having repeatedly threatened local people with their 'pistols' in the build-up to the incident which had made matter worse.[80] Intelligence reports show that the HKP, with the assistance of the army, had been able to 'capture stocks of offensive weapons' despite resistance to police raids. Importantly, the Hong Kong government was keen to demonstrate that 'any exercise by British troops was for any purpose other than that of exercising control and maintaining law and order'. However, a future military strategy had been thought through by this stage to allow for a shoring-up of the British position in Hong Kong. This included the reinforcement of the garrison 'to maintain the confidence of both the police and civil population'; visits by navy and air force units; use of additional helicopters, and, continued 'R and R' visits by US service personnel on leave from Vietnam.[81] Despite this, occasional flare-ups continued along the border screen until late 1967. The abduction of two Chinese constables on 29 September and of Inspector Frank Knight at Man Kam on 14 October led to intense negotiations between Beijing, Hong Kong and London. In the event, Knight 'escaped captivity' on 20 November and the two constables were deported on 26 November.[82] A border agreement between both parties was signed in November 1967 which allowed for a number of bridge closures along the border and made an ex-gratia award of HK$75,000 to farmers living within the border area who had not been able to cultivate their crops.[83]

Conclusion

The HKP were essential players in following the government line on containment of the 1967 disturbances. Eates stated that 'the police did not loose control in the urban areas though were stretched at times . . . the presence of a body of troops was a good deterrent to disorder, even though they did not take action.'[84] However, the police/military network that lay behind was undoubtedly an important part of the overall law and order structure. In a quest for political settlement within the colony, the Hong Kong government needed to prevent the total breakdown of law and order. The presence of the military during police handling of a disturbance was increased police morale and by extension public confidence in the HKP. Although it was the police, in the first instance who were charged with preventing the unlawful use and spread of violence by the public — in other words 'holding the ring'. With the lessons learnt from the both the 1956 and 1966 riots — the police had vowed never to repeat those earlier mistakes — the HKP had perfected their crowd and riot control techniques. This came about through the use of highly trained PTUs coupled with an increase in the overall size of the force. The degree to which the police operated with restraint is questionable and the evidence suggests that greater use was made of paramilitary rather than civil styles of policing. This has suggested that pressure policing as a civil rather than colonial mechanism of policing was something of a myth. The HKP, in line with any colonial constabulary, projected an image of restraint and co-operation. The reality was that the police could rely on the PTUs, auxiliaries and, if necessary, the military. Certainly, policing the 1967 disturbances was different within rural areas. The border area saw both internal and external security issues reaching potential boiling point where the army assumed overall primacy, demonstrating the difference between the policing of rural and urban areas. Yet curiously on 9 June 1967, the colonial secretary, writing on the question of 'force levels' in Hong Kong noted that any decision to withdraw one major unit from Hong Kong should be 'shelved for the time being' though the matter would need to be reconsidered in the near future with agreement reached between the Defence and Commonwealth Offices. His suggestion was that by 1975/76 'Hong Kong might build up its police force to an extent that would make the Colony no longer dependent on a military garrison for the internal security task'.[85]

Certainly, in acquiring the prefix 'royal' in the aftermath of 1967, the HKP gained a reputation for excellence both at home and overseas particularly in terms of riot control tactics. The force was used as a testing ground for new riot equipment and subsequently exported its methods (particularly of riot control) back to Britain and elsewhere (e.g. the USA). One example would be in September 1981 when the Association of Chief Police Officers (APCO) in Britain decided that three forces with particular expertise in riot control tactics should be asked to share their experiences with the Metropolitan Police. Richard Quine, director of operations in the Royal Hong Kong Police (RHKP), was sent to London to present *the* 'paramilitary blueprint for suppressing rebellion by Chinese communists, indigenous trade unions or any else who had the nerve to take on the colonial power of the British abroad'.[86] (Another force present at that time was the Royal Ulster Constabulary.) One of Quine's recommendations was the creation of an elite police squad capable of dealing with all types of disorder, crowd control and riot suppression. Without media and public knowledge at the time, the Metropolitan Police took on board these recommendations wholeheartedly. At the same time, cross fertilization in terms of exchange of police officers was formalized through the setting up of what became known as 'Cop Swop' revolving around the idea of bringing localization to the RHKP. Chinese officers would spend a period of time in a UK police force (e.g. the Metropolitan, Sussex, Manchester, Northumberland Police), who would, in exchange, send UK officers to Hong Kong.[87] Though by this stage there was rising public discontent towards the question of corruption that existed within the administrative structures of Hong Kong. The corruption scandals of the 1970s would tarnish the fabled image of the Hong Kong Police amongst the general public that had for a short period of time during and after the 1967 disturbances held it in high esteem.

7
The banking and financial impact of the 1967 riots in Hong Kong[1]

Catherine R. Schenk

By 1967 Hong Kong had already established itself as an important international financial centre, but this status depended on confidence in the rule of law, the continuation of British sovereignty and relative political stability.[2] Beijing's acquiescence to British sovereignty in turn relied partly on the financial services that the colony provided for the Chinese Mainland. These fundamental elements in the continued prosperity of Hong Kong were all challenged during the riots of 1967. This chapter uses previously unpublished archival material from Hong Kong and London to assess the impact of the 1967 riots on Britain's view of Hong Kong's economic prospects, on the Hong Kong banking system, and to illuminate the role of mainland Chinese banks in Hong Kong. The analysis reveals that the economic impact of the 1967 crisis on the banking and financial system in Hong Kong was tightly intertwined with the role that Hong Kong played in the sterling area system as the second largest holder of overseas sterling in the world, as a major supplier of foreign exchange to mainland China, and as a nascent international banking centre. This created tensions between loyalty to the metropole and obligations to the Mainland at a time when confidence in British rule had already been undermined by the Defence Review of 1966 that forced Hong Kong to contribute significantly more to its defence costs. The impact on the banking system brought into question the activities of mainland Chinese banks in Hong Kong, but the resilience of the banking system as a whole to the crisis enhanced confidence in the colony's future, although the market share of the mainland banks declined steadily until the launch of the Open Door Policy.

The riots and Britain's view of Hong Kong's future[3]

The May disturbances came at a critical point in the political as well as economic relationship between the UK and Hong Kong. Britain had already completed the bulk of its decolonization programme, which left Hong Kong as an unusual territory destined for perpetual colonial status because of its position in the Cold

War between China and the West. Along with this realignment of Britain's global role, the London government was also committed to reducing the military reach of British forces both for economic and strategic reasons, and took the decision in the summer of 1966 to begin to withdraw forces from Southeast Asia. By this time Singapore and Malaysia were independent states so Britain's imperial obligation had ended, and once the confrontation with Indonesia was concluded in August 1966, the way was paved for withdrawal.

Complete withdrawal would leave Hong Kong as the only major site for the British military in the Far East. Total UK military expenditure there was estimated at only about £11 million in 1966–67 compared with £86 million in Singapore and Malaysia, but the London government sought to make savings on its overseas expenditure here also. Hong Kong's contribution to its defence had been increased from £1 million per annum to £1.5 million per annum in 1958. In 1964 the colonial government agreed to an additional programme of £6 million in expenditure over six years for capital works associated with the garrison, bringing the total to about £2.5 million per annum. They also reimbursed the UK government for military and naval land brought back into civilian use. However, the Ministry of Defence calculated that the cost of troops stationed in Hong Kong for internal security was about £5.5 million per annum and this fell well below Hong Kong's contribution.[4] In August 1966, the governor of Hong Kong was asked to meet the costs of internal security locally. The issue of greater expenditure on British forces by the colonial government was widely debated in Hong Kong and prompted accusations that Britain was abandoning its imperial obligations to a colony that was still burdened by low per capita incomes and resettlement commitments. For example, in the Legislative Council, Kan Yuet-Keung, chairman of the Bank of East Asia, argued that the opportunity cost of greater defence expenditure was lower social spending and that

> if the money were to be used for the further development of our social services, the resultant benefit, both to us and indirectly to Britain, would be far greater; for it would be in Britain's interest as well as our own that this colony continues to enjoy social stability.[5]

The strong resistance in Hong Kong to increasing its contribution led the Chancellor of the Exchequer James Callaghan to warn in October 1966 that 'the Hong Kong government would be prepared to take so little of the burden of the stationing of British troops in Hong Kong that it might become necessary to withdraw the troops as no longer militarily viable' and he asked for advice on Hong Kong's likely reaction and the economic impact on the UK.[6] This shows how strained the relations had become and that contingency planning had begun in London in the months before the riots.

In the end, London's firm commitment to cutting overseas expenditure forced Hong Kong's hand. The colonial secretary went out to Hong Kong and by early

December had agreement from the majority of the unofficial members of the Executive and Legislative Councils and the governor to meet the British demands. From April 1967 the colonial government would spend a total of about £5 million per annum on four units of the British garrison that could be claimed were for local defence. This amounted to nearly half of UK defence expenditure in the colony and was nearly five times the annual expenditure to date.[7] London also wanted to reduce the number of personnel by pulling out a major unit of soldiers, but was persuaded by the governor, with the Commonwealth secretary's support, not to take this step because it would adversely affect public sentiment at a time when the disturbances in Macao were reverberating in the colony.

Within the context of these strains in the London–Hong Kong relationship, the impact of the riots on the economic and political prospects for Hong Kong was a key part of the British and American assessment for the colony's future. Both the Americans and the British believed that the greatest threat was not immediate invasion, but the possibility that the People's Republic of China (PRC) would pursue a low level but sustained campaign to weaken Hong Kong's viability and Britain's political authority. This would ultimately allow the Chinese Communist Party (CCP) to rule there without direct military confrontation.

In these assessments, the events in Macao were considered a potential model for what might happen in Hong Kong although there were also crucial differences between the two cases. In July the Central Intelligence Agency (CIA) reported to the US president that Beijing was unlikely to provoke a war, but would rather 'erode the position of the Hong Kong authorities and thus prepare the ground for an effort by the local communist apparatus to assume de facto control over Hong Kong in a year or so — on the pattern of the Macao takeover last winter'.[8] However, the risks to Hong Kong were mitigated by the commercial and financial advantages that Hong Kong provided for China, which Macao did not share. As well as providing international banking services, China ran a rising trade surplus with Hong Kong from 1960 to 1967 and the colony was the source of about £875 million in sterling for China, amounting to one-third of China's foreign exchange earnings, which were particularly vital for grain imports.[9] The greatest immediate danger from the riots was to business confidence, on which Hong Kong's future prosperity and continued usefulness to China depended. The CIA concluded that '[w]e do not believe the loss of Hong Kong would be a serious psychological blow to Britain or to the Labor [sic] government'. There would be some emotional protest 'but most Britons would accept it philosophically as an inevitable part of the winding up of Empire to which all political parties long have been at least resigned'. They concluded that the British 'already have faced the fact that their position is militarily indefensible and that they can remain only so long as Peking sees their presence to its advantage'.[10]

The reaction in London seems to concur with this assessment. The Foreign Office believed that the PRC continued to see advantage in the colonial status of

Hong Kong and had no immediate plans to establish sovereignty.[11] The economic benefits of Hong Kong to the Mainland were stressed, both as a source of foreign exchange and because of the colony's 'valuable role in developing China's commercial relations with the Free World.'[12] Given his preoccupation with the health of the UK balance of payments, the chancellor of the exchequer asked for a fresh assessment of the implications of an economic breach between the UK and Hong Kong.[13] If all trade were severed, the Treasury concluded that the loss to UK exports would not be 'enormous — at most a few tens of millions — and the effect on the trade balance and our balance of payments smaller still'.[14] The possibility of imposing exchange controls on Hong Kong had already been considered (because of the free exchange market operating there) and it was concluded that there would be little advantage to the UK of doing so now. At the end of May, the cabinet was reassured that the situation was easing and that the Hong Kong government and police had handled the situation well. The Commonwealth secretary reported 'some indication that the mainland Communist leaders were concerned at the mishandling of the situation by the local Hong Kong Communists'. The foreign secretary reported that the UK representative in Shanghai had been effectively expelled and that he had considered expelling the New China News Agency from the UK but thought this might lead to further retaliation in China.[15]

Thus far, the reaction in London was sanguine but the escalation of hostilities in July prompted the prime minister to commission a report on 'the action which should be taken if our position in Hong Kong became untenable'.[16] A high level and secret ministerial committee, chaired by the chief secretary to the Treasury was set up to report to the Queen and prime minister.[17] The leadership of the committee emphasizes the importance of economic factors in Britain's assessment of Hong Kong's future. With the debacle in Macao in the forefront of their minds, ministers concluded that there should be a complete withdrawal of British sovereignty in the wake of coordinated Chinese aggression. Officials concurred that there was no prospect of useful negotiations with the Chinese and that contingency planning for evacuating Hong Kong should begin immediately.[18] Only Henry Jenkyns of the Department of Economic Affairs dissented. He recommended negotiating with China and envisaged sharing responsibility for Hong Kong during a transitional period rather than a 'hasty and chaotic withdrawal'. Drawing a distinction between the situation of Hong Kong compared to Macao, Jenkyns stressed that Britain's bargaining power included Hong Kong's sterling assets, the usefulness of Hong Kong to China for trade, and the possibility of an earlier surrender of leases and ceded territories before 1997. By exercising these negotiating strengths the UK might 'salvage what we could of lives, trade, relations with China over a generation or two, and something which seems to me to add up to self-respect over the longer rather than the shorter term'.[19] He was outvoted and on 24 July ministers tasked officials in the Treasury, Bank of England and Board of Trade to report on the financial implications of abandoning Hong Kong.

Given Hong Kong's large holdings of sterling (£364 million in May 1967) and the precarious state of the sterling exchange rate, a crucial part of the government's analysis was the threat to the value of the pound if this sterling was dumped on the market by Chinese occupiers. During the summer, the Treasury, Bank of England and Board of Trade concluded that Hong Kong's sterling assets could be frozen within twenty-four hours, so they did not pose a threat if they fell into Chinese hands. Indeed, the frozen balances 'might ultimately be used as a bargaining weapon in a settlement with a Chinese occupying authority'.[20] No fixed assets would be removable from Hong Kong, but capital flight was likely to ensue if the disturbances were prolonged. The report concluded that the Hong Kong government should be drawn into consultations about possible responses to capital flight if disturbances revived in the longer term. The Bank of England was particularly keen to speak to the financial secretary, J. J. Cowperthwaite, about the potential for a longer-term drain of capital if business confidence did not return, but the Treasury warned that 'it is vital, that absolutely no hint should be given to Mr. Cowperthwaite that we have been considering contingency plans for the event of an evacuation'.[21] In his meeting with the Bank of England in mid-September, Cowperthwaite claimed the tensions in Hong Kong had dissipated and dismissed long-term planning as inappropriate for Hong Kong's uncertain environment.[22]

As the crisis receded in the autumn, the momentum for contingency planning fell away. The Rogers Working Party returned to the longer term and concluded that the riots had shaken business confidence and therefore 'the greater likelihood may now be a gradual decline from now on'.[23] Further planning was constrained by the need for absolute secrecy since 'if any hint emerged that evacuation was being contemplated this would have the most grave effects on the confidence of the Hong Kong population and on the continued viability of the colony in face of Chinese pressure. These effects could well include damage to Hong Kong's economy and financial stability, which in turn could lead to a run down of her sterling balances.'[24] Note the continued stress on the vulnerability of sterling to unrest in Hong Kong. In September, ministers considered sending an extra battalion of military to Hong Kong to cover the Chinese New Year period, but the Ministry of Defence argued that the situation did not call for further action.[25] Active contingency planning was abandoned by the end of the year, although the special ministerial committee on Hong Kong's prospects continued to meet sporadically.

In sum, the riots in Hong Kong came at a time when the colony was viewed as an inconvenience in terms of Britain's overall imperial strategy. The disturbances prompted concern in London, mainly over the impact on Britain's trade and the sterling exchange rate, but the deliberations revealed equanimity to the abandonment of Hong Kong in the context of Britain's withdrawal 'East of Suez' and the contraction of Britain's imperial commitment.

Monetary impact

Figures 7.1 and 7.2 show the movement in some key banking and monetary data. Given Hong Kong's free exchange market, losses of political confidence in the colony generated a flight of capital as well as a rise in the demand for currency. The decline in deposits was greater than the increase in the note issue, which gives some measure of capital flight from the colony and a simple measure of monetary contraction of about 5.5 percent, which was particularly acute in July when China retaliated against the UK. Hong Kong-owned deposits in US banks doubled during 1967 to reach US$200 million although this was also influenced by the devaluation of sterling in November.[26]

In May/June 1967 capital flight took place, particularly through the free market in US dollars, leading to a brief surge in the US$ rate in Hong Kong as is shown in Figure 7.3. This was not unprecedented and was relatively short-lived.

The Financial Secretariat made estimates of the net money transferred in and out of the colony on a monthly basis based on movements in currency issue and bank balances, and these are presented in Table 7.1, which shows a net outflow for the year of HK$703 million. The estimates also show that the capital flight was not reversed so that the net outflow for the year as a whole was about the same as the net outflow for the three crisis months alone.

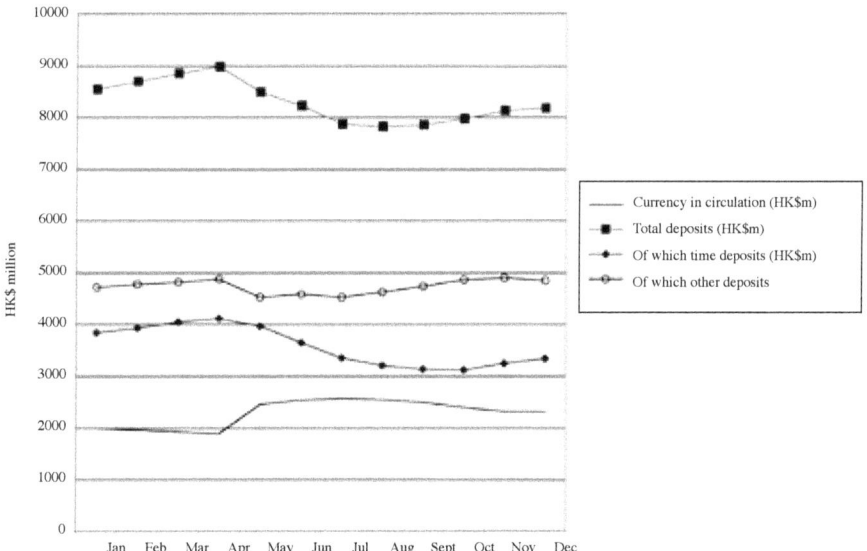

Source: TNA FCO59/442.

Figure 7.1 Monthly banking statistics for 1967

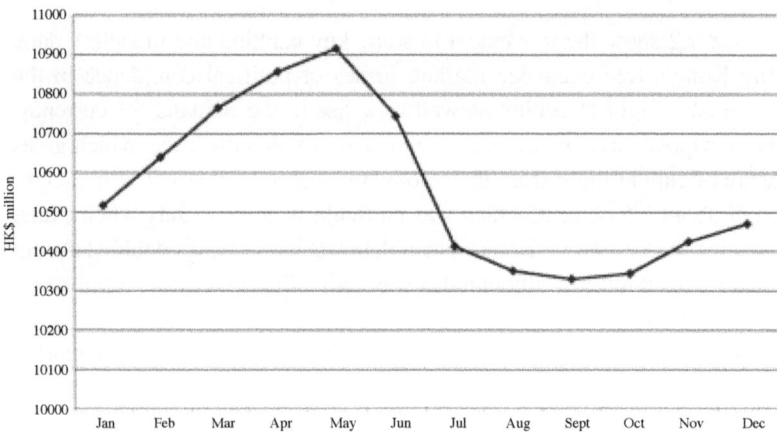

Figure 7.2 Deposits plus notes in circulation: 1967

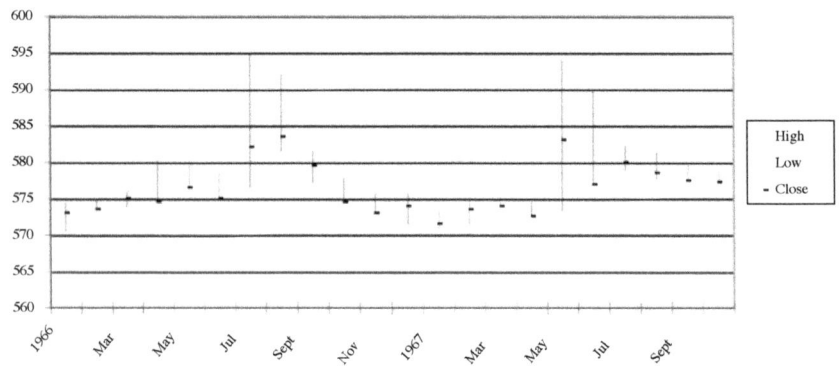

Figure 7.3 Free US$ TT market rate in Hong Kong 1966–October 1967 (HK$/US$100)

In contrast to capital flight through the US-dollar market, the riots also prompted a very brief surge in inward remittances from overseas Chinese back to Hong Kong, mainly through the Chartered Bank shown in Figure 7.4. The assistant financial secretary reported that 'my own guess is that Chinese in Malaya and Singapore, where there is a strong KMT element and incidentally many branches of the Chartered Bank, remitted passage funds for quick getaway to their friends and relatives in Hong Kong as soon as left-wing troubles began'.[27] If this is true, then they were reassured over the next few months as remittances fell well below their seasonal levels (the peak for remittances was usually at the start of the year coinciding with Chinese New Year).

Table 7.1

Net money transferred in and out of Hong Kong in 1967 (HK$m)

	IN	OUT
January	123.613	
February	64.071	
March	13.071	
April	52.931	
May		207.975
June		337.276
July		158.526
August	147.809	
September	70.115	
October	67.552	
November	304.720	
December	7.723	
NET		702.926

Source: HKRS 163-1-3275. Including transfers into foreign currency notes.

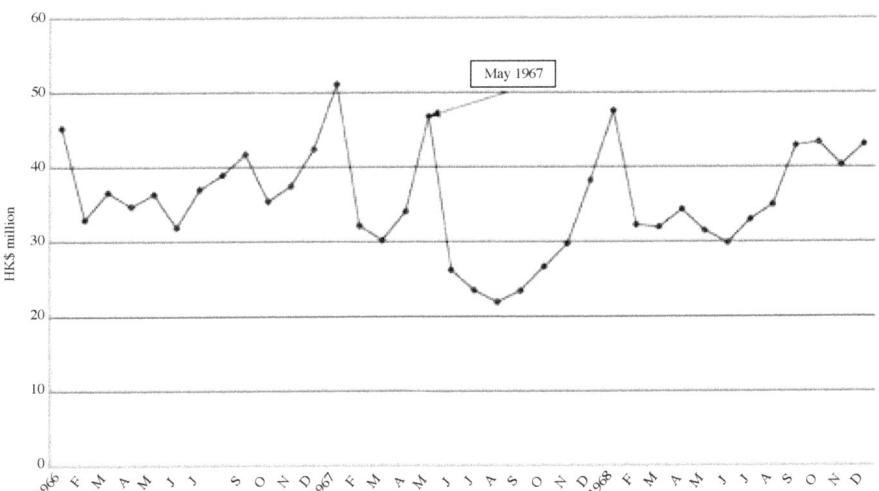

Figure 7.4 Overseas remittances to Hong Kong 1966–68

Data show identified remittance from overseas Chinese through authorized banks, Kwangtung Provincial Bank and the Post Office.

A more important result of the rise in demand for local currency was an emerging shortage of sterling in the colony. Since every Hong Kong dollar note issued had to be backed by an equal amount of sterling deposited in the government's Exchange Fund, the emergency note issue sparked a large demand for sterling by the HSBC. The security sterling market in London was closed by the chancellor of the exchequer on the eve of the crisis in April 1967, cutting off the main supply of sterling that the HSBC had used to meet the orders from the Bank of China, cover issue of extra Hong Kong dollar notes, and to maintain adequate reserves in London. This drove the Bank to the free market to buy US dollar, converting them to sterling, but this market had tightened up due to capital flight and hoarding.

The demand for cash due to the disturbances required an increase of HK$600 million (£37.5 million) in the local note issue from May to July (of which HK$80 million was issued in the first week of June). The HSBC negotiated a deal with the government that this emergency issue would be redeemed at par and so avoided the usual losses on the redemption of Certificates of Indebtedness. Although there were warnings of a monetary crisis, the flexibility of the system, which operated primarily through the HSBC, allowed the demand for cash to be met without threatening public confidence. Underlying these operations, however, were technical problems that profoundly affected Hong Kong's position.

As seen above, the economic contribution that Hong Kong made to the Mainland was a main argument that encouraged a sanguine attitude in London to the riots. The shortage of sterling prompted the HSBC to warn that it might not meet its obligations to sell sterling to the Bank of China. N. H. T. Bennett of the HSBC identified this as 'the most pressing problem that faced us and the Government at the moment' since if Hong Kong could not supply China with its required sterling, Hong Kong would be of 'no economic benefit to them' which would undermine Hong Kong's viability.[28] Sterling receipts from Hong Kong amounted to one-third of China's foreign exchange earnings and financed 30 to 40 percent of China's imports from 1964 to 1970.[29] Figure 7.5 shows the rapid increase in the amount of sterling sold to China in the run-up to 1967 and Figure 7.6 shows the monthly drop in sales during the summer of 1967.

The HSBC hoped to get support from the Bank of England and the British government to back the expanded note issue.[30] Two years earlier, during the 1965 banking crisis the Bank of England had pledged £20 million of support and actually flew in £5 million Bank of England notes to Hong Kong airport at the height of the crisis. Also in 1965, sterling was declared legal tender to forestall the monetary contraction from the banking crisis. In the end, the notes were not circulated and the publicity surrounding the arrival of the cash achieved its goal of easing panic, but the HSBC hoped a precedent had been set for UK support in case of monetary crisis. Although the Bank of England was asked to plan for a similar action in 1967, they initially declined. Instead, the Hong Kong government asked the HSBC to pledge their own British government securities as backing for the note issue, to

114 Catherine R. Schenk

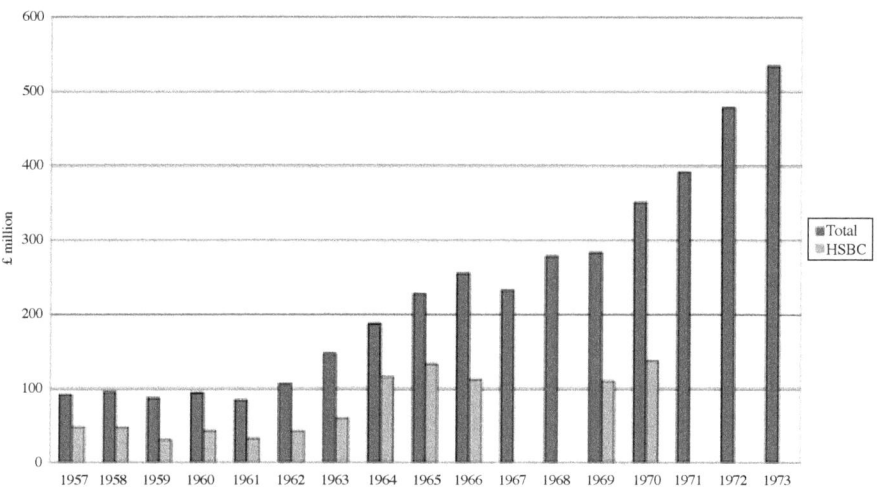

Source: 1957–67 HKRS163–1–2055, HKRS163–1–2600. The sources for the data for 1968–73 are explained in Leo Goodstadt, *Uneasy Partners* (Hong Kong: Hong Kong University Press, 2005), pp. 233–4. HSBC data: 1957–66 GHO201, 1967–70 GHO366, HSBC Group Archive.

Figure 7.5 Sterling sold to China against HK$ (£ million)

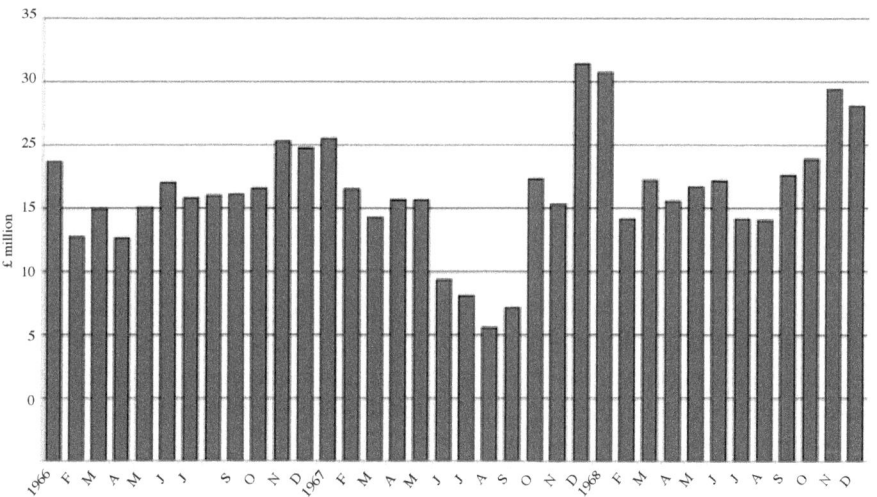

Source: HKRS 163–3–168.

Figure 7.6 Sales of sterling to PRC banks against HK$

which Knightly replied 'our securities were part of the bank's reserves as a whole and were not available to meet a crisis inflation of the Note Issue. I have always thought there was a trap attached to this Note Issue role of ours'.[31] The financial secretary, Sir John Cowperthwaite, happened to be in London and he took the opportunity (with the support of the Bank of England) to suggest that Hong Kong dollar deposits by banks could be used as cover for the note issue since this was legal under existing legislation, but a fiduciary issue was not in the end required.[32] Instead, support came from the Hong Kong government. At the end of June, they deposited £10 million for 'liquidity reasons' on seven-day deposit, thereby increasing the HSBC's London sterling account from £42 million to £52 million.[33]

Meanwhile, the use of public relations to cool depositors' panic was employed in ways similar to the 1965 bank runs. On 19 May the front page of the *China Mail* showed a photo of the manager of the HSBC in front of a pile of HK$20 million in cash with a quote that there was 'plenty more where this came from'.[34] The inference was that the bank was not likely to run out of cash and so dishonour depositors. Four days later the *South China Morning Post* reported on its back page that twenty cases of sterling notes had arrived from the UK by air. They were greeted by anti-riot police and escorted to central Hong Kong. Again, the exercise was aimed at stemming any fears of the liquidity of the banking system and so to ease the pressure of deposit withdrawals. Unlike the more recent case of the run on the Northern Rock in the UK in 2007, depositors appear to have been quickly reassured by this evidence of external support and the queues outside banks quickly disappeared. As the demand for notes eased off, the note issue did not need to be expanded much after the first week of June. Only a further £5 million worth of emergency issue was required, and in the second half of the year notes began to be redeemed so that by the end of 1967 a further HK$240 million (£15 million) were returned. HSBC was thus able to ride out the storm at the expense of their reserves in London with some transitional support from the Hong Kong government.

In summary, the defence review closely followed by the communist disturbances led to a reassessment of Britain's commitment to Hong Kong. Passing a substantial burden of the cost of local troops to Hong Kong raised hostility between Hong Kong and London on the eve of the riots. The disturbances then emphasized the fragility of Britain's tenure in Hong Kong and the possible loss of the colony was considered with some equanimity, although it was not in the end necessary. The financial consequences were not long-lasting; business confidence was soon restored and no monetary crisis ensued. There were, however, longer-term consequences for the Hong Kong banking system.

Impact of the riots on the banking system

As noted above, the political disturbances and the prospect of mainland intervention in Hong Kong led to a public rush for liquidity in the form of withdrawals of bank deposits for cash, which was hoarded or exchanged for gold and US dollars. On 19 May 1967 the *Cheng Wu Pao* newspaper reported that the HSBC Sheung Shui branch in the New Territories had opened its doors for only one to two people at a time from 9 a.m. in order to reduce the pace of withdrawals (and possibly to discourage people from waiting in queues). Depositors were later formed into groups of five to make withdrawals. Chartered Bank branches in Mong Kok were reported to have imposed similar restrictions.[35] The governor of Hong Kong advised London that these events were due to reports of an imminent invasion from the Mainland in the local left-wing press, but the panic was quickly eased partly by reassuring radio broadcasts to the public and the newspaper articles reported above. As a precaution, legislation to limit bank withdrawals was drafted but not in the end required.[36] The level of deposits continued to decrease across the board, but the rate was sustainable and no banks failed as a result of bank runs. Liquidity of the banking system dipped during the disturbances but never approached the low levels of the 1965 banking crisis, when many banks fell below 25 percent. Liquidity (liquid assets as a percent of deposits) of mainland-controlled banks fell 7 percent from 76 percent to 69 percent in May 1967, local banks' liquidity fell from 45 percent to 42 percent and foreign banks from 44 percent to 42 percent. These were all well in excess of the statutory 25 percent minimum liquidity. Nevertheless, the detail of the fall in bank deposits was considered a highly sensitive issue for business confidence in Hong Kong and the Banking Commissioner Leo Cole resisted publishing any deposit statistics throughout 1967 until they had recovered to their April 1967 level. In the end, this was not achieved until May 1968.[37]

Unlike deposits, the crisis had no discernable impact on the overall level of advances that banks made to borrowers. This was the result of a deliberate strategy led by the HSBC to retain confidence in the colony, and was linked to efforts to inhibit capital flight. On 26 May N. H. T. Bennett of HSBC noted that

> our own position is such that many of the advances on our books are tied so closely to the economy of the Colony that it is virtually impossible to restrict them or rather to reduce them to any degree. If in the present lull we detect any efforts on the part of borrowers to increase their facilities from us in order to remit funds out of the Colony, then this must be resisted . . . we must equally be alert for those industrialists whose facilities from us are already up to the limit and who may in the next few months attempt to siphon off profits from their business and remit these abroad rather than repay their indebtedness to the bank.[38]

In August 1967 business opinion was further strengthened when the government agreed to take up 25 percent of the cost of the cross-harbour tunnel, thus resolving uncertainty about the funding of the project. In October, representatives of HSBC and Hang Seng made public announcements in the local press that they were carrying on 'business as usual' in their lending in order to reassure business confidence.[39]

Table 7.2 shows that while overall advances to customers in Hong Kong declined less than 1.5 percent during 1967, mainland banks and foreign banks did retract their lending. This was offset by a six-percent increase in advances by the HSBC which was by far the largest single lender in Hong Kong and indeed exceeded the value of advances by all the local banks combined. All the decline in advances took place from July 1967 after the Chinese retaliation, rather than in May when the disturbances in Hong Kong began. The data also show that the Chartered Bank followed the general pattern for foreign banks despite its greater commitment to the colony as an issuer of local currency notes.

Table 7.2
Percent change in bank advances, December 1966–December 1967

Local	−1.12061
Mainland	−13.584
HSBC	6.075007
Chartered Banks	−5.47286
Other Foreign	−5.64099
TOTAL	−1.35187

Source: HKRS 163–1–3274, 163–1–3275.

Figure 7.7 shows that lending rates charged by HSBC rose during 1967, but were not increased during the crisis, indeed the Best Lending Rate fell by 0.5 percent and only increased in November in response to the devaluation of sterling. The interbank lending rate spread increased during 1967 but the seasonal New Year demand for cash early in the year had a bigger short-term impact than the riots.

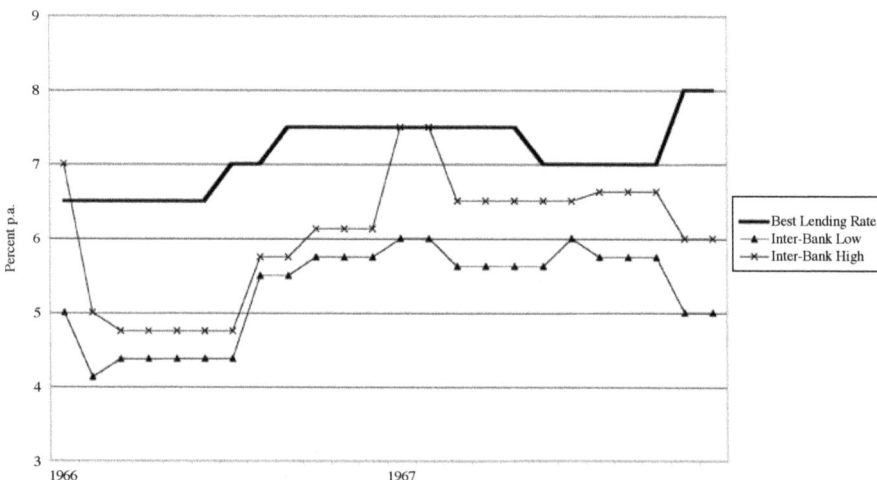

Figure 7.7 Hong Kong lending rates: Monthly 1966–67

Table 7.3
Value of bank deposits (HK$ '000s)

	1966	1967	% Change
Local banks	2295.8	2446.2	6.6
Unincorporated (4) banks	4.0	3.6	−10.9
HSBC	3133.2	2725.8	−13.0
Foreign banks	2351.2	1969.5	−16.2
PRC-controlled banks	1309.5	1016.8	−22.4

Table 7.3 shows that overall, bank deposits were 10 percent lower at the end of 1967 compared with the end of 1966. The largest withdrawals were from mainland-controlled banks, which fell 22 percent over the year. Conversely, there was a net increase in the bank deposits held at local Hong Kong-controlled Chinese banks.

Why should depositors be more concerned about the prospects for mainland banks? These banks were well known to have much higher liquidity ratios than local Chinese banks. Indeed, the local banks had been exposed as fragile and poorly managed in a major banking crisis in February to April 1965, merely two years earlier. Several local banks had failed during this crisis, leaving their depositors with substantial losses. As part of the crisis, Hang Seng Bank, the largest locally registered Hong Kong Chinese bank had to be taken over by HSBC to save it from failing. Mainland-controlled banks did not suffer from the governance problems that plagued local banks, they were not engaged in speculative lending to the property and stock markets, nor were they involved in insider lending to local business groups in ways that weakened the asset structure of many local banks. The rush out of the mainland banks was more logically related to depositors' judgement of the vulnerability of these deposits to political pressures (such as seizure by the mainland government or forced closure by the Hong Kong government) and to the perceived weakness of their assets given the growing social and political turmoil on the Mainland.

Figure 7.8 shows the percentage changes in each month, confirming that the local banks were hit severely in the first month but then began to recover their deposits by August. The HSBC began to recover the following month but the Chinese mainland banks and foreign banks continued to lose their deposit base. The panic peaked for foreign and mainland banks during July, when the British consulate was sacked in Beijing.

Figure 7.9 allows some greater texture to interpret depositors' behaviour and attitudes to various category of bank. The data show the level of deposits in November 1967 compared with April 1967. This shows that although the immediate crisis had receded, depositors continued to be less enthusiastic about time deposits, preferring to keep their money in more liquid form. While overall, by November the

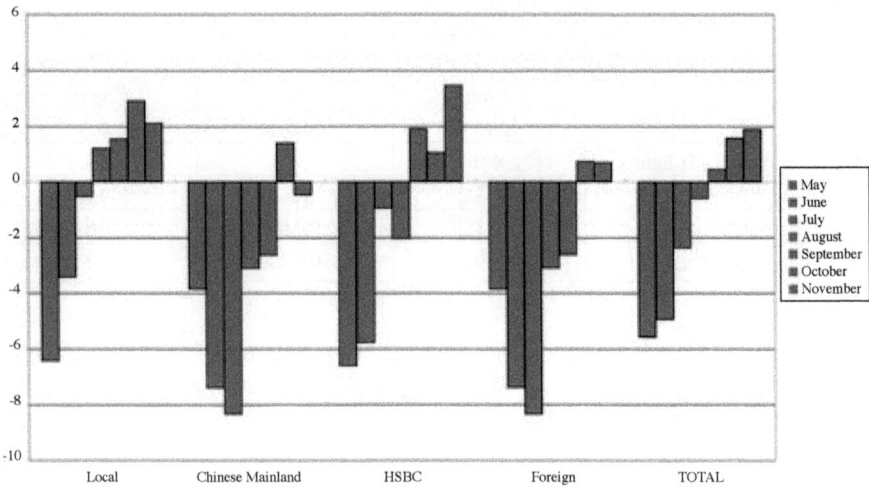

Figure 7.8 April–November 1967: Monthly changes in deposits (percent)

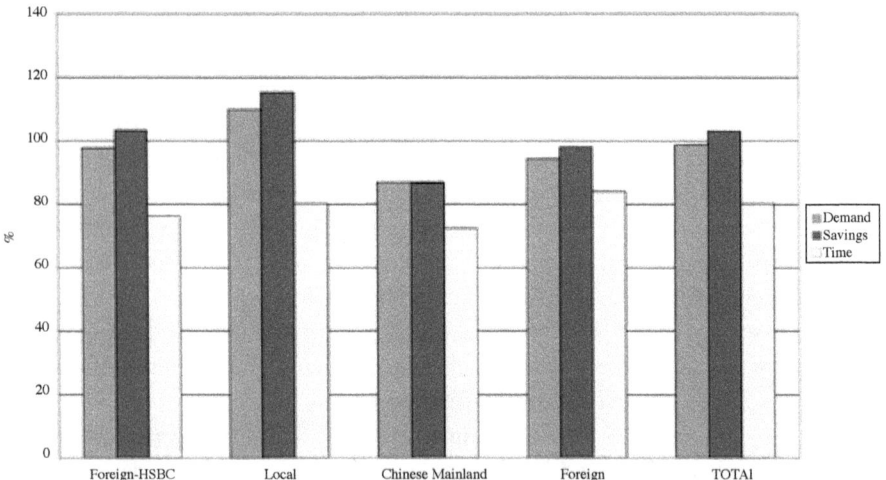

Figure 7.9 Value of deposits in November 1967 as percent of April value by type of deposit and type of bank

level of savings accounts and demand deposits had recovered for foreign banks and the HSBC, this was not true for the mainland Chinese banks. What the data suggest is a shift for short-term deposits from banks identified as mainland-controlled to local, Hong Kong Chinese-controlled banks.

With regard to local banks, there is no statistical relationship between the size of the bank (as measured by total deposits) and the fall in deposits in May 1967. Nevertheless, the three local banks that lost more than 10 percent of their deposits in this month were among the smallest four banks by size of deposit. On the other hand, the three banks that gained deposits during this month of crisis were also relatively small banks. When deposits recovered from August, there is no evidence that larger banks were taking in deposits from smaller banks. Figure 7.10 shows the range of performance by the twenty-seven local banks in May. By September 1967, only five banks had not recovered to hold at least 80 percent of the deposits they had before the crisis. Yau Yue Commercial bank stood out since their deposits were still only 43 percent of their April level by this time, but they had been under the control of HSBC since September 1966 when the bank was deemed insolvent due to bad loans and their deposits had been falling ever since and continued to do so through 1967 until the bank was closed in 1969.[40] Two of the smaller local banks even managed to increase their deposits by over a third from April to September.

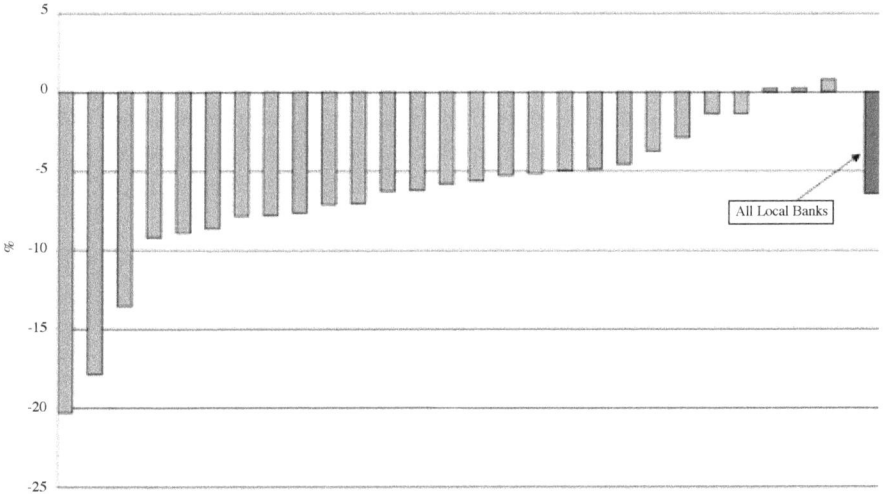

Figure 7.10 Percent change in deposits of local banks during May 1987

The analysis so far suggests that the activities and performance of the mainland-controlled banks are of particular interest during this period. As the Hong Kong administration noted, 'The Bank of China is quite open about the political affiliations of the [mainland controlled] banks' so they were clearly categorized by the public.[41] Table 7.4 shows that among all the nationalities of banks that owned property in Hong Kong, the PRC banks' assets were the most valuable, even ahead of British banks. They had a strong physical as well as financial presence in the colony that was linked to their political allegiance.

Table 7.4
Value of bank premises by nationality of bank, October 1969

Banks incorporated in	Value of premises HK$m
People's Republic of China	55.2
United Kingdom	43.3
USA	4.9
Southeast Asia	4.5
EEC	2.1
India	0.5

Source: GCM Lupton, Deputy Economic Secretary to Dr EF Gerlach, OECD Development Department, Paris, 29 October 1969. HKRS163/1/3277. Not all banks owned their premises; the Japanese, German, Korean, Philippine and Pakistani banks operated in rented

In 1967, there were twelve banks controlled by the PRC, many with multiple branches in the colony. They included the Bank of China, other banks registered on the Mainland, and banks registered in Hong Kong but known to be controlled by the PRC. The Bank of China was undoubtedly the most politically influential PRC bank in Hong Kong, but Nanyang Commercial Bank (locally registered in Hong Kong) had the largest local deposits and advances. Figure 7.11 shows the growth in total assets and deposits of Nanyang Commercial Bank from its published balance sheets. The rate of growth was interrupted by the communist disturbances in Hong Kong in the spring of 1967 that affected all PRC banks adversely, and it took several years to recover its position.

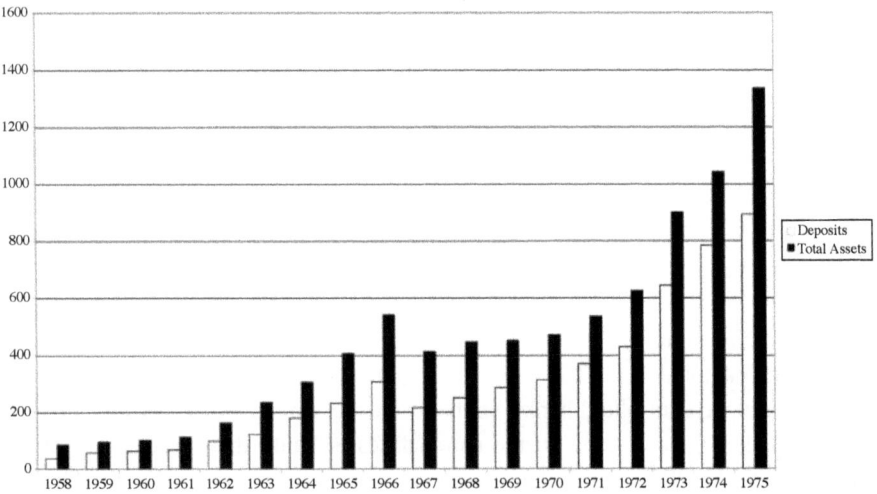

Source: Nanyang Commercial Bank annual reports

Figure 7.11 Nanyang Commercial Bank deposits and total assets (HK$ million)

Based on archival data, Figure 7.12 shows the rise in deposits and advances for the PRC banks in Hong Kong from 1964 to 1972. After growing quickly at the beginning of this period, deposits and advances declined in 1967. It took two years for the mainland banks to recover the 1966 level of deposits, but the rate of increase then rose and by the end of 1972 mainland banks in Hong Kong held HK$2 billion (US$354 million) of deposits. The fastest growing banks after 1967 in terms of deposits were Sin Hua Trust and Kwangtung Provincial bank, both of which (along with Nanyang Commercial) had significant branch networks in the colony. In both 1964 and in 1972 these three banks accounted for over 40 percent of total mainland banks' deposits in Hong Kong, although their share dipped below 40 percent in the intervening years. In terms of local advances, Sin Hua Trust and National Commercial Bank together accounted for about one-third of advances by mainland banks.

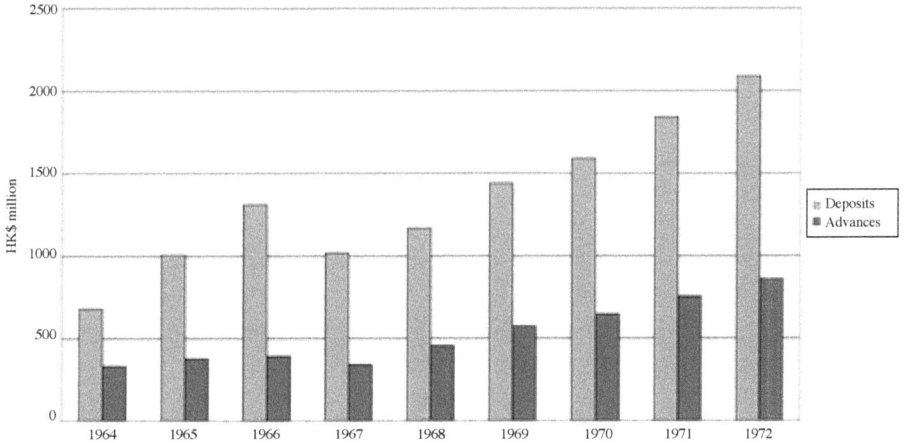

Figure 7.12 Mainland Chinese-controlled banks in Hong Kong

During the period April to September 1967, a total of HK$306 million was withdrawn from PRC-controlled banks. Within this overall picture of decline, however, Table 7.5 shows that there was a variety of experience. In the first month, during May 1967, the Bank of China's deposits actually increased by HK$7.5 million (3.3 percent) while every other mainland bank lost deposits (the loss to the group as a whole was 4 percent or HK$51.5 million). The Bank of China also suffered the least decline overall in deposits from April to September 1967 (12 percent compared with 23 percent for the group as a whole, with an average decline of 25 percent).

Table 7.5

Percent change in deposits of mainland-controlled banks: April to September 1967

Bank of China	−12.5798
Bank of Communications	−19.7427
Kwangtung Provincial Bank	−19.9599
China and South Sea Bank	−23.1397
Nanyang Commercial Bank	−24.1788
Sin Hua Trust, Savings and Commercial Bank	−24.8661
Po Sang Bank	−26.9285
Kincheng Banking Corp	−27.2306
Hua Chiao Commercial Bank	−28.1598
Yien Yieh Commercial Bank	−30.2031
China State Bank	−32.6053
National Commercial Bank	−34.4146
TOTAL Mainland Banks	−23.0807
AVERAGE Mainland Banks	−25.3341

Source: HKRS163-1-3275. Data are for 'true deposits' i.e. excluding interbank deposits.

Figure 7.13 shows that although the value of deposits recovered from late 1968, the mainland banks did not keep pace with the rapid growth of Hong Kong banking in subsequent years. After peaking in 1966 at 14 percent before the May riots, the share of deposits held in mainland-controlled banks declined steadily to below 9 percent by the end of 1972.[42] It appears that after making significant initial progress, confidence among depositors in the mainland-controlled banks never recovered from the disruptions of 1967 and the ensuing political strife on the Mainland. By 1981, however, after the Open Door policy was in place, mainland-controlled banks restored their share of deposits to 14 percent and increased their share of advances to the historically high level of 15 percent.[43]

Figure 7.14 shows the decline in more detail using monthly data, showing that the slower growth rate was due to a stagnation in the value of time deposits, which were the most severely affected in 1967. While other demand deposits grew from mid-1970, savings accounts grew more quickly and steadily. Still, these rates of increase did not keep pace with the overall growth of the Hong Kong banking system in these boom years.

It was suggested above that confidence in these banks should reflect confidence in their assets, so what were the mainland-controlled banks doing with the funds collected in Hong Kong? The ratio of advances to deposits was much lower for the mainland banks than for any other category of bank, which should have enhanced

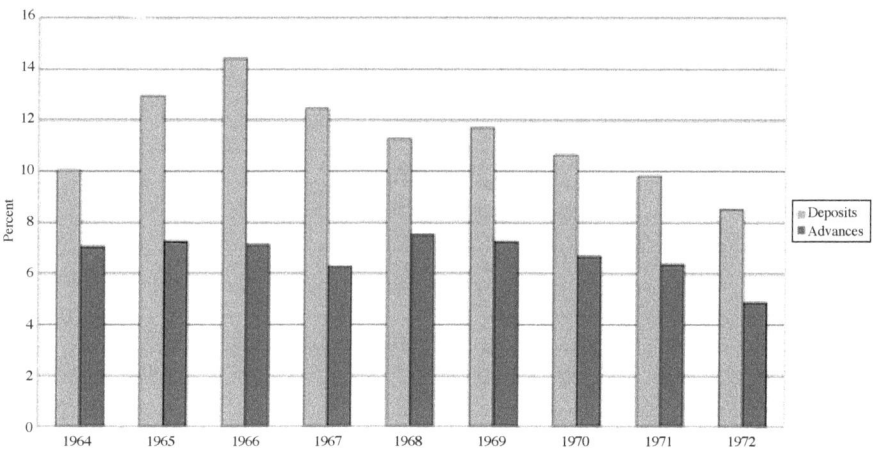

Figure 7.13 PRC banks in Hong Kong: Market share

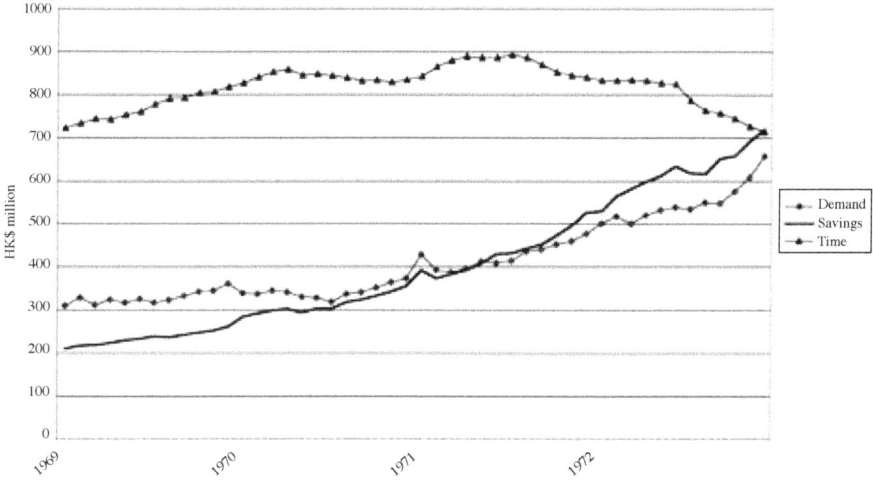

Source: HKRS166-9-371.

Figure 7.14 Mainland Chinese bank deposits

confidence in the reliability of deposits. However, dangers arose from the nature of the resulting high levels of liquidity. In January 1966, 80 percent of the overall liquidity of Chinese mainland banks was held overseas in bank balances and money at call. The other 20 percent was held in cash and net bank balances in Hong Kong. About 80 percent of these overseas liquid assets were held in China and the rest mainly in London.[44] Net claims on the mainland amounted to about 38 percent of the

Table 7.6
Hong Kong banks' claims and liabilities to the Mainland, 1967 (HKD million)

	Claims	
	PRC	Other Banks
April 1967	745.908	2.236
June 1967	721.886	1.757
October 1967	709.538	1.901
November 1967	708.53	1.792
Jan 1968	799.098	2.159
	Liabilities	
	PRC	Other Banks
April 1967	137.371	18.576
June 1967	165.521	15.981
October 1967	146.814	11.908
November 1967	149.328	13.11
Jan 1968	150.277	12.043
	Net Claims	
April 1967	608.537	−16.34
June 1967	556.365	−14.224
October 1967	562.724	−10.007
November 1967	559.202	−11.318
Jan 1968	648.821	−9.884

PRC banks' deposits in Hong Kong, and 124 percent of local advances, suggesting a substantial transfer of funds from Hong Kong across the border.

The impact of the crisis on cross-border flows between Hong Kong and the Mainland is suggested in the data available for Hong Kong banks' claims and liabilities on the Mainland. These mainly represented deposits in China (liabilities) and deposits received from Chinese entities such as head offices on the Mainland (claims). Table 7.6 shows movements in these balances during 1967. This data confirm that the mainland banks were by far the largest participants in this cross-border activity. During the crisis, they withdrew claims on the Mainland and increased their liabilities to meet demands for cash from their depositors in Hong Kong. Other banks in Hong Kong had small net liabilities on the Mainland, which decreased during the crisis and their cross-border activity did not recover as quickly as the mainland banks from the crisis. By the beginning of 1968, however, the impact of the crisis had been more than reversed and the mainland-controlled banks in Hong Kong resumed their accumulation of claims on the Mainland.

In summary, the crisis of 1967 showed the resilience of the banking system to external political crisis. Unlike 1965 when the weakest local banks were targeted by nervous depositors, the decline in deposits was manageable because it was shared across all categories of banks initially, and in the longer term it was focused on the highly liquid mainland-controlled banks. The archive data presented shows the importance of the links with the Mainland in the activities of these banks, which undermined their reputation with depositors when there was a threat of political conflict between the PRC and Hong Kong.

Conclusion

This chapter has highlighted the importance of considering the economic consequences of the 1967 riots both for how the British government viewed Hong Kong's future and their commitment to this last bastion of empire, and also for the Hong Kong banking and monetary system. The riots came at a time of estrangement between Hong Kong and London after the defence review of 1966, which prompted the British to consider the consequences of abandoning Hong Kong. This pessimistic outlook was reinforced during the disturbances and Britain believed that business confidence would be undermined and that this would gradually erode the economic viability of the colony. The riots certainly did generate a shock to confidence as is evidenced in the data presented on bank deposits, money supply, remittances and capital flight but these effects were short-lived. In 1968, Hong Kong recovered its dramatic growth rate. One lasting outcome was the relative decline of PRC-controlled banks in Hong Kong. They suffered most from the loss of confidence in 1967 and never recovered their market share until after the open-door policy in the 1980s.

8
The riots and labour laws:
The struggle for an eight-hour day for women factory workers, 1962–71[1]

David Clayton

Chapters in this volume refine our understanding of the causes of the 1967 disturbances. The focus of this chapter is different. It examines the effects of the riots on policy-making. It addresses the first part of a historical consensus, one that has been held for a generation: that the riots (of 1966, but more particularly of 1967) were a 'watershed' that reconfigured 'Hong Kong politics'. Thereafter 'wave after wave' of 'collective actions'[2] weathered away opposition to social reform, and in 1971 with the arrival of a new, reformist governor, Sir Murray MacLehose, the tide turned in favour of welfare-state building.[3] This chapter argues that, before the arrival of MacLehose, any foundations on which a welfare state could be built were extremely shallow. It uses the case of reforms to laws governing women's work. The empirical focus is on a very particular policy intervention: how the colonial state sought to reduce the hours of factory work undertaken by women. This is, however, a pertinent case. For those earning their living from the production of manufactured goods in Hong Kong during the1960s, this was a highly controversial intervention. As the first section describes, it was also one with a long and contested history.

The chapter divides into four parts. The first part provides a potted history of regulations governing the hours of women's factory work, ending in 1967 with the granting of an entitlement to an eight-hour day. To provide further context the second part describes the actors, structures and processes which, according to existing accounts, directly and, in the case of the riots, indirectly shaped labour policy-making. Parts III and IV chronicle labour laws regulating the hours of work for women before and during 1967. Part V assesses to what extent elite and mass attitudes towards women's work shifted in the aftermath of the riots. It speculates that, in the years immediately after the riots, many female workers colluded with employers to undermine the spirit of the eight-hour law. The final section sums up and sets down an agenda for further work in the field.

Legal regimes governing the hours of women's factory work, c. 1920–71

Four legal regimes governed women's factory work.[4] The first, which lasted from the 1920s to the late 1930s, began during a period of rapid industrialization, one characterized by the growth of working-class radicalism. The 1925–26 General Strike-cum-Boycott, which paralysed the local economy and demonstrated the marked impact that anti-imperial, nationalist and socialist ideologies could have on local political cultures, forced the local administration to intervene to a greater extent in the working lives of ordinary people. However, before the war, governmental responses to mass social and political pressures were piecemeal and inconsistent. Progressive laws emerged to regulate the industrial employment of children and to ban women in factories from working the night shift. These marginal social gains must, moreover, be offset by significant social losses. Government efforts to suppress radicalism eroded many of the customary protections enjoyed by workers, notably their social right to form mutual support groups (guilds and secret societies) and to strike.[5]

The late 1930s to the mid-1950s was a period of social and economic change in Hong Kong. There was mass migration from a war-torn China, and from the early 1950s, extremely rapid industrialization. With communism in the ascendancy in China, there was a heightened risk of social revolution in Hong Kong. However, despite colony-wide industrial unrest in the early 1950s, industrial relations were relatively quiescent. During this period, the main dynamic was the emergence of a welfare-orientated Colonial Office that encouraged the colonial administration to reform its labour policies so that they conformed to those in Britain. During this second regime, British policy set down a two-part framework for Hong Kong: modern (legally recognized) and moderate (social democratic) trade unions were to be encouraged and, where necessary, the state was to regulate working lives more extensively, notably by protecting groups of workers (such as women) who were poorly represented by trade unions. This policy was slowly implemented in Hong Kong. At the end of the 1940s, Hong Kong adopted modern trade union law, which gave labour organizations legal protections — if, that is, they registered with the state. British governments hoped that labour movements in the colony would, now that they enjoyed the backing of modern trade union law, enter into collective agreements with employer organizations to regulate wages and working hours, and sever their links with mass political movements in China (and Taiwan). This did not come to pass. Trade unions recruited a small proportion of the working population (about 10 percent), and an extremely small proportion of the industrial workforce. They also fractured politically. Most aligned either with the Guomindang or with the Chinese Communist Party. Corporatism, a structure of state-sponsored and quasi-democratic relationships between representatives of organized labour and capital, had failed to take root in industrial Hong Kong.[6]

The failure of British-style structures of industrial relations in Hong Kong meant that towards the end of the second period, far greater weight was attached to the second component of metropolitan labour policy; that is, the use of statute law to set minimum standards for groups of workers. This pressure to legislate to protect Hong Kong workers intensified from the late 1950s due to the rise of protectionism. This caused a change of regime. During this period, British business organizations, trade unionists and social reformers complained that Hong Kong workers were being exploited and that, consequently, trade between Hong Kong and the rest of the world was 'unfair'. This created a powerful political dynamic, the shape and impact of which will be explained more fully in later sections.[7] This was a period of legislative change, brought about by the structures of international politics. In 1959, the existing pre-war ordinance governing night-work by women was amended to introduce a statutory limit on the maximum hours of factory work undertaken by women: ten hours a day, and sixty hours per week.[8] In 1962, all factory workers gained statutory paid sick days and paid annual leave. These piecemeal legislative interventions by the colonial state on behalf of select groups of workers would not have occurred without pressure from British governments.

The fourth regime began, like the first, with social unrest in Hong Kong: the riots of 1966 and 1967. After this 'watershed', the speed of legislative change accelerated. Labour laws in Hong Kong began to converge with those in the West. In December 1967, in the immediate aftermath of the riots, new statutory limits were introduced. From then on, women could only work for a maximum of forty-eight hours per week and eight hours per day. In 1968, a new Employment Ordinance was passed, which, by codifying and extending existing statutory protections, became the 'primary source of legislative protection for Hong Kong workers'.[9] The standard way of viewing this process of legal convergence is that it formed part of a wider political strategy that aimed to 'close the gap' between the colonial government and the people.[10] This was a period when new institutions were established to improve communications between bureaucrats and the average person (social elites always had good access to power in the colony) and formulate and implement progressive social policies. According to the existing accounts of social policy, this period laid down some solid foundations for MacLehose. This reformer sought to transform relations between the state and society during the 1970s. Regime change between 1967 and 1971 was, so the standard story goes, the result of local processes.

As this chapter demonstrates, this thesis needs to be qualified with respect to labour laws. The labour legislation of 1967 and 1968 was not drafted and enacted overnight, that is, in response to the radicalism of 1967. Metropolitan pressures were still critical under this fourth legal regime. The riots strengthened the position of social reformers in London and Hong Kong. Moreover, before the arrival of MacLehose, there is no strong evidence that social attitudes were shifting. Mass and elite attitudes towards the three institutions — markets, cultures and laws — ordering working lives in Hong Kong were deeply entrenched, as Part II now demonstrates.

Labour policy-making: Some actors, some structures, and some processes

Until 1967 three groups of actors made labour policy in Hong Kong: bureaucrats based in Hong Kong and London, employer groups, and a select number of workers' representatives.

Bureaucrats, working for the British and the colonial state, can be subdivided into benevolent and pragmatic types. The benevolent promoters of progressive labour laws worked in the Colonial Office and in the Hong Kong Labour Department. These individuals sought to create institutions that would, they hoped, minimize conflict between labour and capital. They promoted trade unionism, intervened during industrial disputes, gathered information on working conditions, and drafted and policed labour laws setting minimum standards of working conditions. Within the Hong Kong secretariat, however, there were also pragmatists concerned that these interventions would impose burdens on the state and damage the local economy. Sir John Cowperthwaite, financial secretary (1961–72), for example, was a highly influential figure within the Hong Kong secretariat, a man of 'considerable intellect and integrity'. He was pragmatic. He may also have been idealistic. This was a man with a 'Gladstonian' world view.[11] According to one historian, he was of the 'Hong Kong school' of economics, a natural heir to the nineteenth-century Manchester school, and a bed-fellow of the 1960s Chicago school.[12] He believed that 'free' markets would deliver development.

During the 1960s, as debates raged within Hong Kong, about how the colony's 'free' labour markets should be regulated by the state, the positions adopted by governors fluctuated. Neither Robert Black (January 1958 – April 1964) nor his successor David Trench (April 1964–November 1971) can be labelled pragmatic or benevolent. They took up flexible positions that reflected the pressures that they faced; they were straws that bent in the wind. They had, constitutionally, to uphold the metropolitan desire for social justice, but they also had to ensure that any interventions did not damage the growth prospects of the Hong Kong economy. They also had to be aware that any interventions that proved to be unpopular in Hong Kong would be difficult to enforce and might jeopardize the ability of future governors to rule effectively.

Legislating necessitated liaising with business groups in Hong Kong. Time and again, this proved to be a major obstacle to implementing a reformist policy agenda. Most business organizations opposed welfare-state building, which they perceived to be costly — paid for by taxes the incidence of which fell mainly on the property-owning elites. The position of these vested interest groups with respect to labour laws was obstructionist, but there were subtleties that are worth noting. Trade associations representing the interests of industrial capitalism divided into two factions.[13] There was, on the one hand, the government-sponsored Federation of Hong Kong Industries (FED) and on the other the Chinese Manufacturers' Association (CMA) (originally Union). The latter was established in 1934 and, until the arrival of the FED in the late 1950s, it was the only business group that represented the interests of small-scale manufacturers. During the 1960s, both of these groups opposed the introduction of new labour laws which, they argued, would increase production costs and thus either reduce profits or push up factory-gate prices. The CMA refused to liaise with the government on this issue. The FED, by contrast, was more amenable and agreed to government requests to scrutinize draft labour laws. This factionism made enforcement unpredictable (would firms represented by the CMA agree to collaborate with factory inspectors?), and potentially costly (if CMA firms evaded the law might more inspectors have to be recruited?).

A further problem compounded the politics of enforcement. A large proportion of local manufacturing firms did not partake in associational life, and a large proportion of these were small, family-owned and run, enterprises operating in the extra-legal sector. These latter firms employed fewer than twenty workers and did not use centrally powered machinery. They did not, therefore, have to register with local factory inspectors and were not subject to labour legislation. These firms were numerous and in the 1950s employed hundreds of thousands of workers. The organized business community believed that this poorly organized business sector gained a competitive advantage because they were not subject to labour laws. This was one reason why the CMA and the FED were reluctant to agree to any new labour laws. These labour-intensive workshops were, in essence, beyond the reach of labour inspectors (the law) and beyond the contempt of FED and CMA committee men ('self-regulation' by the organized business community).[14] Yet, these were just the type of enterprises that were gaining Hong Kong its reputation as a haven of 'sweatshops'.

To counteract the opposition of employers, governors should have been able to argue that new labour laws were in the interests of workers. The state could also have appealed directly to workers to inform on employers who were transgressing the law, and reduce the costs of enforcement (that is, the regularity and intrusiveness of visits by factory inspectors). However, the views of workers were difficult to evaluate. Benevolent bureaucrats were uncertain whether local workers would support the establishment and enforcement of minimal labour standards. The patchy evidence available to them suggested that workers were opposed to labour laws that threatened to lower their wages, 'suspicious or resentful' of any 'threat' to their ability to earn a living.[15]

Bureaucrats gained a feel for the attitude of workers during exchanges with employers, who spoke on behalf of their employees. Consequently this evidence of popular opposition to labour laws might have been partial or even spurious. However, given structures of employment in post-war Hong Kong, popular opposition may have been entirely rational. Workers in Hong Kong were mainly paid by the piece (by the amount they produced per day), and such workers would have feared that it was the unemployed and under-employed that would have gained from restrictions on their hours of work. A shorter working day meant that they could produce less and hence their take-home pay would fall. Given that industrial trade unions were extremely weak, they may also have feared that, as their hours of work fell, they would not have the political clout to demand higher wage rates, of which more will be discussed in the penultimate section. They may also have known that their ability to work more productively (to compensate for fewer hours) would have depended on investment in new machinery and the introduction of new working practices. In the 1960s there was no guarantee that employers would make these risky investments.

In hindsight, if the pace of legislative change in 1960s Hong Kong was to be rapid, governors would have had to use their power to circumvent employer opposition and persuade workers that restrictions on their hours delivered private gains (more discretionary time) plus public ones (higher employment for all). However, existing political structures seriously shackled Robert Black and David Trench; this is perhaps one reason why neither of them felt able to intervene.

Hong Kong had a 'bureaucratic intervention state' which had 'comprehensive control over the colonial society in matters of legislation, legal judgments, [and] law enforcement . . .'[16] Power was vested with a governor, appointed by the British government, who continued to take instructions from the Colonial Office in London.[17] Metropolitan pressures for social reform could, therefore, force local bureaucrats and elites to legislate against their perceived vested interests.[18] But this was rare. Usually, a system of consultation between local interest groups and local bureaucrats ensured that policy reflected the prevailing values of local elites.[19]

By the 1960s, channels of communication between bureaucrats and business elites had been formalized; advisory bodies, such as the Labour Advisory Board, had been established and business and professional elites were represented on Legislative and Executive Councils. But informal channels of communication remained of significance. Bureaucrats would, before legislating, consult with 'pressure groups and the representatives of different identifiable interests within the community'.[20] According to Scott, the capacity of the colonial state to transform society was duly constrained; bureaucrats were 'relatively autonomous' even though the Hong Kong political system was colonial and undemocratic, the state was constrained by local elites.[21] Before 1967, consulting with elites to gain a consensus behind socially-progressive labour laws was a fraught process.[22]

The politics of industrial reform were further complicated because it was only unions with ties to the Chinese Communist Party that publicly backed regulations on the hours of female factory work. They argued for the extension of 'the standard of reasonable working time' (an eight-hour day) for all workers. They argued that the existing law was 'unfair' and that it had 'aroused' workers.[23] These unions did not, however, represent the majority of the industrial labour force and refused to collaborate with the colonial state. They boycotted the Labour Advisory Board, making this an ineffective channel of communication between state, employers and employees.[24] In 1967, left-wing trade unions only affected the process of labour policy-making indirectly, by encouraging radicalism.

In addition to structural forces, three historical processes also affected how labour laws were made: the 'refugee crisis' of the 1950s, the rise of protectionism, from around 1958 onwards, and the riots of 1966 and 1967. In the period of 1967–1971 under close scrutiny here, all three of these processes reverberated, pulling policymakers one way and then another.

The 'refugee crisis', caused by large-scale inward migration from a war-torn and revolutionary China, had two effects. Firstly, it put a severe strain on the existing (and inadequate) social infrastructure, and forced the government to intervene much more extensively in markets for food and shelter. Secondly, it caused widespread under-employment and depressed wages. Socio-economic conditions gradually improved from the early to the mid-1950s. Industrialization promoted employment and, when migration from China slowed and labour became more scarce, wages increased.[25] Hong Kong had, thanks in part to an effective response by the Hong Kong government, survived a population explosion.

This favourable outcome conditioned government and business thinking into the 1960s. A fear that strong regulations on industrial life would jeopardize economic performance and social stability became pervasive and persistent, lasting into the 1970s. This positioning was understandable and, in many ways, inevitable. It was the outcome of globalization and the presence of relatively free markets for the products that Hong Kong made: garments, textiles, footwear and other light consumer goods, such as toys. Industrialization depended on exporting such low-cost produce to highly competitive Western markets. If strong regulations increased wage costs and factory-gate prices, overseas demand for Hong Kong goods might fall. The rise of protectionism in the West and the riots challenged this mentality, but did not transform it.

From the mid-1950s, Western industrialists, trade unionists and social reformers argued that competition with Hong Kong was 'unfair' because Chinese industrialists based in the territory did not have to meet the direct and indirect costs of Western-style employment regulations.[26] Western governments could have chosen to ignore these arguments, as Western consumers were benefiting from lower prices, but industrial lobby groups were powerful. The rise of protectionism was keenly felt in Hong Kong. A political pattern soon emerged. Pressure from British governments on the Hong Kong government to regulate economic life would intensify before general election campaigns (1957–59; 1962–64; 1968–70) and when voluntary export restraint trade agreements, struck between Hong Kong and British industrialists, were due to be signed or expire (1957–59, 1962, and 1965). These commercial-cum-political cycles map well onto labour policy-making in Hong Kong.[27]

During the 1950s and 1960s, the Colonial Office regularly sent 'labour advisors' to Hong Kong to collect evidence on working conditions. Telegrams were also sent to Governor Robert Black and his successor David Trench. They argued that, if working conditions in Hong Kong were seen to be improving, it would dampen demands for protectionism in Western markets. This shock produced legislation in 1959 and 1962. It also, however, produced a backlash within Hong Kong. Employers and bureaucrats advocated 'free trade', positioning themselves against what they perceived as Western mercantilism. During the 1960s these views became entrenched. Moreover, they were to survive the effects of 1967.

The leading experts on the process of labour law making in post-war Hong Kong agree with Scott that, with respect to the extension of new legal rights to industrial workers, the riots of 1966 and 1967 were a 'watershed'.[28] It was only after the riots that the power of employers and certain bureaucrats to block legislative change was reduced. England, in the first seminal contribution to the field, argued that the riots had a 'major' effect. The report on the riots of 1966 sounded a 'first semi-official warning bell' but 'very little' would have emerged without the confrontation of 1967. These riots, orchestrated by local communist activists and 'an offshoot of the Cultural Revolution', were sparked by labour disputes and fuelled by an 'undercurrent of dissatisfaction'. Consequently, labour relations, a 'sensitive area', were given a far greater 'priority' within government. Draft legislation, which had been 'pigeonholed' for years, was 'dusted off', and enacted. From 1968 there was a 'flow' of legislation. The confrontation provided this 'impetus' because it severely 'jolted' employers, and forced them to embrace a 'new orthodoxy': that labour policy had to ensure that wages and working conditions in Hong Kong were, after Japan, the 'best in Asia'.[29]

Lee agrees that there was 'no great impetus' to extend legal protections to workers before the 1967 riots, and Scott argues that, in the aftermath of the disturbances, the government, realizing that it needed to establish a 'new basis of legitimacy', quickly enacted legislation which provided a 'basis for the more equitable treatment of workers and a platform from which more specific reforms could subsequently be made'.[30] However, both of these authors rightly question the impact of the riots; and so qualify England's position. They argue that employers continued to oppose progressive social legislation, and that there was no fundamental shift in the ethos of the colonial bureaucrat who continued to govern in a 'characteristically pragmatic Hong Kong Government fashion'.[31] The 'refugee crisis' mentality gave primacy to maintaining full employment and entrepreneurial freedoms. As the next two sections demonstrate, this mentality held a strong grip on key actors, before, during and after the riots.

Labour law-making before the 1967 'watershed'

To recap from our earlier discussion, from the 1920s women (and young persons) had been banned from working in factories at night under a Factories and Industrial Undertakings Ordinance and, in 1959, this ordinance was amended to restrict the hours of work for women to ten-hour daily shifts (including set rest breaks), for six days a week maximum.[32] This was an important initiative, affecting social relations of production. In the years that followed, this regulatory regime forced most (but not all) capital-intensive factories (such as cotton-weaving and spinning plants) to move from a two twelve-hour shift pattern to a three eight-hour shift pattern. However, this labour law could have had a more dramatic effect on working lives.

In 1958–59, before the ordinance was enacted, concessions (regarding when the law would be enforced) were secured by employers. Throughout the 1960s, exemptions were granted to employers that allowed their staff to work overtime. The new regime, therefore, hardly impacted at all on the thousands of manufacturers who did not operate 'a shift system of operation'. They made consumer goods, such as garments and electronic goods, demand for which expanded rapidly in the 1960s. Not surprisingly, they became 'the main' group of employers resisting further reductions in the hours of women's work.[33] Unlike more progressive employers in the late 1950s, they refused to collaborate with the colonial state.

During the early 1960s, the Colonial Office became highly dissatisfied with the 1959 ordinance which they perceived to be limited in scope and laxly enforced. Officials believed that during consultations in the late 1950s, Black had agreed to reduce the working hours of women during the 1960s so that ultimately women would enjoy an eight-hour day and a forty-hour week, a convention already adopted throughout much of an industrializing Asia.[34] They saw no reason to delay. The ordinance had to be amended whether 'economic forces' were favourable or adverse.[35] During the 1960s, the Colonial Office increasingly came to believe that the Hong Kong government was reneging on a promise.

The long-term aim of British governments was to extend the eight-hour working day to all Hong Kong workers because once workers were entitled to this universal standard, British politicians could declare that they had met their 'responsibility' for "good government" in Hong Kong[36] British bureaucrats also argued that although regulations on the hours of work would burden employers, these additional costs could be 'offset' by higher rates of productivity when local employers invested in new systems for managing labour.

During the early 1960s, the Colonial Office sent labour advisors and ministers to Hong Kong to present these arguments. In 1960, Lord Perth, the minister of state at the Colonial Office, visited Hong Kong and reached an understanding with Black that by 1962, there would be a statutory 9-hour day and a 54-hour week for women. When this deadline was missed despite intense pressure from London, C. G. Gibbs, a Colonial Office labour expert, visited Hong Kong to investigate why industrialists, workers and colonial officials had put up such resistance.[37] Finding that Hong Kong workers 'treasured' the rights granted to them in 1959, he insisted that Black sign up to a new timetable.[38]

Throughout the rest of 1963, the Colonial Office kept the pressure up. The governor was instructed to resolve an 'unsatisfactory' situation that was encouraging economic 'discrimination' against Hong Kong,[39] and damaging 'the reputation of the colony abroad'.[40] But, much to the disbelief of officials in London, Black failed to act.[41] From April 1964, the Colonial Office briefed Black's successor, Trench, that it was his 'duty' to 'prevent the balance being tilted permanently against the interests of workers', and to overcome the opposition of 'local business interests'.[42] Trench ultimately succeeded, but only thanks to colony-wide rioting. Before then, just like Black, this governor failed to circumvent opposition from business groups.

In the 1960s, Hong Kong employers deployed three arguments when opposing a lower statutory cap on the hours of work. First, it would increase labour costs, pushing up export prices, and make it difficult for local firms to respond flexibly to overseas orders.[43] Second, this law would discriminate against women workers. They argued that women were paid by the 'piece', and therefore, unless there was a costly reorganization of production processes in Hong Kong, their incomes would fall, as their hours of work declined.[44] Third, the large number of Hong Kong employers operating in the extra-legal sector, and thus not subject to statute law, would gain a competitive advantage over them.[45]

Benevolent bureaucrats countered these arguments. They argued that if Hong Kong firms invested in better production techniques, their competitive position could be maintained. But business leaders responded to this rational and plausible stance by arguing that the time was inopportune for making such investments. To reap major productivity gains, they estimated that their costs would have to rise by as much as 30 percent.[46] They claimed that given the 'uncertainties' in international markets — that is, the rise of protectionism — these investments were risky.[47] The presence of firms operating in the extra-legal sector, 'undercutting' progressive firms by evading statutory rules on wages and working conditions, heightened their concerns.[48]

During 1964 and 1965, Trench could have used the government's majority in the Legislative Council to circumvent societal opposition. He could have justified this intervention as in the 'public interest'; that is, a means of delivering social justice and long-term productivity gains. However, if employers had dissented, this positioning might have compromised the informal system of consultation with business interests. If the government had used its influence over appointees in the Legislative Council to enact an unpopular law, it might have opened up serious schisms within the business community. The expatriate European business community operated mainly in the service sector and had less to lose from labour laws. A far higher proportion of the Chinese business community owned and ran manufacturing concerns and had much more to lose.[49] An unpopular labour law may also have driven a wedge between large-scale manufacturers (some of whom had already introduced an eight-hour day for women) and smaller-scale ones that had not. Moreover, without societal consent, the costs of enforcing this (and other labour laws) would have been extremely high, requiring the recruitment of many more factory inspectors.

The Colonial Office, accepting that legislating without the approval of the business community was 'virtually never' done in Hong Kong,[50] initially deferred to the man on the spot. During 1964 and 1965, Trench attempted to broker a deal that would phase in an eight-hour day for women and would grant employers generous exemptions that would allow their women employees to work overtime. He proposed that a new ordinance should grant him significant powers of discretion to withdraw these preferential conditions only as 'economic circumstances' changed.[51] This deal, however, proved to be completely unacceptable to the Colonial Office. It was feared that Trench might fail to take up his 'social responsibility' to protect workers[52] by allowing employers to enjoy 'indefinite' loopholes.[53] This labour law might become a 'paper tiger'. If this labour law was weakly enforced, the notion that trade between Britain and Hong Kong was becoming fairer would become a 'farce'.[54] The British government would be criticized by social reformers and industrial lobbyists.

With the man on the spot failing them again, the Colonial Office recommended that a more prescriptive programme be enacted. This would give Hong Kong employers time to adjust to more stringent regulations. It was proposed that the working day for women be reduced by twenty or thirty minutes per year. There was, however, no firm consensus within the Secretariat in favour of this revised deal.[55] It was, therefore, shelved. The precise views of colonial bureaucrats are not known, but they probably realized that if business groups refused to support it, the enforcement costs would be high and the political fall-out on state-business relations potentially far-reaching.

In the aftermath of the 1966 Star Ferry riots, the Hong Kong government renewed discussion of the 1965 Colonial Office-inspired deal. Social unrest had made a difference because, for the first time, the Executive Council agreed that the 1965 'deal' should be passed to the LAB for scrutiny. The Executive Council comprised 'Unofficials', drawn from the professional and business community. These representatives would probably have felt that some response to the groundswell of popular radicalism was required. This shift was not, however, profound or wide-reaching. The Executive Council insisted that the main organizations representing employers should be consulted. This was a significant prerequisite. It gave employers time to mobilize against the proposal. And they did so. In April 1967, only a month before the outbreak of further rioting, employers rejected the 1965 deal.

According to Trench, employers — still 'suspicious' that the British government was promoting this legislation to 'destroy' Hong Kong's 'competitive position in international markets' — claimed that any additional costs would sharply reduce overseas demand for Hong Kong exports, and subsequently, local employment. Local bureaucrats did not counter these arguments. A 'refugee crisis' mentality still held. They feared that lower export growth would reduce employment opportunities and risk social unrest. They were also discouraged from acting by continued evidence that workers were 'suspicious or resentful' about any 'threat' to their ability to earn a living.[56]

Labour law-making during 1967

In February 1968, in a landmark speech to the Legislative Council, setting out a list of forthcoming bills to improve labour conditions, P. C. M. Sedgwick, the commissioner of labour, argued that 1967 had been a 'momentous year'. There had been, he suggested, a new 'sustained interest in labour matters' and legislative progress had been swift. He cited as proof a 'major item of legislation concerning the welfare of women and young persons in industrial employment'.[57] Radicals would have treated his claim with distain. And so should historians. There had been a minor amendment to an existing ordinance. Sedgwick was not, however, exaggerating. From his perspective, much energy had been expended on this amendment and in 1967, there had finally been progress.

In May 1967, the LAB acknowledged that the recent 'events' had 'left their mark', and that, for the first time, workers and employers agreed that the hours of work in Hong Kong must be brought in line with 'international standards'.[58] But although the riots had created the conditions for a 'general agreement' on lowering hours of work, there were still significant disagreements about how this should be done. Workers insisted on 'generous' allowances so that they could work overtime to maintain incomes, and employers argued for a phased reduction in non-overtime hours, given that the 'current situation' (the state of world demand) was 'untimely'. These positions were equivocal, but sensing that the employers were 'more receptive' to reform, Trench seized 'the opportunity' to push through an amendment to the ordinance. He was, for the first time, confident. He reported to London that there had been a 'significant change' in attitudes towards this 'sensitive subject'.[59] The riots of 1967 had had an effect.

During the summer of 1967, however, as mass protest continued, the process of law-making stalled, to be followed by a series of protracted exchanges between colonial bureaucrats and employers' organizations. Business groups in Hong Kong continued to maintain that they needed to retain their flexibility to respond to the ebbs and flows of their order books, and thus demanded generous allowances for overtime work — of between 100 to 150 hours per worker per year, and in special circumstances of up to 300 hours per worker. Moreover, they insisted that the 48-hour week be phased in over six years.[60] By October 1967, rioting had mutated into terrorism, but a deal still had not been struck. This is when metropolitan pressure proved to be critical.

Throughout 1967, metropolitan pressure came from three sources: the Colonial Office, as expected; social reformers such as J. Greenhalgh, the general secretary of the International Textile and Garment Workers' Federation; and ministers of parliament notably Ernest Thornton (Labour, Farnworth, Bolton). A coalition similar in make-up to the one that had formed in the late 1950s had emerged. These individuals and organizations felt vindicated. They had argued for ten years that the root cause of social unrest in Hong Kong had been 'sweated', labour conditions.[61]

From their perspectives, only interventions by the colonial state to protect workers would bring social stability. The tinder for firebrand radicalism had, they argued, still to be removed.

The Colonial Office seized the opportunity presented by new dialogue between employers and the colonial state. In October, another well-travelled labour advisor, G. Foggon, arrived in the colony to hammer home a subtle metropolitan line that had been articulated over the wires since May: although the 'present troubles' were 'political and not social in origin', it would be 'wrong' of Hong Kong bureaucrats and business leaders to assume that 'the material and social conditions of the Hong Kong working population have limited relevance to the future problem of stability'; indeed, the 'slow tempo of improvement in labour standards in the past eight or nine years' had sent out a message to the young that they would not have 'an opportunity' to share in the 'fruits' of 'growth' and that they must, as a last resort, take to the streets to secure social justice.[62]

The presence of Foggon in Hong Kong strengthened Trench's negotiating position. In October, a specific proposal was put to the employers, one that would, the government hoped, meet their demand for a phased programme but also define more precisely the new entitlements of workers. It was suggested that each year from 1968 to 1972 half an hour should be knocked off the working day, to bring forth the eight-hour day for women. Significantly, and for the first time since reform of this ordinance had been under discussion, Trench also agreed that, in the event of continued opposition from the employers, the amended ordinance would be 'forced through' the Executive and Legislature Councils. This would have set a dangerous precedent, and it was this threat (rather than the riots *per se*) that was the handmaiden of legislative progress. To avoid a dangerous precedent, bureaucrats and business leaders conjured up a modified deal, one that granted more extensive concessions to business elites.

Soon after the riots ended, women workers gained a legal entitlement to an eight-hour working day and their weekly hours were capped by statute at forty-eight hours. However, due to sustained pressure from employers, these rights were to be phased in over five years, and certain employers could, once they had been granted permission from the state, persuade women to work up to 300 hours of overtime per year.

Turning the legal entitlement to an eight-hour day into a paper tiger: The regime governing the hours of factory work for women, 1967–71

The efficacy of state regulations on working hours, during the period 1967–71, depended on the level of societal consent and on the quality of the state's enforcement regime. The factory inspectorate had responsibility for monitoring evasion. It fined employers that transgressed the law. Its ability to enforce the law would have been enhanced if workers had reported to factory inspectors when employers asked them to break the law. Collaboration between workers and inspectors, however, was limited. It was highly risky for individuals to act alone. If their employers discovered their identity, they could well have lost their jobs. Membership of trade unions could have protected workers from such discrimination. Trade union officials could have raised grievances with inspectors. Even the Special Branch of the Hong Kong Police admitted that communist unions were the 'only' mechanism for workers to air a grievance.[63] The weakness of the trade union movement removed one of the preconditions for an effective enforcement regime. Trade unions represented a tiny proportion of factory workers, and in the years immediately after the riots, the most effective ones (those aligned to the Communist Party) lost members and influence.[64]

Enforcement did not just depend on the courageous non-unionized worker risking unemployment by reporting transgressions to factory inspectors. In postwar Hong Kong, there was a long tradition of unco-ordinated bargaining. Since the 1940s, Labour Department officials had recorded numerous cases of workers stopping work *en masse*, usually for a short period (a few hours, or a day), to protest because their employers had transgressed a customary code, or failed to increase wages. These workers were not members of a trade union. Their actions were not led by trade union leaders. This was unco-ordinated bargaining. Since the 1940s, this form of industrial relations had been supported by the colonial state which acted as a third party during disputes between workers and their bosses. This history of struggle (which is yet to be told by historians) may have given women workers the institutional capacity to enforce the law, to protect their legal entitlement to more time off.[65] Young women workers recruited into industrial employment late in the 1960s would have learnt from their elders how to protest, and they would have known that the Labour Department would have supported their demands that the 1967 law be upheld.

Although women workers had the capacity to secure, via unco-ordinated bargaining, their new entitlement to an eight-hour day, there is no evidence to suggest that they did so. British policymakers expected that the average working day would fall gradually; that, over a three to four-year transitional period, overtime hours would fall from a legal ceiling of 300 hours per person per year to less than 100. Evidence is patchy on this subject, but it suggests that metropolitan expectations were not met.

By 1970 Hong Kong employers were reporting growing labour shortages, and so applications by employers for exemptions to allow women workers to do overtime were on the rise; 31,492 women undertook overtime in 1967, increasing to 58,212 in 1969. This trend alarmed labour advisors in Britain. They feared that their plan to reduce overtime to 100 hours per person per year would not succeed.[66] Many employers were also evading the law, not bothering to apply for exemptions. By the end of 1970, Anthony Royle, the parliamentary under-secretary of state in Ted Heath's Conservative government, was so disgruntled with the enforcement regime that he sought to implement a 'blue print' for a revamped inspectorate.[67]

An effective enforcement regime would, however, have been costly to implement because economic structures were encouraging wide-spread evasion of the law. It was the market (via 'the scarcity of labour') and custom (via 'the individual bargaining power of the worker') that set the going rate for overtime.[68] Consequently, employers had a strong incentive to evade the law. The bottom line for them was that women were paid less than men. Firms wanted to employ women for as many hours as possible. Their order books were full. Clothing and electronic firms operating one daily shift required women to work a long day to meet tight deadlines to ship goods overseas. Demand for light consumer goods was seasonal. The hours women worked tended to exceed the legal limit during boom months. Firms either had to apply for exemptions, or to come to an understanding with workers that factory inspectors would not be informed about excessive overtime. Most workers would have accepted such an implicit and illicit deal: they wanted more income and were willing to work for longer hours. These small firms did not, moreover, have a contingency strategy. Even if they had a stable order book, and access to the capital necessary to buy more machinery, they could not introduce a shift system because women were banned from working at night. In essence, they evaded the law to prevent a loss of orders, employment and income.

The economic fundamentals were different for large-scale textile firms spinning and weaving cloth. Since the early 1960s most of these firms had operated three eight-hour shifts. They could not, consequently, ask women to work overtime. From the mid-1960s, however, they had been faced by tightening labour markets, which increased labour costs. In response, they began to lobby for a relaxation to the ordinance prohibiting women from working at night.[69] They wanted to cut their costs by employing more women. In February 1970, Trench publicly proposed that this ordinance be amended.[70] Most Hong Kong officials believed that this change was in the 'public interest'. It was accepted that capital-intensive factories faced labour shortages and required more hours from their dexterous women workers.[71] It was accepted that they needed more flexible 'cost structures', to shore up the colony's 'competitive position' at the time when Taiwan and South Korea were beginning to export in larger volumes. The 'refugee crisis' mentality still held sway: 'the most effective safeguard of, and stimulant of improvement in, these conditions [local living standards] has been and remains full employment in the context of rapid export-led growth'.[72]

Bureaucrats, social reformers and business leaders in Britain were dumbfounded by the attitude of the Hong Kong government. For Ernest Thornton, this was evidence that the level of 'social consciousness' in Hong Kong was a hundred years behind that in Britain and that the Hong Kong government had no intention of addressing its 'appalling record' on labour conditions.[73] For J. Greenhalgh, a prominent campaigner on labour conditions in Hong Kong, colonial industrialists were displaying an unbelievable 'arrogance'.[74] The efforts of trade unionists to campaign within Hong Kong for 'more humane' working conditions had failed.[75] They argued, as they had done during 1967, that Hong Kong was 'a sweatshop haven of serious proportions', and warned that there was a grave risk that the 'working people' of Hong Kong would lose their 'faith' in the colonial state.[76] They would, as they had done in 1967, rebel. The Foreign and Commonwealth Office (FCO) was, likewise, alarmed by this piece of legislation. It acknowledged that if the law was amended, Hong Kong employers would dismiss higher-paid male workers and recruit low-paid women workers. It insisted therefore that any discussion of the amendment should be delayed until a metropolitan labour advisor had a chance to investigate local social conditions. Some answers to some new questions were required. Did Chinese women workers want to work at night? If so, would they receive good material rewards? How would employers manage demand for women with children to work at night?

A new pattern of negotiations had emerged. Since the late 1930s metropolitan labour advisors had visited Hong Kong to accelerate the pace of progressive social policy-making. Now, in 1970, it was proposed that British labour advisors should meet face to face with workers, bureaucrats and bosses in Hong Kong to avert legislative change. Since the late 1930s, governors had always granted metropolitan labour advisors the right to investigate local labour conditions. Now, in 1970, Trench refused to allow another labour expert access. The FCO was furious but Trench played his trump card. He argued that he had to legislate quickly because Executive Council members were threatening to rebel over the issue.[77] He was implying, less than subtly, that his ability to govern Hong Kong using the tried and tested methods of working closely with local elites was being put at stake by a FCO scheme to conduct yet another survey into local labour conditions. The FCO, acknowledging that Trench did not need their approval to amend the law, backed down.

A battle had been lost. The war, however, continued a pace. During the last few months of Wilson's labour government, the FCO was still confident that it could reform the way Hong Kong was governed. The new governor-to-be MacLehose, was their man, chosen from within the ranks of its experts on Chinese affairs. They must have realized that he was also a social reformer, a man with courage and convictions. In anticipation of new games to be played, of new requests for the governor to circumvent societal elites, they sent MacLehose a record of these exchanges between London and Hong Kong on the issue of night work for women. This documentation was, as they informed MacLehose, 'another example of the way in which the Hong Kong government goes about its business'.[78] The Colonial Office evidently wanted him to change the way Hong Kong was governed.

Conclusion

Until 1967, self-seeking business interest groups and narrow-minded local bureaucrats blocked the lowering of a statutory cap on the hours of factory work undertaken by women. They argued, in a sustained and forceful manner, that the predicted public (slower economic growth) and private (lower profits) costs of extending employment rights outweighed any potential gains for women (more discretionary time) and for the economy (stronger incentives to invest in higher-value added labour processes). The mentalities of these social and political elites did shift during 1967 but not by much. A shorter working day and working week was contested before and after 1967. The hunches of Scott and Lee are thus correct. The riots did affect social policy-making, but they did not completely reconfigure labour policies. This is not surprising because the positions in which issues had been taken up reflected strongly held beliefs.

There were those in Hong Kong and Britain who believed that the market would fail to deliver economic and social justice for the common people of Hong Kong, which was defined as rising incomes and increasing discretionary time for all. Some of these actors were humanistic; they sought to deal with market failures by promoting communication between organized labour and organized capital, and by using the powers of the colonial state to intervene on the side of the weak, such as women workers. Actions by social organizations (notably British textile and clothing trade unionists and employers), who feared that free trade between Britain and Hong Kong would lower wages and profits and increase unemployment in Britain, strengthened the arguments of the benevolent.

There were actors who believed that market forces aided by Chinese customary codes were delivering equity (through full employment) and, as firms and households saved and raised levels of investment, growth and development. These people perceived laws to regulate hours of work as costly and potentially corrosive, distorting the price mechanism and eroding social networks that regulated women's paid work. These idealists were pervasive in the powerful business community. Most Hong Kong government officials were pragmatists. They were concerned that enacting and enforcing a labour law that was unpopular with employers would have a pernicious effect on colonial statecraft. Before the arrival of MacLehose, benevolent bureaucrats were marginal figures. The events of 1967 actually shored up existing value systems.

During 1967, radicals wanted conflict between labour and capital, and sought the overthrow of a colonial state which, they argued, sided with capitalist interests.[79] For the benevolent, the riots of 1967 signalled that the state had to deal with market failures, and to try, once again, to foster strong, politically non-aligned, organizations of workers that were able to use democratic institutions and lawful means. For pragmatists, however, the fear of social revolution soon waned. The 1967 events had, as they must have realized, failed to change how the ordinary person in Hong

Kong thought. The masses had backed the colonial state and backed away from radicalism. Yet, the 1967 riots had had positive benefits. Left-wing unions lost credibility. There was no social revolution in Hong Kong and the colonial state was not toppled. In the years after 1967, left-wing trade unions returned to their tried and tested methods of gaining support from workers. They aimed to improve the welfare of their members. The 'lessons' from 1967 were quickly learnt.[80] The 1967 riots therefore presented an opportunity as well as a threat. Hearts and minds could be won back. Industrial paternalism could be entrenched. The Hong Kong way of self-regulation of working lives by market forces and by Chinese customs could be strengthened.

This study has opened up bigger issues about the optimal institutional foundations for modern Chinese societies. Should working lives be governed by rules or codes? Historians of Hong Kong must enter into this debate by examining how customary practices shifted in the past. To extend this study, historians should investigate how workers in Hong Kong regulated their working lives. This study has also suggested that the impact of the social unrest on labour institutions should be downplayed. However, were the effects of the upheavals of 1925–26 and 1949–51 equally benign? How precisely did radicalism affect popular attitudes towards markets, states and customs? We need, in short, new labour histories of post-war Hong Kong to be written.

9
Learning from civil unrest:
State/society relations in Hong Kong before and after the 1967 disturbances

Alan Smart and Tai-lok Lui

The 1970s were a decade in which many social reforms were first enacted in Hong Kong. As a consequence, the nature of the political economy and society was substantially transformed. The catalyst for these changes has been repeatedly described as the riots of 1966 and 1967. However, there is profound ambiguity about the precise causation. Most commonly, both years are mentioned; sometimes only 1967 is singled out, and occasionally 1967 is omitted. The two sets of disturbances were very different in their causes, duration and intensity, as well as in the immediate responses they drew and the kinds of societal problems they were perceived by decision-makers to have reflected. Thus, while it is possible that 1966 and 1967 were lumped together as a cause for concern and social reform among those who promoted the reforms of the 1970s, it is also possible that the consequences of the two were quite distinct. The 1966 riots might have prompted the same or similar initiatives even without the reinforcement of the 1967 events. On the other hand, the smaller scale of the 1966 events might have resulted in the concerns fading away without support from other incidents. Even if the reforms were likely to have occurred after the 1966 Star Ferry riots without reinforcement, it might be that the rather dissimilar nature of the 1967 events resulted in significant differences in the character of those reforms. Counter-factual history is always a difficult exercise to engage in, but an analysis of the reasoning behind the reform initiatives in the 1970s may help to disentangle the conceptual ambiguity involved in the pairing of the 1966 and 1967 events in the explanation of social change in Hong Kong during the 1970s.

More broadly, we suggest in this chapter that the response of the Hong Kong government to the 1967 unrest needs to be considered in the context of previous incidents of civil disturbances as well as within a changing political environment. Governmental responses to one disturbance reset the wider political environment and conditioned the emergence of a modified system of governance. However, given that contentious politics is by itself a dynamic social and political process, it does not have to move teleologically in a single direction driven by the underlying social contradictions of the first event of political contention. Changing political agendas and contexts for political contention would continuously reshape the course of political development, and ultimately bring about social and political reforms that had not been anticipated by either the state or political challengers. Omitting many smaller occurrences, major incidents in the post-war era included Kowloon Walled City disturbances (1948), the Tung Tau Comfort Mission riot (1952), Double Ten disturbances (1956), and the Star Ferry fare increase riots (1966). A case can be made that the reforms were more of a response to 1966 than to 1967, which could be dismissed as external provocation, while the Star Ferry riots seemed to reflect local problems that needed to be addressed. John Young suggests that the 1967 disturbances 'eventually removed some of the heat generated by the riot the year before, and as it became more and more Communist controlled, the Hong Kong population lent its support' to the government.[1] On the other hand, David Faure suggests that the government would have been less impelled by the 1966 disturbances to 're-think its relationship with Hong Kong society had it not been for the need to organize support for itself when its authority was challenged by the riots of 1967'.[2]

Space does not permit exposition of the theoretical considerations that underpin our analysis here beyond acknowledging our debt to recent work on the dynamics of contention. Particularly relevant to our account here is their description of its basic approach which requires the analyst to:

> Identify its recurrent causal mechanisms, the ways they combine, in what sequences they recur, and why different combinations and sequences, starting from different initial conditions, produce varying effects on the large scale.[3]

Focusing on a series of events, rather than single events or issues, exposes processes of escalation, gradual shifts in cultural approaches to the situation, and may promote learning from mistakes by all parties.[4] By looking at the dynamics of political contention, we shall see how a change in the course of political development would emerge.

Crucial factors that structured governmental responses to these situations included the geopolitical vulnerability of Hong Kong in the post-war era and the extremely limited involvement of the government in the everyday life of ordinary Hong Kong Chinese. Both factors constrained the government's ability to influence public opinion. Lessons learned from earlier civil unrest helped to condition the emergence of the Squatter Resettlement Programme, the first major intervention in expanding influence through the provision of government services. The Double Ten disturbances, which started in a resettlement estate, demonstrated that public housing provision did not by itself automatically create a sense of civic responsibility. One of the eventual outcomes of the 1967 riots was Governor MacLehose's decision in the 1970s to replace the Resettlement Department with the new Housing Authority, along with other reforms such as the Mutual Aid Committees, in order to build a stronger relationship between the population and the government. The sporadic occurrence of unrest ironically and eventually undermined the fatalistic attitude that the Hong Kong Chinese were unreliable and ultimately loyal to China rather than Hong Kong. At the same time, changing international politics (such as China joining the United Nations and its new diplomatic relations with Western countries) contributed to a change in the perspective of the colonial administration, alerting it to the need to build a new kind of state/society relations in the aftermath of the two major disturbances in the 1960s. More efforts were attempted to promote a Hong Kong identity and sense of commitment to the territory, in part through the expansion of social citizenship in the form of housing and the expansion of free education.[5]

In this chapter we will first discuss the various governmental responses that have been attributed by many observers to the 1966 and 1967 disturbances, and how these were intended to transform a deeply problematic state-society relationship. The following section describes the nature of the relationship between Hong Kong society and its government prior to 1966. The examination of this period raises questions about ideas that the reforms can be explained as simply a consequence of the disturbances in 1966, 1967, or both. Instead, we suggest that they were the final demonstration of governance problems that had repeatedly arisen and which eventually convinced decision-makers that a new approach was in order. We argue that there is a need to consider the impact of the 1967 events in a broader context. The penultimate section draws on recently released documents from the MacLehose regime to attempt to reconstruct the motivations, goals and strategies that underlay the reforms in the 1970s. The conclusion returns to the question of the importance of the 1967 events in prompting the social reforms of the 1970s.

In the wake of 1967

Many of the most 'progressive' reforms of colonial Hong Kong occurred in the aftermath of the disturbances, and particularly during the tenure of Governor Murray MacLehose (1971–82). As Steve Tsang notes, the 'new policy under MacLehose, with its astute publicity campaigns, gradually earned it a caring reputation'.[6] In addition to the ambitious Ten Years Housing Scheme, the government had taken a far more active role in the provision of medical and social welfare services. Also, universal free education was provided for nine years. In this chapter we suggest that these responses were not single-handedly brought about by the disturbances in the 1960s, but were also conditioned by the experience of prior disturbances in the post-war period, including but not limited to those taken place in 1948, 1952, 1956 and 1966 (for an incisive account of these events and a number of other political conflicts, see Lam 2004). These events had exposed the dangers of street violence for a British colony on the edge of China during a period in which decolonization was occurring elsewhere in the world. In this connection, it is important to recognize that the first major attempt to review various state provisions of social services was carried out before 1967. For instance, the white paper *The Development of Medical Services in Hong Kong* and the working party report entitled *Review of Policies for Squatter Control, Resettlement and Government Low Cost Housing* were published in 1964. This was followed by the white papers *Education Policy* and *Aims and Policy for Social Welfare in Hong Kong* in 1965.[7] Following the publication of its first white paper on social welfare by the colonial government, Lady Gertrude Williams, professor of social economics at London University, was invited 'to visit Hong Kong "for the purpose of advising the Government whether a survey of social welfare services in Hong Kong would be feasible and valuable" '.[8] A working party was set up in 1966 to look into matters concerning the idea of establishing some kind of social security system and its report was published in 1967. With hindsight, such official reviews of the changing needs of Hong Kong people and the role of government in provision of services were rudimentary and could hardly be described as signs of a fundamental change in the colonial government's approach to state provisions. Yet, the fact that they were carried out in 1964–65 is indicative of the colonial administration's growing awareness of emerging social needs and the need of building up an institutional structure, despite an emphasis of the contribution of the voluntary sector, in meeting such expectations. Policy review, planning and systematically administered reform initiatives had begun before 1967.

Meanwhile, the archival record also shows that the response to disturbances in the 1940s and 1950s reveals a governmental attitude that was deeply suspicious about the Hong Kong Chinese, assuming that their ultimate loyalties lay with China rather than with Hong Kong or the Crown. For various reasons, repressive options were constrained, and ultimately governmental experience encouraged the adoption of new strategies that would attempt to build bonds between the population and the government. The result was a series of initiatives to expand official capacities to understand what was happening in the urban areas, to incorporate non-elite Chinese into governance structures, and to use redistributive programmes to generate loyalty. However, the explosiveness of the 1966 and 1967 disturbances, with the alarming participation of ordinary working-class youths in the former and its connection with industrial strikes in the latter, brought the colonial government's attention to labour issues. The Employment Ordinance was quickly enacted. Labour reforms including improved health and safety standards, accident compensation, and worker's contracts protection were promised in 1968 and enacted by 1973. The city district officers system was put in place to 'advise the government on the concerns of the Hong Kong citizenry and to carry out the implementation of government policies'.[9] The need to 'close the gap' between the government and the people of Hong Kong was recognized in the official report on the 1966 riots.[10]

New forms of citizenship were developed out of the disturbances in 1967, but we suggest that these initiatives can only be fully understood by considering the prior series of disturbances and the gradual shift in official attitudes after previous approaches failed. Governor MacLehose stated that the creation of 1500 mutual aid committees was 'not only a considerable administrative achievement, but indicates the great need that these organizations fill'.[11] He acknowledged that there was 'indeed, a void: a void which was as dangerous for the Government as it was unwelcome to the ordinary citizen, who was left without means of influencing conditions outside his own door'. While democracy was seen as too risky because of the precarious situation of the colony in relation to the People's Republic of China, other forms of bridging the void were increasingly explored in the years after 1967.

The main question we address in this chapter is how these dramatic shifts in the mode of governance arose. While the 1967 disturbances were clearly a catalyst for political transformations, our suggestion is that it was the previous incidents of civil unrest that conditioned the government for these changes. The 1966 disturbances were of great importance because they could not easily be blamed on outside instigators,[12] as the 1967 riots were, and it seems likely that they would have prompted social reforms even in the absence of the trauma of 1967.

Hong Kong social and political organization before 1966

Hong Kong in the 1950s was a society in which the government had relatively minimal interaction with the mass of the population, although the Chinese economic elite were more closely integrated socially and through incorporation into advisory bodies.[13] Government services such as expenditures on health care were primarily intended for the expatriate population, while ordinary Chinese had to provide for themselves or rely on the philanthropy of associations like the Tung Wah Hospital or the Royal Hong Kong Jockey Club. The interaction between government and people was frequently one of conflict: new controls or rules that infringed upon the customs or economic practices of people in ways that caused anger. While government intervened in many ways in the lives of the Hong Kong Chinese through the legal system and the suppression of anti-colonial activities or social practices seen as unacceptable in Britain, the general tendency was to intervene in Chinese affairs only when and as necessary.

As a free port, the Hong Kong government regularly expressed its commitment to doctrines of laissez-faire, or what came to be known as 'positive non-interventionism'. Tak-wing Ngo argues that the laissez-faire policy was only retrospectively constructed as a framework that supported industrial expansion: previously it had reflected a policy bias against manufacturing that supported primarily British merchant firms.[14] Chiu has argued that the absence of overtly developmental policies in Hong Kong, compared with other countries in the region, is due to the greater political influence of commercial interests compared to industrialists.[15] Although some manufacturers were large employers, the sector as a whole was characterized by a myriad of small and medium enterprises. The most influential tycoons were generally in the areas of trade, finance and real estate, and their influence had had a large impact on the character of Hong Kong's development. Leo Goodstadt offers an alternative interpretation of the attractions of laissez-faire for Hong Kong administrators.[16] That is, non-interventionism provided excuses 'to intervene as little as possible in economic and social affairs',[17] and this in turn was due to a 'siege mentality' where even the best expatriates were distant from Chinese society, and were beset by 'fear of an unruly populace'.[18] Steve Tsang observed that after the Second World War the Hong Kong Chinese began to see pre-war conditions as involving 'too much privilege, snobbery, discrimination, racial prejudice, corruption and absentee exploitation against the local Chinese'.[19] James Hayes, newly arrived in Hong Kong as a 'cadet' (administrative officer) in 1956, describes how even then 'few expatriates had more contact with ordinary Chinese beyond how much or little they got to know of their amah's [housekeeper] families'.[20]

One of the most influential accounts of Hong Kong society is that provided by Siu-kai Lau.[21] Lau saw Hong Kong as structured around utilitarian familism where the Chinese population expected little of the government; instead, they relied on their kin to make a living and resolve the myriad problems they faced as ordinary Chinese in the hard times of early post-war Hong Kong. Because of the traditional Chinese political culture, compounded by the situation of a refugee population, Hong Kong people's values were self-interested, materialistic, and non-ideological. At the same time, they felt no responsibility to be involved in politics, so that clear boundaries were maintained between society and politics. There was a prevalence of political apathy or aloofness which meant that relatively few people took advantage of the venues that existed for political participation and expression. Others have seen this apathy as one of the conditions allowing for the efficient delivery of what services the government actually provided, particularly in the form of public housing. Denis Dwyer, for example, suggests that the greater ability of Hong Kong to resettle massive numbers of squatters compared to its Southeast Asian neighbours was the result in part of the political apathy of the squatters.[22] This attribution of 'apathy' neglects the considerable degree of resistance to squatter clearance in the 1950s and later, and inappropriately reads back into the past the higher degree of compliance once resistance had forced the government to begin resettling rather than simply clearing, thus reducing the degree of resentment that they experienced.[23]

Wai-man Lam offers a devastating critique of Lau's framework. She argues that Lau's conclusions depend on an inappropriately narrow definition of 'politics', and are contradicted when one takes an empirical look at the amount and intensity of political action in the 1950s, 1960s, and 1970s.[24] She documents many conflicts in the 1950s, when the 'refugee' mentality should have been at its height, that were both considerable in scale and importance for subsequent developments. Moreover, she argues that these conflicts were not only about utilitarian issues related to people's livelihood, but also focused on social issues such as marriage rules or instituting Chinese as an official language. She may dismiss the utilitarian and practical emphasis too easily, however. There seemed a sense that ordinary people could not expect too much of the colonial government, and that it was enough that the government did not act in such a way as to undermine their efforts to resolve their own problems. The trouble was that it seemed to repeatedly do so. Protests against fare increase at the Star Ferry and the Hong Kong Telephone Company and the strike against the Hong Kong Tramways Company reflected widespread beliefs that there were too many mutual interests between the government and the utilities.[25] Goodstadt has documented the extent to which laissez-faire principles were not applied to local monopolies or oligopolies, particularly if they were controlled by British firms.[26] As late as in the 1980s, squatters expressed ideas that government actions were particularly unjust if the actions impinged on their ability to make a livelihood (*wan sik*) by themselves.[27]

Much of the process of *wan sik* involved working outside the scope of the officially regulated economy, whether this was in the illegal squatter settlements (numbering at some points over three quarters of a million residents) with their myriad of industrial workshops that did not conform to most of the minimal regulations that applied to business operations at the time, or in the illegal street markets, or the complex networks of subcontracted work without reported income.

Although Lam systematically critiques the idea of Hong Kong as apolitical or apathetic, she concludes that it did experience a 'culture of depoliticization'.[28] High levels of political activism actually 'excited the growth of the culture of depoliticization'.[29] Furthermore, to the extent that civil society was weakly developed, this was partly the result of governmental attitudes and actions related to the culture of depoliticization. In the early post-war period, the Hong Kong government did not believe that most Hong Kong residents felt themselves to be 'Hong Kong people' in any significant way. Instead, they saw them as 'sojourners' residing temporarily in the colony for reasons of economic advancement, and whose ultimate loyalty was to China rather than to Hong Kong.

Official beliefs in the unreliability of the Chinese can be seen in a whole range of policies and actions.[30] One that is particularly relevant to Lau's thesis of political aloofness is the Societies Ordinance, adopted in 1949 to prevent subversion by either CCP or KMT sympathizers.[31] The Ordinance was related to Hong Kong's strategy for survival in the 1950s: while finding itself 'vulnerably placed amidst the conflict of the superpowers and unable to afford becoming a flash point, Hong Kong tried to minimize such risks by ignoring the Cold War'.[32] It was able to do so because all of the Great Powers preferred to avoid a showdown there. In this context, the 'basic threat to the colony's security' arose from the contest between the Communists and the Kuomintang which could undermine its balancing act. As a result, only a policy of neutrality and suppression of political activity from both sides would preserve Hong Kong's security.[33] Thus, political repression (at a time when Hong Kong was seen as a place of freedom on the frontier of communism) could be justified as a necessity for the survival of freedom.

In the early post-war period, the British colony of Hong Kong was very reluctant to provide social services. Yet by March 1963, there were 462,582 people living in government-constructed resettlement estates, with total public housing costs amounting to HK$177,745,000.[34] This was the prelude to the 1970s expansion of public housing under MacLehose. The paradox of the rapid expansion of expenditure on squatter resettlement by a government that stressed laissez-faire is amplified by officials' deep distrust for the squatters who were eventually settled, since they were seen as even less deserving and trustworthy than the general Chinese population of Hong Kong. This surprising development, which has had so much impact on the territory's subsequent development,[35] can best be understood as the result of governmental inability to eradicate squatters' occupation of land badly needed for development. This inability was itself the result of the diplomatic vulnerability of a colony perched between the geopolitical ambitions of Washington and Beijing. Multi-storey squatter resettlement emerged from a series of squatter fires and the attendant political problems that they created. Unsuccessful early efforts eventually produced a learning curve that prompted the adoption of an initially very inexpensive, high-density multi-storey resettlement programme.[36]

The government hoped to manage the resettlement estates in such a way as to create a degree of gratitude, responsibility and civic consciousness among their residents.[37] The 1956 riots, which started in Li Cheng Uk Estate, suggested that this was not developing to the extent that the government might have hoped. The poor management practices in the resettlement estates were at least partly to blame.[38]

The crucial question is how Hong Kong's government moved from this mode of distrust about its population, and grudging expenditure on housing of the absolute minimal standards, towards energetic efforts at creating civic engagement and responsibility among its population in the 1970s, including a major expansion in the coverage, quantity and quality of public housing. Even if the 1967 riots played a role, they do not seem to have been sufficient on their own. Instead, it is the whole sequence of disturbances and other challenges to the regime that created a situation where significant reforms seemed unavoidable, or at least desirable. The greater impact of a series of crises — compared to a single event, however massive, in generating institutional learning — has been asserted in the general literature on social mobilization[39] and has also been demonstrated specifically for post-war Hong Kong.[40] Wai-man Lam argued that after 1966:

> The simmering public rage simply waited for another delicate moment before erupting again. There is much evidence that the 1966 riots

precipitated not only the 1967 riots, but also the ensuing student and social movements. Through these bloodstained experiences, society was growing more articulate and was straying away from the principle of political moderation.[41]

The colonial government eventually learned that their inadequate responses to past crises had been convincing increasing numbers of Hong Kong people that the continuation of the status quo was unacceptable and intolerable. In the next section, we turn to evidence from the archives about what lessons Governor MacLehose may have learned from these events, and what other considerations influenced the initiation of reforms in the wake of 1966 and 1967.

The MacLehose years

As we have emphasized in the previous sections, there were both continuities and discontinuities in terms of the response of the colonial state to Hong Kong society before and after the disturbances in the mid-1960s. It was most evident in the departing governor David Trench's second last despatch to the secretary of state for foreign and commonwealth affairs and the new governor Murray MacLehose's first to London.[42] In his despatch dated 23 April 1970, Trench gave an overall view of Hong Kong's developments in 1969 and then noted, referring to an issue very likely to have been of concern to London after the 1967 disturbances, 'The local Communists have continued their long term campaign to increase their presently very limited support within the Colony to a point where they can hope to dominate us . . . Their concentration on a long term strategy of winning new adherents will tend to preclude any serious brushes with authority in the short term.'[43] He then concluded with two important observations. First, on the significance of the government's social programmes:

> The people of Hong Kong have responded to the favourable economic climate with their usual high degree of enterprise and hard work, and most are enjoying a well-earned improvement in living standards. With all this inevitably comes increased expectations and a growing, but not as yet very widespread, concern for the less privileged who for one reason or another cannot share in this prosperity. For its part, the Government is pressing on with a wide range of programmes in the social service area, as well as in the more concrete field of improvements in the general environment. We are aiming at a steady improvement in the Government's performance at the level at which it has direct impact upon ordinary people, and as close a correlation between public policy and public opinion as sound administration permits . . . Indeed, while 1967 was a year in which many plans had to be delayed and 1968 was a year in which these plans had to be dusted off and momentum regained, 1969 has seen many of them brought to fruition or far along the road towards it. [44]

The paragraph above echoes our earlier note on the response of the colonial administration to successive disturbances and political contentions. The awareness of the need of addressing ordinary people's expectations seems to have predated the disturbances of the mid-1960s. While the two major disturbances might have forced the colonial government to take immediate remedial actions, social reform initiatives had their deeper roots in a growing awareness of the inadequacies of earlier practices.

Second, Trench had also taken note of Hong Kong vulnerability and how its very existence depended on the maintenance of confidence:

> Nevertheless, Hong Kong socially, politically and economically is pre-eminently a community that depends on confidence. On all three points we are vulnerable and it is essential that, with the backing of Her Majesty's Government in the United Kingdom, the Government of Hong Kong should continue, albeit with the minimum of provocation, to be firm in resisting any encroachment on the interests of the people. A loss of confidence could only too easily be generated by the successful exploitation of social and administrative problems by the Communists, or an erosion of our export markets by overseas interests.[45]

This point on popular confidence seemed to be an issue on which Trench had placed much emphasis. In a report (dated 17 February 1971) prepared by J. R. A. Bottomley, summarizing the key points of his conversation with the governor when he visited Hong Kong in early 1971, this issue was again brought to London's attention:

> What I think I should record is the fears expressed to me by the Governor that we were gradually eroding his capacity to retain the confidence of the people of Hong Kong. He was referring in particular to the pressures imposed on him for the release of Chinese Communist prisoners, and the insistence of the British Government for wider reasons on the acceptance by Hong Kong of economic measures regarded by the Hong Kong authorities as detrimental, coupled with our continued refusal either to assist in projects like the extension of the Airport or to allow Hong Kong the freedom to use its bargaining power in its own interests (again, for example, over the use of the Airport).
>
> Sir D. Trench said an important element in the Hong Kong situation was the confidence felt by the mass of the people there that the Hong Kong Government were willing and able to protect the interests of the inhabitants of the Colony. If that confidence were too badly eroded, it would become impossible to govern the Colony without a great deal more use of police action and other kinds of force, which the British Government would obviously be reluctant to have to employ.
>
> The Governor was inclined to question whether we took sufficient account of this kind of consideration when formulating our policies.[46]

By confidence, Trench was referring to both the people's confidence in the colonial governance capability and the colonial regime's ability to convince the people that it could deliver policies to safeguard their interests. The latter was the key condition to bring about the former (as an outcome). This, in turn, relied upon London's willingness to recognize the interests of Hong Kong society. Trench, who seemed to have a rather uneasy relationship with the Foreign Office,[47] raised his critical remarks before stepping down from his governorship. What is relevant to our discussion here is that Trench's remarks point to the colonial administrators' growing awareness (and, given Hong Kong's colonial status, the difficulties) of actively responding to the local people's demands and expectations. He suggested that the colonial framework, particularly the practice of subordinating the interests of the colony and its people to those of the metropole, became a source of problems and concerns as far as effective local governance was concerned. He was clearly aware of the emergence of a local political and social agenda in Hong Kong. More importantly, future effective governance critically rested upon the colonial administration's ability to meet the challenge from Hong Kong society.

MacLehose was equally conscious of this confidence issue. Trench had held to the Colonial Office tradition of the governor having considerable autonomy as 'the man on the spot' and sent the Foreign Office his despatches on an irregular basis. MacLehose, however, given his background in professional diplomacy, openly expressed his intention of maintaining close contact with London. As we shall see in the following discussion, which is largely based upon his first Hong Kong annual despatch,[48] dated 1 January 1973, the question of confidence was central to his work of administration, planning and governance. He began his annual reporting by highlighting the vulnerability of Hong Kong to external forces: 'Though Hong Kong's stature may have changed the hard facts which govern its existence have not. Its four million inhabitants and their government are still dependent on the one hand for their livelihood and revenue on the growth of export industries, and on the other for their very existence, on the policy of the Chinese Government.'[49] The China factor that he emphasized came to constitute an important component of his overall picture of how to govern Hong Kong. However, it is important to note that the China factor in MacLehose's perspective was less of a source of internal political threat or challenge to the colonial authority (as found in the 1967 disturbances, or earlier in the Comfort Mission riot of 1952), but centred more on China's role in determining Hong Kong's longer-term political future. China was then undergoing rapid changes in its participation in international affairs and organizations, returning to social and political order and leadership from the stormier days of the climax of the Cultural Revolution, and rebuilding diplomatic relations with the Western world. Such changes created a new environment for working out new visions of planning for Hong Kong's social development. Indeed, as early as late 1971 when MacLehose was preparing the documents on 'The Guidelines for the Governor Designate, Hong Kong', he noted that '[w]e must work out policies in Hong Kong consciously designed to prolong confidence and so gain all possible time for conditions to emerge in China in which a favourable negotiation would be possible. Conversely we must avoid actions and administrative procedures in Hong Kong which tend to highlight the diminishing term of the Lease.'[50] He then continued: 'Hitherto the Hong Kong Government has believed that the security risks involved in forward planning were greater than any advantages derived from it. My own view is that the balance of advantage now lies in initiating a highly secret but thorough look at the future. While I do not think the critical period will commence before the second half of this decade, the planning process will have to start now.'[51]

MacLehose returned to this question in his review of his first year of governorship in the annual despatch. Apparently, this focus on prolonging confidence and preparing for subsequent negotiation with China over Hong Kong's future had come to constitute the overarching perspective of his social reform initiatives:

> Though I myself may take a more sombre view, and may have constantly in mind how to keep the population's confidence undisturbed, and how to gain time and cohesion against the pressure that may come, whether by design or mischance, I don't think this is the view of Hong Kong at this time. People are more concerned with conditions of life for themselves and their children and with their prospects of betterment.
>
> This makes the social policy of the Hong Kong Government and what is done to improve living conditions of particular significance for the Colony's future. Moreover I find that in the last ten years the population has become much less fatalistic about conditions of life and more expectant of Government. . . . While this increased awareness and expectancy represent a potential danger to the government if it acts beneath public expectations, it also offers opportunity to the Government if it sets out to meet them and is believed to be doing so. The increased awareness and expectancy, if met, could generate a civic pride that could not have been stirred amongst the more fatalistic and apathetic and desperately preoccupied refugees of 20 or even 10 years ago.[52]

In this connection, MacLehose went on to explain his political calculations in launching major projects in public housing, education and social welfare services:

> For these reasons, and in any case on its merits, in the course of 1972 Government drew up and announced long term plans: . . . These programmes were all logical developments of policies already in practice. But their simultaneous announcement, with its implied determination to put a term to the make-shift conditions created by the influxes of refugees in the 1950s and early '60s was a calculated move intended to focus the attention of the population on Hong Kong as their home, and on the Government of Hong Kong as their government.[53]

Summing up his overall review of his work in 1972, MacLehose contextualized various government initiatives in a broader framework of changing state/society relations:

> One feature that strikes me as salient is that though Hong Kong is the home of over 4 million who have to a greater or lesser extent rejected China, a large proportion have not fully accepted Hong Kong. A new generation is growing up – 55% of our population is under 25 – and is demanding more from Government, often rightly. Like any other government this one must govern by consent and must do so without the aid of the electoral system. If that consent is to be retained, not only must legitimate demands be satisfied, but the population must be conceived that such satisfaction is genuinely the objective of Government. The need is not only for administrative action producing physical results; there is also a need to secure the active confidence of the population. We cannot aim at national loyalty, but civic pride might be a useful substitute.
>
> This can be achieved only by corporate effort, and such a concept is new to Hong Kong where the tradition has been for people to do only more or less what they are told by Government and otherwise . . . to be as little bothered with corporate affairs as possible. I think that from now policy must aim to make both the elite and the masses feel, as they felt in 1967, that Hong Kong is an entity to which they belong, and the place they wish to live in.[54]

As we have noted earlier, MacLehose had reformulated the overarching perspective of how Hong Kong was to be governed. Like Trench, his starting point was popular confidence. But unlike Trench, he saw the confidence issue not so much one of effective governance after two major disturbances but as involving a longer-term development of a new kind of state/society relations. Taking another look at the colonial administration under MacLehose in the light of the above discussion, we are sceptical of the stereotypical description of MacLehose as a benevolent social reformer and his governorship as a period of fundamental transformation of colonial rule.[55] While it is true that MacLehose was conscious of the need for building popular confidence in order to cope with an uncertain political environment when Hong Kong was expected to be in confrontation with China in the years approaching 1997, this does not necessarily mean that he was eager to launch drastic reforms even at the risk of antagonizing the colonial bureaucrats and the established interests of the capitalist economy. It is beyond the scope of this chapter to dwell upon the determinants of policy initiatives undertaken by the colonial administration under MacLehose's governorship. Elsewhere, one of us has discussed the impacts of British politics, particularly in the form of union lobbying and political pressures from Britain's trading partners, on policy changes concerning labour conditions and welfare.[56] Suffice it to say, the stereotype of MacLehose's governorship as benevolent colonialism may mislead one to overstate the readiness of the colonial state to take the initiative of promoting reform from above. MacLehose reframed the practice of the colonial administration by highlighting the political preparation for future diplomatic manoeuvres. But the scale and scope of his policy initiatives were shaped by political concerns. Sometimes, pressures from London prevailed. On other occasions, the colonial state's assessment of emerging social needs and people's rising expectations played its part in determining the policy outcomes. In brief, politics, be it local contention or calculation from the perspective of the metropolis, matters in the shaping of policy changes under colonialism.

MacLehose's contribution was therefore not so much about being a social reformer, but rather that he had introduced a new framework for British colonial rule in Hong Kong. He described his government as 'a Government in a hurry'[57] as it had to race against time in building civic pride among the local Chinese in a colonial context before the question concerning the future of Hong Kong was put onto the table for diplomatic negotiation. He had moved beyond the aftermaths of both the 1966 and 1967 disturbances. In fact, as we have emphasized throughout our discussion, he had gone back to the fundamental issues of colonial governance — how the colonial government was going to develop its relationships with the governed, especially in view of repeated political actions in the past and rising expectations in the years to follow.

Conclusion

The 1967 disturbances could be, and were, treated as externally provoked and as failing to achieve significant support from the average members of Hong Kong society. Given this, it initially seems surprising that broad and significant social and governance reforms were adopted in its wake. If the responses revealed the loyalty of Hong Kong people, why did they need to be placated with expenditures and policies which were at odds with dominant laissez-faire ideas that were seen as crucial for Hong Kong's success? We suggest that the responses only make sense in the context of past disturbances and the challenge that they presented to the colonial regime. Without the 1967 events, it seems likely that the 1966 disturbances would also have encouraged substantial reforms. The 1952 event had indicated the way in which riots might threaten Hong Kong's stability due to its vulnerable diplomatic and geopolitical situation. In fact, fears about the unreliability of Hong Kong subjects had created a situation where the expansion of government involvement in the direct provision of housing was the most viable way of solving the squatter problem and making land available for conventional development. The 1956 riot showed that residents of resettlement estates were not automatically more docile and loyal than squatters. The kind of support emergent during the 1967 disturbances was clearly not that of active political support that would give the colonial government an opportunity to develop hegemonic rule and leadership. Rather, it was more of a kind of passive support, backing the colonial authority in view of a communist threat and the resultant political uncertainty. In this regard, what was exposed by the 1967 disturbances was actually the fragility of the colonial regime. Like the 1966 riots, discontents and unrest could easily spark off widespread political contentions in 1967. The colonial government was unsure of the extent of political support from Hong Kong subjects. It was due to this awareness of a lack of active political support that Governor David Trench discussed the issue of public confidence. It was upon this ground that various measures were launched after the 1967 disturbances to promote public confidence in colonial authority.

Were the events of 1967 the last straw to precipitate social reforms that had long been under consideration, or were they the primary driving forces for transformation in the colonial government's approach to managing social affairs? Further research is necessary for answering this question. Our tentative analysis here points to a view that those reforms launched immediately after the year of 1967 formed the basis of broader and grander governmental efforts to be found in the so-called MacLehose decade. When MacLehose took up his governorship, he had a different political framework in mind. He was conscious of the political uncertainty of the colony and found it important to boost public confidence and to secure hegemonic leadership before China raised questions concerning Hong Kong's political status. The kind of public confidence he had in mind was different from Trench's conception which was primarily an immediate response to a crisis situation. MacLehose believed that it was necessary to win the active political support of the ordinary people and to develop a sense of belonging among them. He understood that the colonial regime would only secure a firm grasp for its rule when the ordinary people were convinced that Hong Kong was to become a better living environment for them. His reform programme was, therefore, one with a broader political objective than what was launched to cope with a particular crisis. His hegemonic project was a response to, as we have argued in this chapter, a longer and deeper sense of political distrust among the ordinary people. He attempted to change the political distrust that was revealed in repeated political contention in the colony. His programme departed from the 1967 events, but instead of stopping at coping with crisis, it moved on to a hegemonic political project of building identification, cooperation and loyalty.

Section III

Testimonies

1967: Witnesses remember

Robert Bickers and Ray Yep

On 27 May 2007, 150 people crowded into an auditorium at City University Hong Kong to hear those prepared to share memories of their experiences of the events of 1967. The idea of the organizers was to place the academic studies which formed the heart of the workshop in their place: the events were still recent history and there were clearly many in Hong Kong who had participated in or witnessed them, or whose experience of living in those difficult times was strong. The event had been advertised in the press and on radio, and it drew a very large crowd. Many younger people came, which is probably a testament to growing interest in an episode about which there has mostly been a sustained public silence. There were also many in the audience of an age to have strong memories of 1967. Some of those who spoke indicated their willingness to do so in advance, others came from the floor. All were restricted to a short time — eight minutes — to allow as many voices as possible to be heard.

The transcripts below have been translated, but are otherwise entirely unmediated. Three speakers have left no contact details for us or did not respond to our requests for permission to reproduce their comments. Some came prepared, with notes and materials, but other speakers reacted spontaneously to each other's assertions or interpretations. Some spoke from very fixed positions; the politics of others had mellowed with time. Yet, the event was constructive and polite, although real anger and real fear were communicated by many of the speakers. The event was in and of itself an important moment in the public history of 1967. We reproduce the transcripts below to remind ourselves that the year 1967 does not belong to historians, and that while opinions and memories can differ sharply, it is possible to sustain a constructive debate about what happened, and about the place of these events in the history of Hong Kong and Hong Kong society.

These first-person accounts have made three important contributions to the project of understanding the events in 1967. First, these materials remind us an important dimension of history: an awareness of the past that is personally felt.

These speakers connected the events in 1967 with their personal experiences or traumatic encounters. Their accounts are not simply testimony to the emotions unleashed during the months of turbulence, or a window for deciphering the meaning of the event for the local population, they are also contrasting accounts of personal reflections that are forceful reminders of the multiplicity of standpoints on historical events. The task of history writing may thus warrant a more collaborative project and it should not be a process monopolized by experts or academics who are primarily working on archives and official records. The enthusiasm of this self-selected group hints that there may be a prospect of 'bringing the people in'. Second, these vivid accounts of personal trauma reveal the intensity of violence unleashed in 1967. While the discussion remained restrained and moderate, speakers of different backgrounds launched similar attacks on the opposite camp highlighting memories of brutality and senseless violence. It is, however, the fear for his own safety and that of the younger brother in his care, of a teenage boy missing the last bus home before curfew hour that provides the most powerful hint of the rupture to normality caused by the events in 1967. His fear of indiscriminate shooting by the police is certainly ungrounded, but such fear in an innocent boy with no political background is a vivid reflection of the chaos of the time. This certainly was no 'flea-bite', as Sir David Trench described it twenty years after the events.[1] A related question is, with ordinary law enforcement reinforced by draconian measures in the form of Emergency Regulations and highly determined to contain disturbance, why did the left-wing supporters show no sign of deference? This brings us to the most important lesson drawn from these 'witness accounts' — the domestic character of the 1967 events. For most British observers, the official judgement was that the whole episode was nothing more than a spin-off of the Cultural Revolution and there was no domestic explanation or even justification for the riots. The various accounts here seem to suggest otherwise. Common to most stories told in the forum was a sense of frustration and social tension on the eve of the 1967 riots. These personal reflections point to the possibility of spontaneous involvement of local population as a protest against social injustice and limitations of colonial rule, a perspective which colonial officials simply discarded as irrelevant and misguided.

We need to make it clear that we are not presenting these statements as oral testimony of a kind that would properly satisfy an oral historian. Our inspiration was the witness seminar series run by the Centre of Contemporary British History at London University since 1986, but while those bring together the key actors in the events under discussion, we aimed instead to capture echoes in 2007 of the voices that we were not finding it easy to locate in the paper records of 1967. They suggest that there is real potential for an oral history of the events of 1967 and their afterlife, and more than that they suggest that there is a real need for this to be done. The interests of the speakers cross over many of the debates which had emerged in the scholarly workshop, as can be seen, but also discussed areas we had not considered. We do not intend to suggest that they are a comprehensive, representative, systematic, or definitive set of participants, but they offer much for us to reflect on. We have added notes explaining some of the incidents referred to, but otherwise we have left our witnesses to speak for themselves. We are grateful to them.

Speaker 1: Chow Yik （周奕）, *Wen Wei Po* reporter

My name is Chow Yik. I was a reporter on *Wen Wei Po* . . . Firstly, I would like to thank Dr Yep for inviting me to this conference to talk about my real-life experience. As he has mentioned just now, he did not give us any restriction or instruction for my speech. He just said to me, 'Let's talk about what happened during your time as a reporter in 1967.' I feel very honoured to be here to speak to you all. What is the 12.3 Incident in Macao all about? I covered that story. I think I know more about this than Dr Yep. I was there and many of my cameras were robbed. Someone also stole my tripod. I probably want some compensation for my loss.

I personally witnessed all the developments: the 12.3 Incident in Macao, the Star Ferry disturbances, and eventually the San Po Kong incident. These were all my reporting assignments. For people at the grass root, we describe what happened as an anti-British/anti-colonial struggle. Now many people call it the 1967 'riots'. Let's not argue about it. I will only tell you about what I saw. During the whole period of 'struggle', *Wen Wei Po* had instructed me to stay away from the office. The atmosphere was horrible at that time and we did not return to office. I had to be prepared for arrest. But I will put this aside for the time being. Because of my reporting duties, I had witnessed much of the course of the incident. Many people were beaten up; they bled. You have probably heard about the San Po Kong case, and were told about the numerous bomb explosions during that time. This is definitely an exaggeration. There were not that many bombs. It was illegal to put bombs. What I want to tell you is that we should know what happened between the San Po Kong dispute and the waves of bomb attacks. Several TV channels interviewed me recently. Yesterday Phoenix TV interviewed me; the interview will be broadcast at 7.15 p.m. tomorrow. In the interview, I said people should be aware of the unfolding of events in May, starting from the San Po Kong Incident to the Garden Road Incident. On the Garden Road Incident, Cheung Ka Wai asked in his book, 'Who lies?'[2] Cheung does not really understand this point. Who lies? The three people injured during the Garden Road incident are still alive. Here is a photograph of them bleeding. You may all find this photo book very precious.[3] During the Garden Road incident, the police used violence and beat people.

And I also want you to have a deeper reflection on the bloodshed on 22 June 1967. A general strike was planned on 23 June. On the eve of the strike, the colonial government sent out a large contingent of police and broke into the premises of the Hong Kong Plastic Workers' Union (港九樹膠塑膠業總工會). One unionist was shot; four bullets went into his body. The police besieged the union premises and many tear gas canisters were fired as well. I was there as a reporter but I could only observe and take pictures from a distance. At that time the chairman of the Union, Fung Kam Shui, led members of the Union and rushed down the stairs together. He escorted other members downstairs twice. He recalled that as long as a human shadow was seen, the police downstairs would shoot their machine guns. The police had already besieged the Union, why didn't they let people come out? Why did the police have to shoot the people with machine guns? They only wanted to create an intimidating mood on the eve of the general strike. Dozens of members of the Union were arrested, and two of them were beaten to death in the police station. Do we know these bloody incidents? I believe that you don't. Many of the Union members whom I know had their homes searched through. It was natural for the industrial workers to have some tools at home. Unfortunately, these tools were seen as offensive weapons and an excuse for arrest.

There was a bizarre phenomenon during that period. Some newspapers, strangely, lied. The colonial government published and gave out some pamphlets. Whoever had these pamphlets at home was charged for possessing subversive materials and would be sentenced to three months' imprisonment. Some of my friends asked me, 'Why do you still hide these?' I replied, 'I am ready to be caught at any time.' It did not really matter whether you had done anything at all. I thought I would be arrested anyway simply because I worked for *Wen Wei Po*. At that time I worked with two young colleagues and we tried to continue our reporting away from the office. The paper did not give us specific instructions and we worked independently. I had to rely on my journalistic experience and my reading of stories covered in *Wen Wei Po* and *Ta Kung Pao* to decide what to write about. But we didn't contact the paper directly. Instead, when we were ready, we called them and the paper would send someone to pick up the report from us. I can tell you it was a very special situation, and in a way it is similar to life that was under the rule of the Guomindang before the Liberation; we were always prepared to be arrested. I hope you would take notice of these. I have published a book; there were three reprint editions in one year.[4] The book is also available in public libraries. I hope you all would know the truth. Why would there be such happenings? I only want to tell you what I saw.

Speaker 2: Ling Man Hoi（凌文海）, son of a leftist school headmaster

Ladies and gentlemen, I did not intend to speak, but Chow Yik has put down my name. I believe that there are many missing gaps in the narrative of Hong Kong history. Nowadays, much has been said about 'collective memories'. I think everyone should reflect on this 1967 incident. We do not have to decide who did right and who did wrong. Talking about the year 1967 today is, in fact, rather sensitive. I am a politician holding public office. I just want to share some of my personal experience with you today.

Just now, Mr Tam (Chi Keung) has said that the 1967 riots were related to the 12.3 Incident in Macao. I agree with his view totally. It is because both incidents were a result of the Cultural Revolution — the product of the fanaticism of Mao Zedong thought. At that time I was about 18 or 19 years old and had just graduated from secondary school in 1966. After graduation I taught in a left-wing school. My father was the headmaster of a primary school in the New Territories as well. It was the time when the riots started. I do not wish to use the term 'riots'. Instead, during that time we had a phrase describing the episode: 'May Storm' (五月風暴). I think this is more appropriate. 'Riots' implies that we were rebels or leftists (左仔), and we made troubles. I do not think calling the incident 'riots' is fair. I do not want to engage in the debate on who was responsible for the violence as raised by Chow Yik a moment ago. But I would like to point out that there had been a reign of 'white terror' in Hong Kong ever since the founding of the People's Republic of China in 1949. The colonial government, with the assistance of the Special Branch, had maintained a close watch on patriots like us who supported the PRC and the Chinese Communist Party. When I was young, my home was searched by the police three times. It usually happened at night. A group of Western and Chinese officers dressed in casual wear would knock on the door. Once they got in, they would check everything we had in our house. I was very young at that time; I leaned against my mother and looked at my father's pale face when the house was being searched. This is what I mean by 'white terror' in Hong Kong. It was oppression and the government wanted to control our thinking and behaviour. I also remember that every time when the search was over, *Wen Wei Po* was nowhere to be found in our house and we would only read *Sing Tao Daily* for the next two or three months. These are my recollections of those frightening moments.

Two of my relatives were victims of violence during the 1967 riots. One of them was my uncle, who was a victim of the 5.22 Incident as shown in Chow Yik's photograph. On that day, people protested outside the Government House. My uncle was one of them and was assaulted so seriously that his body was covered in blood. He sat outside the entrance of Hilton Hotel on Garden Road and this is shown in the photograph. After looking at these photographs I recalled a lot.

Another victim was my father. He was the headmaster of a primary school in Sai Kung. I do not understand why the colonial government wanted to arrest him. He was arrested on the night of 15 July 1967. A lot of police officers surrounded our house and the front gate was destroyed. The date of arrest was chosen on the ground that it was the school graduation day on the 16th. Rumour had it that my father had planned to run away, but the police calculated that he might not flee until the graduation ceremony was over. I was not at home on the night of my father's arrest. I was a teacher in a leftist primary school at that time. It was a school holiday as examination was over in mid-July. I was at the Tram Workers' Union (電車工會) office that night. At that time, development of the riots was discussed at the Union office every day. I went there with a few teachers and we performed dancing and singing for the workers as a token of support. I knew nothing about my father's arrest until the following morning when I read a newspaper headline which said: 'The headmaster of Sai Kung School arrested'. Then I knew something bad had happened. My family recalled that when my father was taken away from the house, some police officers also stole some valuables, like gold rings from us.

Eventually, my father was brought to Mount Davis.[5] At first, we could not find where he was. We only located his whereabouts when we went to the police headquarters. From the relatives of others who were also detained by the police, including Fu Ki (傅奇) and Shek Wai (石慧), I finally found out the place where my father and other detainees were locked up. Only one visit was allowed each week. We had to register at the Special Branch and they drove us to the building at Mount Davis. I am not sure if the building is still there. Inside we took it in turns to meet our relatives. My father told me later that for the first two or three months, he was locked in a room with a fluorescent lamp which was never switched off. He was isolated from the others and there was no clock in his room. This deprived him of the sense of time and orientation. My father had not been seriously beaten up, yet this arrangement was also a form of torture. When I visited him, there was a fence between us in the room, with a policeman watching us. He also complained that it was very cold at night. He was only given one blanket, though he was granted another one later. We complained on his behalf. The officer replied that we could supply him with extra clothes if we wanted, but there would be no extra blanket. In the end, we tried to get around this by making a 'special jacket' for him. We used a very thick blanket and cut it into a jacket-shaped stuff.

We were victims of the 1967 riots. My father was released after a year and a half. I guess this was a result of the negotiations between London and Beijing. Before his release, we had tried very hard to get him out. To everybody's surprise, my father suddenly returned home one day. The colonial government drove him and his luggage to Sai Kung and left him there. My father came home barefoot and the entire family was stunned. There was a warning letter in his luggage though. The colonial government claimed in the letter that they had the right to arrest my father again at any time. We organized some 'mass movement' as a safety measure. In the next few days, friends and relatives were invited to our house and had meals with us because we were afraid that my father would be taken away again. In fact, the letter was just used to scare us. However, we did find strangers peeping at us from time to time; I knew they were policemen.

This is what happened to me during the riots. You do not need to decide who is right and who is wrong. But I believe that my family were victims; we were oppressed during the whole process.

Speaker 3: Luk Kai Lau (陸啓鎏), police officer

Just now there is a speaker who said he can easily identify police officers. Just wonder if he can tell that I was a policeman as well. Here today, we do not intend to argue who is right and who is wrong in history. I know that many people at that time were victims. Not only were they victims, we policemen were victims too because we were used as 'political tools'. Take the recent WTO conference, for example. The police was ordered to the frontline. Yet this does not mean that we did it out of our own will; we do not have a stand, but we have to take orders. However, we are not going to talk about that today. Today I wish to share with you why we policemen could maintain our morale in 1967. How could we perform our duties and maintain order and stability? I am 63 years old this year and I am a retired police officer. I was 'lucky' as I started my career as a policeman on 1 April 1965. So, I could witness the riots in 1966 and 1967. I was involved in the incidents in (the artificial flower factory) in San Po Kong, Hilton Hotel, Government House and Kiu Kwun Building (僑冠大廈) that Mr Chow just talked about. This was because I was a member of the Bayview Company (銅鑼環防暴隊). In retrospect, I am really grateful for the help of the Auxiliary Police at that time. We fought together and only with their assistance did we manage to stabilize the situation. At that time we were all youngsters. I entered the police force in 1965. And by the time the riots started, I was only 21 or 22 years old. During that time all the young police officers were reassigned to the Police Tactical Unit. Our Company was reassigned PTU Reserve, which maintained standby status all the time ready for any order for action from the police commissioner. With all the young officers drafted into frontline action, how could we protect the police stations and our families at the dormitories? The Auxiliary Police did a great job here and as a result we did not have to worry about our families when we went to work.

The political storm hit Hong Kong in 1967. There was no diplomatic channel for the colonial government to negotiate or bargain with the communists. The leftists in Hong Kong were fanatical and determined and we confronted the rioters on a daily basis. Take, for example, the experience near the China Products Company on Johnston Road, Wanchai. Street lights were off along the entire road. The rioters yelled through loudhailers: 'Down with the yellow dogs! Down with the white-skin pigs!' (打倒黃皮狗！生劏白皮猪！) Containers with acidic chemicals were thrown at us from above. There is no need to argue about whether the leftists started the violence. I hope, one day, we will have more time and peace of mind so that we can all sit down and discuss this matter. All this is now history and there is no need to argue about who did right and who did wrong. Still, I hope we could discuss this further and find a better understanding or account of the events.

A related question is why did the Hong Kong police force handle riots better than the Macao police force? Perhaps it was because the colonial government of Hong Kong was more skilful in manipulation. First and foremost, our police officers were victims. We were told to maintain self-restraint when confronted by the rioters. When I worked at the Government House, I belonged to the Police Tactical Unit. We were ordered to keep all our heavy gear inside the building, and we did not carry guns. When the demonstrators approached us, we held hands together and tried to fend them off. The demonstrators confronted us and shouted with their loudhailers close enough to touch my nose. And in order to run quickly, we all wore canvas shoes. These shoes did not offer any protection and when the people stepped on our feet, it really hurt! People can see the whole event from different perspectives. And the way we police officers see it is probably different from the demonstrators. We did not complain at that time. But I would like to emphasize that I was not a soldier. If we did not have a sense of justice and responsibility and believe in what we were doing, we could simply walk away from the force. But most of my colleagues did not do so.

The riots broke out in the period of water rationing. Water supply was limited to once in four days. We always worked long shifts and had to stay in the station for a week at a time. Amusingly, as we did not take baths very often, our woollen socks stank. In fact, they could stand like a Christmas tree if we took them off and placed them on the floor. Many of us had athlete's foot as a result. The pepper spray we had was used as a sort of disinfectant! Does anyone know about this? Probably not. It is like during the recent WTO event in Hong Kong, not many of us are aware of the fact that the policemen have been running around with heavy equipment on their backs for thirty hours. In my generation, we are lucky to have the support of the business sector and local people. They knew that the survival of Hong Kong was dependent on the morale of the police force. It was touching to see them giving us soft drinks, sandwiches and cakes when we finished our job outside the Hilton Hotel. After the 1967 riots, the business sector set up an education fund and raised $6 million for the children of policemen. Both regular and auxiliary police can enjoy this benefit. It was a huge sum of money at that time. My children made good progress, thanks to the fund. I am very pleased and grateful.

We tried to tolerate the provocations of the demonstrators as much as possible and some people wondered why we police did not fight back. It was because our self-restraint gained us support and sympathy, from both the citizens and the media. The silver lining of the 1967 riots was the improved public image of the police force. We received more trust and support from the people than before. I think it is easier to be a policeman in my time than now, as media attention is everywhere today. They can make a meal of anything you do these days.

Speaker 4: Luk Tak Shing（陸德成）, dockyard worker

Ladies and gentlemen, I would like to talk about what I saw and experienced during the 1967 riots. I was a trainee at the Swire dockyard in 1967 and also a unionist. On the day the workers in the San Po Kong Artificial Flower Factory were arrested,

I had planned to go and visit the factory with a few of my colleagues to show our support. We had planned to bring them some bread. But once we reached Tai Yau Street (大有街), I immediately realized that the police were soon going to arrest people. It was forty years ago but I still have a vivid memory of the episode. Whenever I talk about this, I still get very emotional. I saw two policemen grabbing a worker's arms while the third policeman hit the man's chest very hard with the baton. The baton was two to three feet long. That worker spat blood immediately. After forty years I still remember this incident vividly. Many people witnessed this too, including workers at the Tai Yau Street factory. The workers who saw this in the upper floors protest by throwing down cups and glass bottles. I do not know whether that worker had died on that day or not. What a poor guy!

The second thing I want to talk about was my arrest. After the strike began, I joined the Swire Dockyard Union (太古船塢工會). The Union asked me to concentrate on union affairs and step down from work. I was arrested on a Sunday. Before the arrest, there were already some hints of its coming. At ten o'clock that morning, many police cars were deployed from North Point to Chai Wan. Some of my colleagues warned me that the police would probably search the Union soon. But others thought that we had nothing to worry about and that it was not a big deal to be searched. Besides, most searches were launched at night, so we were really off our guard.

At the time, many workers were bachelors and they usually went back to the Union for lunch. By around noon, we found the whole Shau Kei Wan area was surrounded by the police with helicopters, speed boats and police vehicles everywhere. The police eventually came and five unions — Swire Dockyard Union (太古船塢工會), Swire Automobile Union (太古車廠工會), Metal Industries Union (五金支會), Oil Paint Union (油漆支會) and Seamen's Union (船家友支會) — were searched. The workers were not armed and were soon arrested by the police easily. But after we had been arrested, the anti-riot squad started charging at us indiscriminately. I remember this very clearly. They did not even care whether we had resisted or not. They took us to the corner of the street and took turns to hit each of us with the bottom of their long guns. I forgot how many times I was beaten. All I knew was that my back was swollen. They did not care who you were; they just beat everyone. Later the police claimed that we were arrested on the grounds of unlawful assembly. We were only having lunch on the union premises. But the police testified that we were holding a meeting and singing at the time of the arrest. What is the problem with singing? In fact, we had not sung; we only ate.

I believe that the outbreak of the 1967 riots had external and internal causes and also immediate causes. The external causes were the Cultural Revolution and the 12.3 Incident in Macao. These developments nurtured a rebellious spirit among the Hong Kong people; they started complaining about colonial rule. However, external causes alone were not enough to trigger off the riots; internal causes played a key role here. At that time there were a lot of social tensions and corruption was rampant in Hong Kong. My mother was a hawker. What was the life of a hawker? Every day the policemen on patrol (花腰) asked her for a dollar, and the hawker control officer (韭王) did the same. What could you do? You dared not refuse as they could arrest you the next day, and you could lose all your money and have your goods confiscated. Nowadays hawkers are luckier than we were; the hawkers used to earn only five or six dollars a day. This was what I saw. Other social hardships included serious unemployment and under-provision of welfare. Ethnic inequality was apparent. The difference in status between Westerners and Chinese was huge. Basically all the middle-ranking managers in foreign-owned companies were Westerners, let alone the government. These were the internal causes.

The immediate cause was the artificial flower factory labour dispute. It was just a labour dispute, so why should it involve the deployment of the riot squad? Can you tell me the reason? Someone said the suppression was down to the bombs laid by the leftists, but I think this really depends on how you see things. In the beginning, there was no bombing. But then we witnessed the violent suppression of the workers in the San Po Kong Artificial Flowers Factory and the demonstrators on Garden Road. It was followed by the general strike, searches of unions and many more workers getting beaten up, arrested or even killed. What could we do under these circumstances? I think we could only use violence in the face of this violence (以暴易暴). Li Yee (李怡) published an article a few weeks ago which used the apposite term, 'suppression first, riots later' (先鎮後暴).[6] I would say it is more appropriate to describe the 1967 riots as 'anti-Britain and anti-violence' (反英抗暴). I think that while the disturbances might still have been triggered by external developments, without the police oppression, they would never have been as intense as they were. This is what I wanted to say.

Speaker 5: Ng Huen Yan（吳萱人）, civil servant

I would like to thank Cheung Ka Wai who persuaded me to come to this forum. First of all, let me show you a 'treasure' that I have kept for forty years. This is a sample of a 'mosquito newspaper' (蚊型報) — something very famous during the riots. There is also a fake hundred dollar note. Why was there such a banknote? It was because the Hong Kong currency was significantly depreciated during that time and this 'banknote' was a mockery of the colonial government's indifference to the interests of Hong Kong. Many criticized devaluation as robbery of the wealth of Hong Kong people. This paper is called *The Shock* (衝擊), and this is only one of the several hundred papers circulated during that period.

Recently some young people have organized hunger strikes in memory of the May Fourth Movement; or they see it as an act to honour the May Fourth tradition. We all know that there was a new magazine, *New Youth* (新青年), published during the May Fourth years, which represented the new ideas and enlightenment of that generation. But we may not know that there was a magazine with the same title published in Hong Kong during the riots. Here is a copy of this magazine. Its publisher is the one which published the famous weekly *Youth Garden* (青年樂園) in the 1960s. Its major competitor was *Chinese Students Weekly* (中國學生周報), another popular magazine at the time. *Youth Garden* tried to maintain a low profile and acted as a platform for rational debate during the riots period. It was later banned but it still continued to publish the *New Youth* as its supplement. The young people today may find the politicized nature of the magazine difficult to comprehend; in most issues of the magazine, you could always find Chairman Mao's 'highest directives' on the front pages.

Why do I bother to show you these valuable publications? I think we need a new perspective for understanding the 1967 riots. I have great sympathy for the workers and journalists who were involved in the political struggles during 1967. I have some friends who were close to the left-wing camp and were arrested as well. I am not one of them, although I was always a radical. I cannot think of any reason to be a rightist. I believe the 1967 riots was a 'Hong Kong version of the new international radical youth movement' (全球青年激進運動香港版本). Why did I call this a youth movement? Let's go back to the magazine, *Shock,* which I mentioned earlier. For this generation of young people who are preoccupied with the computer, they would find it hard to understand how difficult it was to publish a magazine in the 1960s. We used very primitive technology — writing on carbon copy, carving of the typeset by hand, and so on. But there were hundreds of similar papers being circulated among the young people at the time. *Wen Wei Po* published a full page of articles that were selected from these papers every day and the column was very popular.

I believe if we want to really understand the nature of the 1967 riots, we must look into these materials. Where did these papers come from? They were all published by young people and these young people came from all sorts of backgrounds. They came from different ideological backgrounds or political stances; they were students from English-language schools, patriotic schools, government schools, and evening schools; some had no formal education at all. What was the motivation behind the involvement of this great mass of young minds in these publication efforts? I personally believe that regardless of their backgrounds, young people in the 1960s were all pondering the prospect of social reform. The wave of social changes did not come out of the blue. First, it was a response to the international radical movement of the time. I will leave that aside for the time being. Secondly, young people growing up in the 1960s were confronted with the question of China's status in modern history. It is an undeniable fact that China was defeated and humiliated a hundred years ago and as a result, we all had to live under undignified order of colonial rule in Hong Kong and Macao. As mentioned by another speaker earlier in this forum, social contradictions were intense in the 1960s. I agree with this because I have lived through this period.

I was a junior civil servant in 1967. Let me show you an invaluable document. It is a certificate of appreciation signed by David Trench, the governor. I was praised as a good civil servant because I did not take part in the riots — I did not take a single day off during the period. This is illustrative of the oppressive stance of the colonial government. If you were not absent from work, you were a good employee and you got a prize. This 'certificate' is just a photocopied letter and you can even produce one by yourself. Also at that time, if you were a junior staff, you were expected to join the Government-Military and Medical Staff Union (政軍醫工會). This is a left-wing union for Chinese staff, but I was not a member. Young people were the most conscientious group. They were most sensitive to social injustice and inequality, and they wanted changes. They would rise up if they had the chance. If not, they would probably regret it for the rest of their lives.

Let me briefly say a few words on the anti-colonial history of Hong Kong. In 1952, there was an incident that led to the great discontent of the leftist camp. There was a fire in Shek Kip Mei. After the People's Republic of China was founded in 1949, the political order became complicated in Hong Kong. The mainland government wanted to send a delegation to Hong Kong as a sign of sympathy and support for the victims. This is what many historians called 'the Reunion Incident' (迎親人事件). There were 200,000 to 300,000 local people gathered at the Tsim Sha Tsui station to receive the delegation. However, the colonial government responded by suppressing the event high-handedly. It also dissolved thirty-five cultural bodies and youth organizations immediately. This was a severe blow to the left-wing camp. Such a wound contributed to the outbreak of the riots fifteen years later. There were two other incidents which had nothing to do with the local communists, but had paved the way for the 1967 riots. The first one is the 1966 disturbance that erupted as a result of the Star Ferry fare increase. Another one happened ten years earlier and this was the riot in Tsuen Wan in the New Territories. It is strange that not many people mention the event now. Newspapers at that time described the incident as 'the troublesome October' (十月多事之秋). Involvement of the pro-Taiwanese force was the main cause of its outbreak. Yet, the fact that it took place in Li Cheng Uk and Shek Kip Mei, two large resettlement areas in Hong Kong, was illustrative of grass-roots social tensions. These contradictions are the key factors behind the final outbreak of the riots in 1967.

This is a very meaningful event. Time is limited and let me conclude. I would like to ask those from the left-wing camp to reflect on their responsibility and see if they did any damage to public order during the riots. We can only overcome the trauma if they do so. In addition, only if we place the riots in the context of social movements, can we have any meaningful exploration into this matter.

Speaker 6: Lam Yuet Tin （林月田）, Primary school student

My surname is Lam. I was in Primary 6 in 1967. I would like to first describe how life was like at that time. It was difficult to get a job and even if you wanted to be a shopkeeper, you needed to have some store-owner to provide endorsement for your application. The daily salary was around four to five dollars. There was no labour law and workers had to work every day and overtime work was routine. Corruption was rampant with dirty policemen offering protection for prostitution and gambling businesses. You could find gambling stalls and opium dens everywhere. Even the firemen would only provide help if you gave them money (有水放水). The British were always in a superior position and for the brightest Chinese the top job you could get was a deputy position in a government department. We needed to send a letter in English to apply for a telephone connection. Police abuses were common and the sight of hawkers being beaten up by officers was common. Many people were living in squatter settlements and medical services were seriously undersupplied. It was common to find five to six families of more than twenty people living in a small flat of 600–700 sq. ft. Illegal reconstruction inside the unit was a common practice to fully utilize the limited space. Usually, these extra fixtures were wired in order to prevent people from falling out. There are four people in my family and we lived in an attic. We shared one bed with my parents sleeping at one end and my sister and me occupying the other. Because of all these hardships, many people hated the colonial government and joined the trade unions. Trade unions provided cheap medical services and the affordable goods available at the Chinese products companies were very popular as well.

Let's talk about the confrontation in the San Po Kong factory. I have in my hands here copies of *Ming Pao* covering these stories. I was taking my primary school examination that day. A teacher told me a few days before the examination that there would be a strike in San Po Kong Artificial Flowers Factory, and encouraged us to show our support. We arrived there around noon. I cannot remember the exact name of the street. There were about twenty workers standing by the wall, surrounded by fifty to sixty supporters. We put our school bags aside and started putting up posters on the wall. There were many people trying to show their support to the workers. At about two o'clock, we realized that the police had started to gather around the area. We were just primary school students, the forty of us there. This is a photo taken forty years ago. I am the one on the second right in the picture. We were twelve or thirteen years old. We held hands together and walked towards the riot squad. I was a bit worried in the beginning as the policemen were armed with rifles, tear-gas guns and cork bullet guns. Although these cork bullets were made of wood, they could still get through your skin if you were shot straight on. Even if they shot at your limbs at a 45-degree angle, it still hurt badly. Some were even covered with metal caps. We stood there for a few minutes. We were very frightened and some of us started shaking. Someone started singing songs like 'unity is strength' (團結就是力量) and these helped lift our spirit. After about ten minutes, the police began shooting wooden bullets and throwing tear-gas bombs and we started running away. One of my classmates, a small girl who was about eleven or twelve years old, was hit with a cork bullet. We brought her to a union's clinic on Jordan Road and the treatment took the whole day. I believe the police no longer use these wooden bullets. Many other people were hurt as well, including reporters of Xinhua News Agency and *Wen Wei Po*.

This incident aroused a furious response from many people and provoked more protests. People were angry with the police's brutality towards the students and young people. And again in late May, many unarmed old people were beaten up by the police outside the Hilton Hotel. It is also reported on page 7 of the newspaper which I am showing here. Look, the people were bleeding and were seriously injured. I was only eleven and twelve years old at that time. After that incident, Beijing protested. They should pay for what they had done. If you beat us, we should fight back. The police was very cruel. After they arrested the demonstrators, they would lock them up in the office of the Criminal Investigation Department (CID) and beat them up. They even forced the arrested to drink salty coffee and water with hair in it. My Chinese medicine adviser tells me that this stuff can cause incurable damage to your body. The victim would continue coughing until he died. It was brutal. This was savage torture.

When the police searched the Whampoa Dockyard Union (黃埔船塢勞聯工會), the secretary of the union was beaten to death by them. His surname was Ho and he was the husband of my teacher. Another worker whose surname was Tin was also killed. This was followed by curfew. Any gathering of three people or more would be regarded as illegal assembly. Many people were arrested and unions were searched. Chung Wah School (中華中學) was shut down, and so was *Tin Fung Daily* (田豐日報), *New Evening News* (新夜報) and *Hong Kong Commercial Daily* (香港商報). Schools were searched and many documents were taken away. Around 1,000 people were illegally detained in concentration camps on Mount Davis Road and Chatham Road. The concentration camp in Chatham Road is in Tsim Sha Tsui. Many students were imprisoned for distributing pro-leftist bulletins or putting up posters. It is true that five officers were killed during the gunfire in Sha Tau Kok, but one should also realize that there were casualties among the Chinese as well.

Speaker 7: Chan Chi Kong（陳祠光）, police officer

Fortunately I can say a few words. Otherwise, what happened in 1967 would simply be regarded as 'anti-suppression and anti-colonial' acts (反英抗暴). I believe that the last speaker has just repeated what he heard from the others. What I am going to share with you is my personal experience. I was a policeman. I joined the auxiliary force after I graduated from school. On the first day of the San Po Kong incident, I was ordered to the scene. In fact, we were not prepared for action. Some people argued that the police planned in advance to tackle the demonstrators, but this is simply not true. The truth is there was a lot of confusion and nervousness among the officers when called into action; we were at a loss. I was on duty in the 'control room' in the Mong Kok police station that night. The order for action caused a lot of confusion and we did not even manage to maintain proper communications and coordination. How could you say that this is premeditation or well-planned persecution?

Just now, one of the speakers mentioned that there were no real bombs (真菠蘿) during the riots. I simply cannot agree with this. I was later transferred to the regular force. One day in October, we managed to arrest someone who had just laid a bomb at a roundabout right outside the Palace Theatre (麗宮戲院) in San Po Kong. His name was Ng Kin Piu (吳堅標). He was a member of the Rubber Labourers' Union (樹膠工會) at Whampoa Street (黃埔街) in Hung Hom. He revealed that he had been given $300 to plant the bomb. He was also paid $300 a month to join the general strike. You could find a hole punched on his identity card, and this was the sign they used to prevent those who were being paid from working elsewhere. The bomb he set off was a powerful one. The flames from the explosion reached the second floor of a building. He was lucky. I really wanted to let him run away so that I could have the excuse to shoot him.

People also talked about tortures like forced drinking of 'hair water' (頭髮水) inside the police station. Did we beat them? Yes, we did. But was there time to serve them with 'hair water'? There were usually scores of people being arrested at the same time; we were simply very busy. It is lucky for me to have the chance to uncover the truth to you. We should not forget the Sha Tau Kok incident as well. It happened on 8 July. Five policemen died; three were Chinese and two were Pakistanis. It was the mainland side that shot at us. I knew the man who started all these troubles. His name was Wan Kwok Hang (溫國恆), a member of the Sha Tau Kok Anti-Persecution Committee (沙頭角鬥委). He was later criticized for this by the leftist camp as well. Everyone has the right to judge what is right and what is wrong according to his or her perspective and values. Everyone has his or her own sense of justice. But you just cannot ignore or distort the facts and take it simply as part of the decolonization process.

Speaker 8: Wu Tin Leung (胡天亮), teenager, 14 years old

I think the general reason for social chaos is the reluctance of capitalists and business firms to share the fruits of economic growth with the general public. It was the same in Hong Kong in the 1960s. Industries started to develop in the sixties in Hong Kong. Workers had to endure long working hours, yet they could hardly make ends meet with low wages and rising inflation. As a result, they became more and more discontented and their anger could be easily triggered off by minor incidents. Any small incident could provoke an emotional outburst. It is not the political reason alone that matters; the economic reason is also crucial here. Hence after the 1967 riots, the government decided to set up the Home Affairs Department in order to provide the local people with a channel for expressing their grievances.

Let me respond to a few points mentioned earlier by the speakers here. I can still remember what my father told me about the riots when I was young. It was about the riots in 1956. He told me that a son of a shoe repairer whom he knew was missing. The boy had told his father that he wanted to buy some bread around Nan Cheong Street (南昌街), near Lai Chi Kok Road (荔枝角道). But he never came back. There was a rumour that he was arrested by the police and beaten to death inside the station. All kinds of tortures were used, including beating with fists and forcing someone to drink hair water. I do not know what had really happened, but this is what my father told me. Oral history is also part of history, isn't it? I could not verify this, and cannot really tell whether it is true or not.

Let me also share with you some personal experiences. I was fourteen years old when the 1967 riots broke out. One night, my younger brother and I was on our way home after visiting our uncle. We lived in Ngau Tau Kok (牛頭角) at that time. At that hour, only a few buses were running. We had to take Bus No. 2B to travel from Sham Shui Po to Ngau Tau Kok. The No. 2A service had already stopped. How could we get the bus? We had to walk a long way from the Sham Shui Po Pier to Ruby Restaurant (紅寶石餐廳) on Prince Edward Road. It was about eight o'clock and I thought, 'Gosh, it is nearly nine o'clock and it will be curfew soon.' At that time, we heard that the police would kill anyone violating the curfew indiscriminately (格殺勿論) and if we were found in the street, we would be dead. We were really afraid and it was already past eight by then. I did not worry that much about myself, but I had with me my little brother, and he was a kid. So what could I do? I was terrified. We therefore tried to jump the queue — something I was very good at. We eventually managed to get on the bus. We found many people trying to get on the bus at the Ruby Restaurant stop. The bus company staff tried to restore order and urged the passengers on the bus to get off. Someone spoke through the speaker, 'If you just need a short ride, say if you live in Kowloon City or Choi Hung Estate (彩虹邨), please leave the bus now. Many No. 13 buses will come very soon. Please leave space for those on a long journey.' No one was willing to get off the bus. 'What if no bus was coming, right?' I thought. I told my younger brother that even if we lived in Kowloon City, we wouldn't get off the bus. The scene was illustrative of the anxiety of people at that time; everybody was anxious to get home soon. This is my personal experience.

The other thing I want to talk about is corruption. I worked as a clerk in the government in 1973. I worked in the West Kowloon Magistrate's Court. On a day in late October 1973, I saw a policeman buying newspaper. He left a ten-cent coin to the hawker but the hawker was completely stunned. He jumped back from his stall and did not dare to take the money. I found this episode absolutely unbelievable and wondered why the hawker was so frightened. It tells me something about corruption in those days. This is what I witnessed. I have not exaggerated. Of course, as a 14-year-old in 1967, I witnessed far less than the other speakers. But I guess that there are many young people in the audience and thus it is worth sharing my experience with you here.

Speaker 9: Yip Mo Chiu（葉霧超）, confrontation prisoner

I was a victim of the 1967 riots. On the night of my arrest, I was at home after work. I lived in a stone house in Holy Cross Village (聖十字徑村) in Shau Kei Wan. I lived on the second floor. There were two other boys of my age living on the ground floor. Suddenly, the door was kicked open and the Police Tactical Unit rushed in. They shouted, 'All men come out!' I was a man, and I went out without much hesitation. I thought I had not done anything wrong and had nothing to hide, so there was nothing to worry about. This turned out to be a big mistake and the beginning of a lifelong stigma. I was arrested. The two boys living downstairs were also arrested. They were taken away in an even more embarrassing manner. One of them was taking a shower, and when he was taken away, he was wearing nothing but his underwear. There was a riot squad van waiting for us at the corner. Once we were ushered in, we were beaten up. Just now the other speaker said that the police did not have time to serve people with 'hair water' (頭髮水). This is not true. We were forced to drink this stuff in the police station. They tortured us in other ways as well, like stepping on our toes and hitting our knees with a hammer. We were all beaten up, one by one. One of the older guys was beaten up so badly that he passed out and fell onto the floor. Fortunately, he survived. We were transferred to the detention centre the following day and there were more physical abuses. We were ordered to line up and squat, with our hands on our head. The policemen, who were wearing boots, then kicked our spines heavily. Eventually, we were brought to the court and were charged with violating the curfew order. I was given a one-month sentence term.

We were then taken to the Stanley Prison where we were called 'YP' and we were assigned to the 'YP' dormitory. Everyone was assigned a number. If you did not respond when your number was called, you would be hit by the policemen's elbow. I still remember my number vividly, it was 26564. I still remember this after forty years. Why? It was a number for your whole life. You will never forget it. Because at that time, if you forgot it when you woke up, you would be beaten up. In the prison, we were served congee every Wednesday. It was a horrifying experience when I took it for the first time there. There was snot in the congee. Would you eat it? We could not eat it in the beginning. But then we had to get used to it, or else you starved. On the other days, we had boiled potatoes, yellow beans and pumpkins.

I was locked up in prison for a month. Unfortunately, there was no public holiday during my term there, which means that there was no 'discount' for my sentence. I remember that I passed one Dragon Boat Festival in the prison. After we were released, we were still frightened. It has been forty years now, yet we were still wary of crowds as it reminds us of that traumatic experience. Even after forty years. Those policemen were inhumane and brutal. They wanted to beat us up all the time. People were arrested for obscure reasons. Someone in my cell was caught when he was just playing football and other people got arrested when they were taking an escalator. What kind of law was this? I could only tell myself that I was unlucky.

Notes

Chapter 1

1. See for example, Yang Jianhua et al., *Xianggang chong Beizhan dao Huigui* (Hong Kong: From colonial rule to reunification) (Fuzhou: Fujian Renmin Chubanshe, 1997); Yuan Bangjian (ed.), *Xianggang Shilue* (A concise history of Hong Kong) (Hong Kong: Mainstream Publisher, 1987); Steve Tsang, *A Modern History of Hong Kong* (London: I. B. Tauris, 2004), pp. 183–90. An exception is John Carroll, *A Concise History of Hong Kong* (Lanham: Rowman and Littlefield, 2007; Hong Kong: Hong Kong University Press, 2007), pp. 150–60. By way of contrast one contemporary analysis still worth reading is William Heaton, 'Maoist Revolutionary Strategy and Modern Colonialism: The Cultural Revolution in Hong Kong', *Asian Survey*, 10:9 (1970), pp. 840–57.
2. John Cooper, *Colony in Conflict: The Hong Kong Disturbances May 1967–January 1968* (Hong Kong: Swindon Book Co., 1970), p. 9.
3. Ibid., p. 284.
4. Jin Yaoru, *Zhonggong Xianggang zhengce miwen shilu* (Secrets and facts of the Chinese Communist Party's Hong Kong policy) (Hong Kong: Tinyuan Press, 1998).
5. Gary Cheung, *Xianggang liuqi baodong neiqing* (Inside story of the 1967 riots in Hong Kong) (Hong Kong: Pacific Century Press, 2000).
6. Zhou Yi, *Xianggang zuopai duozhengshi* (History of left-wing struggle in Hong Kong) (Hong Kong: Leeman Press, 2002).
7. Liang Jiaqun et al., *Baodong mixin* (Secret stories of the riots) (Hong Kong: Hong Kong Economic Press, 2001).
8. Good chronologies are to be found in Cooper, *Colony in Conflict*, and Gary Cheung, *Xianggang liuqi baodong neiqing*.
9. Oxford, Rhodes House Library, Mss.Ind.Ocn.s.337, 'Transcript of interviews, 23 and 24 April 1987, given by Sir David Trench, Governor of Hong Kong (1964–71), to Dr Steve Tsang, and edited by Sir David Trench' (hereafter Trench interview, 1987).
10. Tsang, *Modern History of Hong Kong*, pp. 183–90.
11. Carver's note: TNA, FCO 40/95, Carver to CDS, MOD, 21 July 1967.
12. TNA, FCO 40/118, Sir Arthur Goldsworthy to M. D. I. Gass, 8 September 1967.
13. Xu Jiatun, *Xu Jiatun Xianggang huiyilu* (Xu Jiatun's reflection on Hong Kong affairs), Vol. 1 (Taibei: United Press, 1994), p. 40.

14. One work which places Hong Kong in that context is C. R. Schenk, 'The Empire Strikes Back: Hong Kong and the Decline of Sterling in the 1960s', *Economic History Review* 57:3 (2004), pp. 551–80.
15. John Darwin, 'Hong Kong in British Decolonisation', in Judith M. Brown and Rosemary Foot (eds.), *Hong Kong's Transitions, 1842–1997* (Basingstoke: Macmillan, 1997), p. 16. Amongst the oddities outlined by Darwin: lack of significant constitutional evolution, of a Hong Kong nationalism, of demands for self-rule, and in terms of its economic prosperity, the absence of international or other pressure for four decades after 1945 for retrocession, and its 'complete absence as a topic of British political debate' before 1984; ibid., pp. 16–17.
16. Wm Roger Louis, 'Hong Kong: The Critical Phase, 1945–1949', *American Historical Review* 102:4 (1997), pp. 1052–84.
17. Peter Hinchcliffe, John T. Ducker and Maria Holt, *Without Glory in Arabia: The British Retreat from Aden* (London: I.B. Tauris, 2006).
18. Louis, 'Hong Kong: The Critical Phase', p. 1053.
19. J. H. Smith, 'Trench, Sir David Clive Crosbie (1915–1988)', *Oxford Dictionary of National Biography*, Oxford University Press, 2004 [http://www.oxforddnb.com/view/article/64160, accessed 7 May 2007]. There was nothing to worry about, former governor Sir Alexander Grantham assured 'The Times Diary', Trench had prior experience of sorting out such affairs in the Solomons, when 'he was sent to sort out some trouble... when the natives were attacking Europeans and burning houses'; *The Times*, 16 May 1967, p. 10.
20. Obituary, *The Times*, 2 March 1983, p. 14.
21. Georgina Sinclair, *At the End of the Line: Colonial Policing and the Imperial Endgame, 1945–80* (Manchester: Manchester University Press, 2006).
22. Robert Bickers, *Britain in China: Community, Culture and Colonialism, 1900–49* (Manchester: Manchester University Press, 1999), p. 142.
23. See, for example, Beverley Hooper, *China Stands Up: Ending the Western Presence, 1948–50* (London and New York: Allen and Unwin, 1986); Thomas N. Thompson, *China's Nationalisation of Foreign Firms: The Politics of Hostage Capitalism, 1949–57* (Baltimore: School of Law, University of Maryland, Occasional papers, 1979).
24. Saki Dockrill, *Britain's Retreat from East of Suez: The Choice between Europe and the World?* (Basingstoke: Palgrave Macmillan, 2002).
25. Zhou, *History of left-wing struggle in Hong Kong*, pp. 231–2.
26. FCO 40/114 Hong Kong Police Special Branch Report, Ref. GEN/14/368/138, 24 October 1967.
27. New evidence has been sketchily emerging of People's Liberation Army (PLA) threats to the colony in 1967: 'Revealed: The Hong Kong invasion plan', *Sunday Times*, 24 June 2007, although the accepted view is that the PLA acted to prevent any incursions, although not as blatantly as it did in Macao; Allen S. Whiting, 'The Use of Force in Foreign Policy by the People's Republic of China', *Annals of the American Academy of Political and Social Science*, 402:1 (1972), pp. 61–3.
28. Trench interview, 1987.
29. TNA, CO 1030/1107, 'The Governor of Hong Kong to the Secretary of State for the Colonies', ref: CR 14/2041/57, Telegram No. 1712, 12 August 1960.
30. See, for example, C. F. Yong and R. B. McKenna, *The Kuomintang Movement in British Malaya, 1912–1949* (Singapore: Singapore University Press, 1990).
31. TNA, FCO 40/88, 'The Confrontation with Communists in Schools', ref. T. S., 1/3/1168/47, 7 December 1967.

32. TNA, FCO 40/88, Hong Kong to Commonwealth Office, Telegram No. 1779, 28 November 1967.
33. TNA, FCO 40/88, Hong Kong to Commonwealth Office, Telegram No. 1785, 29 November 1967.
34. John Cooper, *Colony in Conflict*, p. 97.
35. Richard Clutterbuck, *Riots and Revolution in Singapore and Malaya 1945–1963* (London: Faber and Faber Ltd., 1972); David Anderson, *Histories of the Hanged: Britain's Dirty War in Kenya and the End of Empire* (London: Weidenfeld and Nicolson, 2005).
36. TNA, FCO 40/105, 24 September 1967.
37. Gregor Benton, 'Chinatown UK v. Colonial Hong Kong: An Early Exercise in Transnational Militancy and Manipulation, 1967–1969', *Ethnic and Racial Studies* 28:2 (2005), p. 337.
38. Heaton, 'Maoist Revolutionary Strategy and Modern Colonialism', p. 846.
39. Richard Ross and Phillip Davies, *Inheritance in Public Policy: Change without Choice in Britain* (New Haven: Yale University Press, 1994).
40. Ian Scott, *Political Change and the Crisis of Legitimacy in Hong Kong* (Hong Kong: Oxford University Press, 1989), p. 39.
41. Leo Goodstadt, *Uneasy Partners: The Conflict Between Public Interest and Private Profit in Hong Kong* (Hong Kong: Hong Kong University Press, 2005), p. 20.
42. Benton, 'Chinatown UK v. Colonial Hong Kong'.
43. Scott, *Political Change and the Crisis of Legitimacy in Hong Kong*, p. 81.
44. Robert Bickers, 'The Colony's Shifting Position in the British Informal Empire in China,' in Judith Brown and Rosemary Foot (eds.), *Hong Kong's Transitions* (London: Macmillan, 1997), pp. 33–61.
45. Goodstadt, *Uneasy Partners*.
46. Heaton, 'Maoist Revolutionary Strategy and Modern Colonialism', p. 840.
47. Benton's work also draws clear links between the 'legacy in the New Territories of radical nationalism' dating from the Pacific War, and radicalism in 1967 in Britain's Chinese community, many of whom had come from the New Territories; see Benton, 'Chinatown UK v. Colonial Hong Kong', p. 335. See also his *The Chinese in Britain: Economy, Transnationalism, Identity* (with Edmund Terence Gomez) (Basingstoke: Palgrave Macmillan, 2007).
48. Oxford, Rhodes House Library, Mss.Ind.Ocn.s.340, 'Transcript of interview, 10 February 1988, given by Arthur Frederick Maddocks, Political Advisor to the Government of Hong Kong (1968–72), to Dr Steve Tsang'; Trench interview, 1987.

Chapter 2

1. Zhou Yi, *Xianggang zuopai douzhengshi* (History of left-wing struggle in Hong Kong) (Hong Kong: Leeman Press, 2002), pp. 231–3.
2. TNA, FCO 40/45, Hong Kong to the Commonwealth Office, 7 May 1967, Telegram No. 553.
3. TNA, FCO 40/45, Hong Kong to Secretary of State of Commonwealth Affairs, 11 May 1967, Telegram No. 947.
4. TNA, FCO 40/49, Hong Kong Government Report on 'Current Communist Disturbances in Hong Kong', 3 August 1967.
5. Jin Yiuru, *Xianggang wushinian yiwang* (50 Years in Hong Kong) (Hong Kong: Jin Yiuru Memorial Foundation, 2005), p. 122.

6. Qi Pengfei, *Deng Xiaoping yu Xianggang huigui* (Deng Xiaoping and the Return of Hong Kong) (Beijing: Xinhua Chubanshe, 2004), pp. 19–52.
7. TNA, FCO 21/204, Ref. FDI/6 W51, 15 June 1967.
8. TNA, CAB 191/17 L.I.C. (Hong Kong) Assessment of the External Threat to Hong Kong, 23 August 1967.
9. S. R. Ashton, 'Keeping a Foot in the Door: Britain's China Policy, 1945–50', *Diplomacy and Statecraft*, 15:1 (2004), pp. 79–94, and James Tang, 'World War to Cold War: Hong Kong's Future and Anglo-Chinese Interactions, 1941–55', in Ming K. Chan (ed.), *Precarious Balance: Hong Kong Between China and Britain 1842–1992* (New York: M.E. Sharpe, 1994), pp. 107–30.
10. Zhang Xichang et al., *Fengluan dieqi: gongheguo de sanci jianjiao gaochao* (Twists and turns: The third wave of diplomacy of the Republic) (Beijing: Shijie Zhishi Chubanshe, 1998), pp. 95–120.
11. K. A. Hamilton, ' "A Week that Changed the World": Britain and Nixon's China Visit of 21–28 February 1972', *Diplomacy and Statecraft*, 15:1 (2004), pp. 117–35.
12. TNA, FCO 21/204, Despatch No. 12, Office of the British Chargé D'affaires to the Secretary of State for Foreign Affairs, Telegram, 6 June 1967.
13. Ibid.
14. TNA, FCO 40/45, Telegram from Beijing Charge D'affaires to the Foreign Office, No. 480, 15 May 1967.
15. Ibid.
16. Ibid.
17. TNA, CAB 134/2945, K(69)1, 28 March 1969, Cabinet Ministerial Committee on Hong Kong, *Hong Kong: Long Term Study*.
18. Ibid.
19. Saki Dockrill, *Britain's Retreat from East of Suez: The Choice between Europe and the World?* (London: Palgrave Macmillan, 2002).
20. James Lilley, *China Hands: Nine Decades of Adventure, Espionage and Diplomacy in Asia* (New York: Public Affairs, 2004). However, one should also note the tension on covert activities in Hong Kong between the Americans and the colonial administration. For details, see Steve Tsang, 'Strategy for Survival: The Cold War and Hong Kong's Policy towards Kuomintang and Chinese Communist Activities in the 1950s', *Journal of Imperial and Commonwealth History*, 25: 2 (1997), pp. 294–317.
21. Chi Kwan Mark, *Hong Kong and the Cold War: Anglo-American Relations 1949–1957* (Oxford: Oxford University Press, 2004); David Reynolds, 'A "Special Relationship"? America, Britain and the International Order since the Second World War', *International Affairs*, 1 (1986), pp. 1–20.
22. Diary Entry, 25 October 1957, Papers of Harold Macmillan, Manuscript Diaries, 1950–66, Mss. Macmillan dep. D.30, Bodlelain Library, Oxford: quoted in Mark, *Hong Kong and the Cold War,* p. 125.
23. Nancy Bernkopf Tucker (ed.), *China Confidential: American Diplomats and Sino-American Relations, 1945–1996* (New York: Columbia University Press, 2001), pp. 196–7.
24. TNA, FCO 40/47, David Trench to the Commonwealth Office, 10 June 1967.
25. FRUS, 1964–68, XXX, China, document no. 263.
26. TNA, DEFE 13/857, Galsworthy to Saville Garner, ref. C/165/5.
27. TNA, CAB 134/2945, K(67)5, 20 September 1967.
28. TNA, FCO 21/191, Note by E. Bolland, Head of Far Eastern Department, Foreign Office, 20 February 1967.

29. 'The Hong Kong University Students' Union Council on the Recent Riot' (17 May 1967), in Ma Ming (ed.), *The Riot in Hong Kong* (Hong Kong: Sky Horse Book Company, 1967), p. 30, and Jack Cater, 'The 1967 Riots', in Sally Blyth and Ian Wotherspoon (eds.), *Hong Kong Remembers* (Hong Kong: Oxford University Press, 1996), p. 107.
30. *Hong Kong Hansard*, 1967, p. 326.
31. Hong Kong Urban Council, *Official Record of Proceedings*, Meeting of 4 July 1967, pp. 131–2.
32. *Hong Kong Hansard* 1967, p. 390.
33. Interview with Edward Eates, Exeter, 28 May 2006.
34. Hong Kong Federation of Hong Kong Industries, *Annual Report 1967*, p. 6.
35. *Ming Pao*, 7 July 1967.
36. TNA, FCO 40/114 Hong Kong Police Special Branch Report, Ref. GEN/14/368/138, 24 October 1967.
37. TNA, FCO 21/192 Hong Kong Police Special Branch Report, Ref. GEN/14/368/3 (3), 15 May 1967.
38. TNA, FCO 40/45, the Commonwealth Office to the Hong Kong Governor, Telegram No. 910, 13 May 1967.
39. TNA, FCO 40/54, the Commonwealth Office to the Hong Kong Governor, Telegram No. 944, 17 May 1967.
40. TNA, FCO 40/54 Hong Kong Governor to the Commonwealth office, Telegram No. 641, 19 May 1967.
41. TNA, FCO 40/45 Peking Chargé D'affaires to the Foreign Office, Telegram No. 483, 15 May 1967.
42. TNA, FCO 40/46, the Commonwealth Office to Hong Kong, Telegram No. 1038, 25 May 1967.
43. TNA, FCO 40/54, Extract from C.O.S. (67) 55th Meeting held on 11 July 1967.
44. TNA, FCO 40/113, from the Officer Administering Hong Kong to the Commonwealth Office, Telegram No. 1151, 2 August 1967.
45. TNA, FCO 40/46, Peking to Foreign Office, Telegram No. 560, 24 May 1967; TNA, FCO 40/46, Hong Kong Governor to the Commonwealth Office, Telegram No. 682, 24 May 1967; and TNA, FCO 40/113 Hong Kong to the Commonwealth Office, Telegram No. 1276, 21 August 1967.
46. TNA, FCO 40/113, Hong Kong to Commonwealth Office, unnumbered telegram, 29 August 1967.
47. Quoted in Edward Rice, *Mao's Way* (Berkeley: University of California Press, 1972), p. 377.
48. TNA, FCO 40/52, Hong Kong to Commonwealth Office, Telegram No. 1876, 18 December 1967, and Telegram No. 1854, 11 December 1967.
49. TNA, FCO 40/51 From JIC London to Hong Kong, 2 November 1967.
50. TNA, FCO 40/114, paper prepared by the Colonial Secretariat, 22 November 1967.
51. In August 1958, Parker Tu, headmaster of the Pui Kiu Middle School, a hard-core communist school in Hong Kong, was deported because of the school's active political indoctrination of students. Hon Wah Middle School, another flagship institution in the communist camp, was ordered to close down for safety reasons in the same month. Zhou Yi, *Xianggang zuopai douzhengshi*, pp. 170–80.
52. TNA, FCO 40/88, 'The Confrontation with Communists in Schools', ref. T. S, 1/3/1168/47, 7 December 1967.
53. Ibid.

54. TNA, FCO 40/88, Hong Kong to Commonwealth Office, Telegram No. 1779, 28 November 1967.
55. TNA, FCO 40/88, Hong Kong to Commonwealth Office, Telegram No. 1785, 29 November 1967.
56. TNA, FCO 40/88, Hong Kong to Commonwealth Office, Telegram No. 831, 29 June 1968.
57. TNA, FCO 40/88, Peking to Foreign Office, Telegram No. 648, 8 July 1968.
58. TNA, FCO 40/88, Peking to Foreign Office, Telegram No. 620, 2 July 1968.
59. Ibid.
60. TNA, FCO 40/88 Hong Kong Commonwealth Office, Telegram No. 855, 5 July 1968.
61. TNA, FCO 40/88, James Murray to Wilkinson, 8 August 1968.
62. TNA, FCO 40/217, 'The Requisition of Ships Order 1955', Hong Kong Department, 5 December 1968; 'The Requisition of Ships Order 1969', Hong Kong Department, 9 October 1969.
63. TNA, FCO 40/114, Hall to Carter, 4 December 1967.
64. Gao Wenqian, *Wannian Zhou Enlai* (Zhou Enlai in twilight years) (Hong Kong: Mirror Books, 2003), p. 232.

Chapter 3

1. For a fuller exposition see Cheuk-yin Wong, 'The Communist-Inspired Riots in Hong Kong, 1967: A Multi-Actors Approach' (Unpublished MPhil thesis, the University of Hong Kong, 2001).
2. Jack Cater was special assistant to the governor between May and June 1967 and deputy colonial secretary (special duties) between June 1967 and February 1968. He was stationed in the colony during the entire period of the riots. Cater interview, 12 October 1999.
3. Cater interview, 12 October 1999.
4. According to Cater, Denis Bray was the 'number two' person in the Special Group. Locking was at that time a district officer in the New Territories West. During the riots, Locking was responsible for the situations in the New Territories. He had 'very good attitudes at work.' David Ford joined the group at the end of July. Cater interview, 12 October 1999.
5. Cater interview, 12 October 1999.
6. Legislative Council, Hong Kong. *Reports of the Meeting of the Legislative Council of Hong Kong, sessions 1968*, 24 January 1968 (Hong Kong: Government Printer, 1968).
7. Stephen Edward Waldron, 'Fire on the Rim: A Study in Contradictions in Left-Wing Mobilization' (Unpublished PhD thesis, Syracuse University, 1976), p. 240.
8. Cater interview, 12 October 1999.
9. Waldron, 'Fire on the Rim', p. 235.
10. Denis Bray, who joined the Hong Kong government as a cadet officer class II in 1950, and retired in 1985 as secretary for home affairs, acting occasionally as chief secretary and governor. Bray interview, 24 April 1999.
11. However, the water came through as contracted, so all the arrangements made for alternative supplies were immediately cancelled. Personal communication with Professor Norman Miners, dated 14 April 1999.
12. Cater interview, 12 October 1999.
13. Waldron, 'Fire on the Rim', p. 236.

14. Bray interview, 24 April 1999.
15. John Cooper, *Colony in Conflict: The Hong Kong Disturbances May 1967–January 1968* (Hong Kong: Swindon Book Company, 1970).
16. 'Government Workers Suspended: Action Taken Following Marine Department Stoppage', *South China Morning Post*, 2 June 1967.
17. Personal communication from Professor Norman Miners, 12 September 2000.
18. Cater interview, 12 October 1999.
19. Ibid.
20. Cooper, *Colony in Conflict*, p. 105.
21. Cater interview, 12 October 1999.
22. Bray interview, 24 April 1999.
23. Cater interview, 12 October 1999.
24. Chen Yangyong, *Kucheng Weiju: Zhou Enlai zai 1967* (Shoring up a shaky situation: Zhou Enlai in 1967) (Beijing: Zhongyang Wenxian Chubanshe, 1999), p. 355.
25. Yao Dengshan was originally an officer in the Chinese Embassy in Indonesia before he was expelled from Jakarta in April 1967. Once back in the Ministry of Foreign Affairs, he set about the task of providing authoritative leadership to the radical forces directed against Chen Yi, who was attempting to shield the conduct of China's foreign relations from the rising tide of internal violence. Wang Li, on the other hand, was renowned for his August-Seventh speech, in which he claimed, '[W]hy can't a 20-year-old become the Minister of Foreign Affairs? We need to capture power now.' See Roderick MacFarquhar and Michael Schoenhals, *Mao's Last Revolution* (Cambridge MA; London: Belknap Press of Harvard University Press, 2006), Chapter 13.
26. Bray interview, 24 April 1999.
27. Jin Yaoru, *Zhonggong Xianggang zhengce miwen shilu: Jin Yaoru wushinian xiangjiang yi wang* (Secret records of China's Hong Kong policies: A memoir of Jin Yaoru, fifty years in Hong Kong) (Hong Kong: Tianyuan Shuwu, 1998), p. 122.
28. Percy Cradock, *Experiences of China* (London: John Murray, 1994), p. 64.
29. Bray interview, 24 April 1999.
30. Wu Kang-min was a member of the 'Struggle Committee' in the 1967 riots. Wu interview, 25 May 2000.
31. Bray interview, 24 April 1999.
32. TNA, FCO 21/204, Chinese policy towards Hong Kong, internal Foreign Office assessment, 16 June 1967. In fact, the only actual support from China was a gift of HK$10 million by the Chinese Trade Union Federation to the Struggle Committee.
33. TNA, FCO 21/65, E. Bollard minute, 15 September 1967, p. 156.
34. *Records of the Hong Kong Legislative Council*, 12 July 1967.
35. 'Paper Reveal Undercover Power Base during 1967 Riots', *South China Morning Post*, 7 June 1992.
36. Bray interview, 24 April 1999.
37. Some of the locations raided by the police were owned and operated by official commercial channels of China. Others were run in buildings leased by the Chinese side. Still others were independent of mainland interest but merely sold Chinese literature and propaganda materials. Waldron argued that the official and semi-official ties of such institutions made the government's action against them potentially more serious than the raids against local leftists, since such actions may lead to Chinese protests. Waldron, 'Fire on the Rim', p. 264.

38. Committee of Hong Kong Kowloon Chinese Compatriots of All Circles for the Struggle Against Persecution by the British Authorities in Hong Kong. *The May Upheaval in Hong Kong* (Hong Kong: Committee of Hong Kong Kowloon Chinese Compatriots of All Circles for the Struggle Against Persecution by the British Authorities in Hong Kong, 1967), p. 38.
39. Bray interview, 24 April 1999. He responded in this way when being asked on his view towards the Hong Kong government's anti-riot tactics.
40. Waldron, 'Fire on the Rim', p. 266.
41. 'Raids on Three Communists Strongholds: Longest Operation Since May', *South China Morning Post*, 1 August 1967.
42. TNA, FCO 21/202, Hong Kong to CO, 21 September 1967, Telegram No. 903. Trench sent this telegram in reply to a Foreign Office telegram, giving details of the assessment of the situation in Hong Kong made by the French Ministry of Foreign Affairs.
43. Jin, *Secret Records of China's Hong Kong Policies*, pp. 149–52.
44. Quoted in Jin, p. 152.
45. TNA, FCO 21/225, E. Bollard minute, Colonial Office official, 19 September 1967, p. 5.
46. TNA, FCO 21/202, Hong Kong to CO, 21 September 1967, Telegram No. 903.
47. Waldron, 'Fire on the Rim', p. 287.
48. HKRS 70-1/313G, Riots 1967, Declarations of Support to Government, 15 May 1967–10 August 1967.
49. The United Nations Association had very few, if any, members. It was formed and run by Ma Man-fei as a platform to publicize his own views. Personal communication with Norman Miners, 12 September 2000.
50. 'Siding with the Strength', *China Mail*, 7 March 1968.
51. 'Riots Warning', *Hong Kong Standard*, 7 December 1969.
52. HKRS70-1/326, Press Library Files, Social Welfare Department, 11 January 1967–7 December 1970.
53. 'Elsie Agrees with Lord Rhodes', *The Star*, 7 August 1967.
54. 'What Opinion Have the Elected Councilors Expressed on Behalf of the Residents', *Tin Tin Daily News*, 7 September 1967.
55. 'Siding with the Strength', the *China Mail*, 7 March 1968. The first half of the places mentioned were residential areas for the wealthy. The latter half was densely populated by the relatively poor.
56. On the concept of legitimacy, see William Connolly, *Legitimacy and the State* (Oxford: Blackwell, 1984); James O'Connor, *The Meaning of Crisis: A Theoretical Introduction* (Oxford: Blackwell, 1987); J. Roland Pennock and John W. Chapman, *Authority Revisited* (New York: New York University Press, 1987); T. H. Rigby and Ferenc Fehér, *Political Legitimation in Communist States* (London: Macmillan, 1982). However, Peter Ferdinand argued that Ian Scott had no clear idea of what the 'legitimacy might be' and Alan P. L. Liu argued that Scott's account of a legitimacy crisis was not very meaningful in the context of the Hong Kong government. See *The American Political Science Review*, 85:3–4 (1991) (book review by Peter Ferdinand and Alan Liu), p. 330.
57. Ian Scott, *Political Change and the Crisis of Legitimacy* (Hong Kong: Oxford University Press, 1989), p. 322.
58. Ibid.

59. The former was used by Dr Patrick Hase, who worked as an administrative officer of the Hong Kong government until taking early retirement in 1996, and the latter by Denis Bray.
60. Scott, *Political Change and the Crisis of Legitimacy,* pp. 36–7.
61. For the difference between legitimacy by performance and legitimacy by procedure, see Samuel Huntington, *The Third Wave: Democratization in the Late Twentieth Century* (Norman: University of Oklahoma Press, 1991), p. 50.
62. Huntington, *The Third Wave,* p. 50.
63. Ibid.
64. Scott, *Political Change and the Crisis of Legitimacy,* p. 327.
65. Ibid., p. 106.
66. Hase interview, 9 May 1999.
67. Ibid.
68. Cater interview, 12 October 1999.
69. *The American Political Science Review,* 85:3–4 (1991) (book review by Alan Liu), p. 330.
70. Personal letter from Norman Miners, 14 April 1999.
71. Scott, *Political Change and the Crisis of Legitimacy,* p. 322. Scott did not define what exactly a crisis was in his 1989 work. For the theoretical discussion, see James O'Connor, *The Meaning of Crisis: A Theoretical Introduction* (Oxford: Basil Blackwell, 1987). In fact, crisis can be defined as 'the moment when a conflict occurred so great that the government cannot deal with it any more, or a situation where conflict, especially political conflict, has become so threatening or dangerous that people are afraid that there will be war or where the government is so heavily attacked that there is serious doubt whether it will continue to exist'. See *Collins Cobuild English Language Dictionary* (London: Harper Collins Publishers, 1993).
72. Norman Miners, *The Government and Politics of Hong Kong* (fifth edition) (Hong Kong: Oxford University Press, 1991), p. 32.
73. Scott, *Political Change and the Crisis of Legitimacy,* p. 104.
74. Ibid., p. 322.
75. Ibid.
76. Cater interview, 12 October 1999.
77. Sir David Akers-Jones was the chief secretary of Hong Kong from 1985 to 1987. He first arrived in Hong Kong as a soldier in January 1945 and began his career in the colonial government in the summer of 1957. Jones interview, 28 May 1999.
78. Cater interview, 12 October 1999. He responded in this way when being asked on his view towards Scott's argument.
79. Personal interviews with a police constable (who refused to disclose his name), 9 June 2000.
80. Bray interview, 24 April 1999.
81. Scott, *Political Change and the Crisis of Legitimacy,* p. 104.

Chapter 4

1. Some of the materials used in this chapter were collected at The National Archives by Ray Yep, to whom I am grateful for sharing copies with me.
2. TNA, FCO 21/235, Hong Kong Tel. to CO, 6 September 1967. For Victoria's move see *The Times,* 28 August 1967, pp. 1, 4.

3. TNA, FCO 21/235, E. T. Davies to I. T. M. Lucas, Central Department, FO, 8 September 1967; Hugh Davies, 'An Undiplomatic Foray: A 1967 escapade in Macau', *Journal of the Royal Asiatic Society Hong Kong Branch* 47 (2008), pp. 115–26.
4. This episode has attracted little attention in English. There is a short account, vague on some detail and chronology, and which is based on newspaper sources in Steve Shipp, *Macau, China: A Political History of the Portuguese Colony's Transition to Chinese Rule* (Jefferson: McFarland and Company, 1997), pp. 89–91. For a fuller treatment see Moisés Silva Fernandes, 'As prostrações das instituições britânicas em Macau durante a "revolução cultural" chinesa em Maio de 1967 e algumas das suas consequências' ('The prostration of British institutions in Macau during the Chinese "Cultural Revolution" in May 1967 and some of its repercussions'), in his *Confluência de Interesses: Macau nas Relações Luso-Chinesas Contemporâneas 1945–2005* (Lisbon: Ministério dos Negócios Estrangeiros, Colecção Biblioteca Diplomática Série A No. 9, 2008), pp. 305–44.
5. TNA, FCO 21/235, E. Bolland to Norman Ions, 28 July 1967.
6. See documents in HKPRO, HKRS 935-2-14, 'China and Macau'.
7. *The Times*, 18 April 1967, p. 5.
8. Quoted in Ian Scott, *Political Change and the Crisis of Legitimacy in Hong Kong* (London: Hurst and Company, 1989), p. 97.
9. Quoted in Fernandes, 'As prostrações das instituições britânicas em Macau', p. 309.
10. C. R. Boxer, *Fidalgos in the Far East, 1550–1770: Fact and Fancy in the History of Macao* (The Hague: Martinus Nijhoff, 1948), pp. 255–62. On images of the colony see also Jonathan Porter, *Macau: The Imaginary City. Culture and Society, 1557 to the Present* (Boulder: Westview Press, 2000).
11. See Chapter 5 of De Leeuw's *Cities of Sin* (London: Noel Douglas, 1934; new editions in 1940 and 1953). Auden's aside — 'And nothing serious can happen here' — occurred in his 1938 poem, 'Macao', first published in W. H. Auden and Christopher Isherwood, *Journey to a War* (London: Faber and Faber, 1939).
12. Wang Zhicheng, *Portuguese in Shanghai* (Macau: Macau Foundation, 2004).
13. TNA, FCO 21/235, 'H.M. Consulate, Macao Return of Consular work for the 12 months ended 31 October 1966'; TNA, FCO 47/24, 'Evacuation (Emergency Planning — Macao', Hong Kong Tel. No. 93, 21 January 1967; K. MacLellan, Canadian High Commission, to E. Bolland, 26 January 1967.
14. TNA, FCO 47/24, 'Evacuation (Emergency Planning) — Macao', Hong Kong Tel. No. 93, 21 January 1967.
15. *The Times*, 2 December 1967, p. 11. For accounts of the 12.3 events see Anthony R. Dicks, 'Macau: Legal Fiction and Gunboat Diplomacy,' in Goran Aijmer (ed.), *Leadership on the China Coast* (London: Curzon Press, 1984), pp. 90–128. (This is a reprint of a survey originally circulated privately in July 1967 as 'Macao: Gunboat Diplomacy'; see TNA, FCO 21/236, 'Macao: Political Affairs Internal. Foreign views on'. Dicks, then a fellow in Chinese law at the Institute of Current World Affairs, was living in Hong Kong. His various monthly reports to the Institute can be viewed at http://www.icwa.org/FormerArticles.asp?vIni=ARD&vName=Anthony%20R.%20Dicks.) Moisés Silva Fernandes, *Macau na Política Externa Chinesa, 1949–1979* (Lisboa, Imprensa de Ciências Sociais, 2006) provides a full survey of events, and his *Sinopse de Macau nas Relações Luso-Chinesas, 1945–1995* (Lisboa: Fundação Oriente, 2000) provides a chronology and reprints of key documents.

16. TNA, FCO 40/71, 'Hong Kong: Political Affairs: Bilateral Relations with Macao', Monthly Intelligence Report, December 1966, Appendix, 'Events in Macao'; Joao De Pina-Cabral, *Between China and Europe: Person, Culture and Emotion in Macao* (London: Berg Publishers, 2000), pp. 72–5.
17. TNA, FCO 40/71, 'Hong Kong: Political Affairs: Bilateral Relations with Macao', Hong Kong Tel. 55, 14 January 1967; CO to Hong Kong, No. 95, 15 January 1967.
18. TNA, FCO 40/71, 'Hong Kong: Political Affairs: Bilateral Relations with Macao', Hong Kong Tel. 68, 17 January 1967.
19. TNA, FCO 47/24, 'Evacuation (Emergency Planning) — Macao', CO to Hong Kong, Tel. No. 123, 19 January 1967.
20. TNA, FCO 40/71, 'Hong Kong: Political Affairs: Bilateral Relations with Macao', 'Submission: Evacuation of Macao', 17 January 1967.
21. Copy of Hong Kong Despatch No. 1164, 23 June 1967 in TNA, DEFE 25/300.
22. De Pina-Cabral, *Between China and Europe*, p. 74; Richard Louis Edmonds and Herbert S. Yee, 'Macau: From Portuguese Autonomous Territory to Chinese Special Administrative Region', *The China Quarterly*, No. 160 (1999), p. 805, n. 14.
23. Fernandes, 'As prostrações das instituições britânicas em Macau', p. 326. In 1964 the Consulate had organized a press briefing to try and quell persistent press attacks on the entry permit system's alleged inadequacies; see Hong Kong Public Record Office, HKRS 41-2-346, 'Immigration Department: Macau Permit Office, Routine Correspondence'.
24. Much of the narrative is taken from Ions' later draft despatch on the episode, composed in early June in London, in TNA, FCO 21/235, paper 54, hereafter Ions despatch, and from Hong Kong telegrams to London collected in the same file. See also the *Times*, 13 May 1967, p. 1. This despatch has now been edited by Moisés Silva Fernandes and partially published as 'A Diplomat Interrupted', *Macau Closer* (15 February–15 March 2007), pp. 40–43.
25. TNA, FCO 21/235, 'H.M. Consul in Macao', Bolland minute, 16 May 1967.
26. Ions despatch.
27. TNA, FCO 21/235, Hong Kong Tel. No. 694, 24 May 1967.
28. *Daily Express* report, 25 May 1967, p. 2.
29. TNA, FCO 21/235, Hong Kong Tels. No. 692, No. 681, 24 May 1967.
30. Ions was satisfied that the hotel staff were spying on him, so he and the Hong Kong government officer with whom he discussed the situation resorted to using that standby code for subjects *pas devant les Chinois*: French.
31. TNA, FCO 21/235, E. T. Davies to I. T. M. Lucas, Central Departmentt, FO, 8 September 1967; George Walden, *Lucky George: Memoirs of an Anti-politician* (London: Allen Lane, 1999), pp. 90–92; Davies, 'An Undiplomatic Foray'.
32. TNA, FCO 21/235, K. R. Welbore Ker (Lisbon) to E. Bolland, 4 October 1967, James Murray, Submission, 'Macao Consulate', 1 December 1967.
33. TNA, CAB 134/2945, Annex, 'The Situation in Macao', 'Cabinet. Ministerial Committee on Hong Kong. Interim Report by Officials', 21 July 1967. The evolution of this report is recorded in FCO 40/77, 'Hong Kong: Territorial (Sovereignty). Future of.'
34. TNA, FCO 40/77, H. N. Hall, minute for Secretary of State, 28 June 1967, 'Hong Kong, Sir David Trench'.
35. *Hong Kong. Report for the Year 1967* (Hong Kong: Government Press, 1968), pp. 1–2. The report was the subject of disagreement between Trench and the Peking embassy:

TNA, FCO 21/193, Hong Kong No. 135, 29 January 1968, and D. C. Wilson minute, 30 January 1968.
36. TNA, FCO 21/192, 'The Communist challenge', Special Branch, Hong Kong Police, 15 May 1967.
37. TNA, FCO 21/204, F. Brewer, 'Hong Kong and China', 18 May 1967. Brewer concluded that while the Chinese 'evidently intended to gain effective, though indirect, control over Macao', their demands in Hong Kong were as yet more limited.
38. 'Probably the Communists have not yet taken the decision to launch an all-out Macau-style attack': TNA, FCO 40/113, Hong Kong No. 600, 13 May 1967.
39. TNA, FCO 40/77, 'The possibility of a British withdrawal from Hong Kong', A. N. Galsworthy minute, 31 May 1967. 'National humiliation' (*guochi*) is of course an important trope in PRC history making. On the subject see Paul A. Cohen, 'Remembering and Forgetting: National Humiliation in Twentieth-Century China,' in *China Unbound: Evolving Perspectives on the Chinese Past* (London and New York: RoutledgeCurzon, 2003), pp. 148–84.
40. TNA, FCO 40/77, 'Extract from minutes of a meeting of the Defence and Overseas Policy Committee held on 25/5/1967'.
41. TNA, FCO 40/77, 'The possibility of a British withdrawal from Hong Kong', A.N. Galsworthy minute, 31 May 1967, after visit to Hong Kong and discussions with Sir David Trench and General Worsley, Commander of British Forces, Hong Kong.
42. Roderick MacFarquhar, 'China gets rough', *New Statesman*, 14 July 1967, p. 40; 'Punch-up diplomacy', *New Statesman*, 1 September 1967, p. 245.
43. *The Times*, 12 May 1967, p. 5.
44. *The Times*, 15 May 1967, p. 4.
45. *The Economist*, 3 June 1967, p. 996.
46. Ian Scott has shown, however, and the chapters in this volume reinforce the point, that in the longer term the crisis catalysed slowly evolving reform across the colonial administration and its practices and assumptions: *Political Change and the Crisis of Legitimacy in Hong Kong*, pp. 105–26.
47. TNA, DEFE 11/754, Commonwealth Secretary to Hong Kong, No. 944, 17 May 1967.
48. TNA, FCO 40/77, 'The possibility of a British withdrawal from Hong Kong', A.N. Galsworthy minute, 31 May 1967.
49. TNA, CAB 134/2945, Cabinet Ministerial Committee on Hong Kong. Hong Kong: Long Term Study, 28 March 1969, para. 87.
50. TNA, FCO 40/77, Cabinet, OPD, Defence Review Working Party, 'Minutes of a Meeting of the Working Party', 26 June 1967.
51. TNA, FCO 40/77, Cabinet, OPD, Defence Review Working Party, 'Minutes of a Meeting of the Working Party', 26 June 1967.
52. TNA, FCO 40/77, Cabinet, OPD, Defence Review Working Party, 'Minutes of a Meeting of the Working Party', 17 July 1967.
53. TNA, FCO 40/77, Herbert Jenkyns to Sir Arthur Galsworthy, 19 July 1967.
54. TNA, CAB 134/2945, 'Cabinet. Ministerial Committee on Hong Kong. Interim Report by Officials', 21 July 1967.
55. TNA, CAB 134/2945, 'Cabinet. Ministerial Committee on Hong Kong', Minutes of a meeting of the committee, 24 July 1967.
56. TNA, CAB 134/2945, 'Cabinet. Ministerial Committee on Hong Kong', Minutes of a meeting of the committee, 22 September July 1967 and attached paper, 'Contingency Planning. Note by the Secretaries', 20 September 1967.

57. Draft OPD paper, 'Contingency Planning: Hong Kong. Memorandum by the Commonwealth Secretary', November 1967, copy in TNA, DEFE 25/300.
58. C. R. Schenk, 'The Empire Strikes Back: Hong Kong and the Decline of Sterling in the 1960s', *Economic History Review* 57:3 (2004), pp. 551–80.
59. TNA, T317/1228, 'Contingency planning: Hong Kong', S. H. Wright, Treasury, minute, 7 December 1967.
60. TNA, CAB 134/2945, Cabinet Ministerial Committee on Hong Kong. Hong Kong: Long Term Study, 28 March 1969, para. 9.
61. TNA, FCO21/204, D.C. Hopson (Peking) Despatch No.12, 6 June 1967.
62. H.A. Turner et al., *The Last Colony: But Whose? A Study of the Labour Movement, Labour Market and Labour Relations in Hong Kong* (Cambridge: Cambridge University Press, 1980), pp. 104–6; TNA, CAB 134/2945, 'Cabinet. Ministerial Committee on Hong Kong', Minutes of a meeting of the committee, 22 September July 1967 and attached papers.

Chapter 5

1. Parts of this chapter draw from sections of my *Concise History of Hong Kong* (Lanham, Maryland: Rowman and Littlefield, 2007; Hong Kong: Hong Kong University Press, 2007).
2. Gary Wayne Catron, 'China and Hong Kong, 1945–1967' (PhD thesis, Harvard University, 1971), pp. 297–300.
3. Catron, 'China and Hong Kong', p. 284.
4. Catron, 'China and Hong Kong', p. 250.
5. For example, *Who Is Guilty of These Atrocities?* (Hong Kong: Ta Kung Pao, 1967), *We Shall Win! British Imperialism in Hong Kong Will be Defeated!* (Hong Kong: Ta Kung Pao, 1967), *The May Upheaval in Hongkong* (Hong Kong: Committee of Hongkong-Kowloon Chinese Compatriots of All Circles for the Struggle against Persecution by the British Authorities in Hong Kong, 1967), *Ying diguozhuyi zai wanhuo* 英帝國主義在玩火 [British colonialism is playing with fire] (Hong Kong: Sanlian, 1967), *Kongsu Gangying diguozhuyi Faxisi baoxing* [Complaint against the fascist violence of British colonialism] 控訴港英帝國主義法西斯暴行 (Hong Kong: Sanlian, 1967).
6. Robert Kotewall's report on the strike, enclosed in TNA, CO 129/489, 24 October 1925, Stubbs to Amery, pp. 433–4.
7. Ming K. Chan, 'Labour vs. Crown: Aspects of Society-State Interactions in the Hong Kong Labour Movement before World War II', in Elizabeth Sinn (ed.), *Between East and West: Aspects of Social and Political Development in Hong Kong* (Hong Kong: Centre of Asian Studies, the University of Hong Kong, 1990), p. 141.
8. This correspondence is contained in the Foreign Office and the Foreign and Commonwealth Office, Far Eastern Department: Registered Files, F and FE Series, TNA, FCO 21/193, 1967–68.
9. *Hong Kong: Report for the Year 1967* (Hong Kong: Hong Kong Government Press, 1968), pp. 1, 111.
10. For a brief discussion of these documents, see Gary Cheung, 'The Secret Handover', *South China Morning Post*, 20 November 2006.
11. Quoted in John D. Young, 'The Building Years: Maintaining a China-Hong Kong-Britain Equilibrium, 1950–71', in Ming K. Chan (ed.), *Precarious Balance: Hong Kong between China and Britain, 1842–1992* (Armonk, NY: M.E. Sharpe, 1994), p. 138.

12. Cheung Ka-wai (Gary Cheung) 張家偉, *Xianggang liuqi baodong neiqing* 香港六七暴動內情 [Inside story of the 1967 riots in Hong Kong] (Beijing: Taipingyang shiji chubanshe, 2000), pp. 16–17.
13. John Cooper, *Colony in Conflict: The Hong Kong Disturbances, May 1967–January 1968* (Hong Kong: Swindon, 1970), p. 10.
14. Chan, 'Labour vs. Crown', p. 139.
15. Robert Bickers, *Empire Made Me: An Englishman Adrift in Shanghai* (London: Allen Lane, 2003), p. 168.
16. For an example of leftist propaganda aimed at students, see *Tongxuemen, tuanjie qilai!* 同學們，團結起來！[Students, organize and rise up!] (Hong Kong: Sanlian, 1967).
17. Chan, 'Labour vs. Crown', p. 139.
18. Kotewall's report, pp. 442–3.
19. Sir Jack Cater, 'The 1967 Riots', in Sally Blyth and Ian Wotherspoon, *Hong Kong Remembers* (Hong Kong: Oxford University Press, 1996), pp. 108–9.
20. TNA, CO 129/489, 10 September 1925, P. P. J. Wodehouse to Colonial Secretary, pp. 193–6.
21. Young, 'The Building Years', p. 140. See also John D. Young, 'Towards a Hong Kong Identity: The Riots of 1966 and 1967', paper presented at the Twelfth Conference of the International Association of Historians, June 1991, the University of Hong Kong.
22. Henry J. Lethbridge, 'Introduction', in *Hong Kong: Stability and Change: A Collection of Essays* (Hong Kong: Oxford University Press, 1978), p. 25.
23. David Faure, *Colonialism and the Hong Kong Mentality* (Hong Kong: Centre of Asian Studies, the University of Hong Kong, 2003), pp. 75–76.
24. Kotewall's report, pp. 431–2.
25. Kotewall's report, pp. 433–4.
26. Chan, 'Labour vs. Crown', p. 142.
27. Cater, 'The 1967 Riots', p. 111.
28. Quoted in Gary Cheung, 'Hong Kong's Watershed', *South China Morning Post*, 3 May 2007.
29. Stephen Edward Waldron, 'Fire on the Rim: A Study in Contradictions in Left-Wing Political Mobilization in Hong Kong 1967' (PhD thesis, University of Syracuse, 1980), p. 21.
30. Leo F. Goodstadt, *Uneasy Partners: The Conflict Between Public Interest and Private Profit in Hong Kong* (Hong Kong: Hong Kong University Press, 2005), p. 147.
31. Quoted in John Rear, 'One Brand of Politics', in Keith Hopkins (ed.), *Hong Kong: The Industrial Colony* (Hong Kong: Oxford University Press, 1971), p. 55.
32. TNA, CO 129/263, 23 August 1894, Ripon to Robinson, reprinted in Steve Tsang (ed.), *Government and Politics: A Documentary History of Hong Kong* (Hong Kong: Hong Kong University Press, 1995), p. 109.
33. TNA, CO 129/268, Robinson to Chamberlain, 16 August 1895, reprinted in Tsang, *Government and Politics*, p. 109.
34. TNA, CO 129/274, Chamberlain to Robinson, 29 May 1896, reprinted in Tsang, *Government and Politics*, p. 110.

Chapter 6

1. 'Hong Kong Defeat of Rioters; High Prestige of Police', David Bonavia, *The Times*, 22 June 1967.

2. European was the imperial term given for 'white' officers who were typically British but could also be drawn from other Commonwealth countries.
3. See Charles Jeffries, *The Colonial Police* (London: Max Parrish, 1952), pp. 28–34. Jeffries was the deputy under-secretary of state for the colonies at this time and made the earliest study of British colonial policing.
4. It consisted originally of ninety-three soldiers seconded from British and Indian regiments.
5. Kevin Sinclair and Nelson Ng Kwok-cheung, *Asia's Finest Marches On: Policing Hong Kong from 1841 into the 21st Century* (Hong Kong: Kevin Sinclair Associates Ltd, 1997); Colin Crisswell and Mike Watson, *The Royal Hong Kong Police, 1841–1945* (Basingstoke: Macmillan, 1982).
6. The Auxiliary Police Force was formed in 1914 and known originally as the Hong Kong Reserve. It was disbanded in 1919 but then re-formed in the early 1920s. In 1941, a special constabulary was formed separate to the Hong Kong Reserve though both bodies were amalgamated in 1957 to form the Hong Kong Auxiliary Police Force.
7. Taken from an interview with Peter Schouten (RHKP, Sen. Assist. Commissioner, Rtd., 1949–78), 10 November 2006.
8. Mark S. Gaylord and Harold Traver, 'Colonial Policing and the Demise of British Rule in Hong Kong', *International Journal of the Sociology of Law*, 23 (1995), pp. 24–26.
9. Taken from an interview with Michael Ko-chun (RHKP, Sup. Rtd., 1950–75), 18 August 2003 and 15 September 2006. Ko-chun was born in Weihaiwei, arriving in Hong Kong in 1950 as a refugee.
10. Taken from an interview with Ivan Scott (RHKP, Sup. Rtd., 1955–1987), 21 May 2001.
11. For detailed discussion see Georgina Sinclair, *At the End of the Line: Colonial Policing and the Imperial Endgame, 1945–1980* (Manchester: Manchester University Press, 2006), Ch. 1.
12. This was particularly true in the late 1940s when the local population saw an influx of immigrants from China, many of whom were 'Nationalists and keen to support the Colonial Government'. Indeed, the 'loyalty' of Chinese police officers recruited from this population was not called into question. Taken from an interview with Ted Eates (Sierra Leone, The Gambia, Nigeria RHKP, Com. Rtd., 1946–1968), 22 October 2007.
13. Eates interview, 23 July 2003.
14. Gaylord and Traver, 'Colonial Policing', p. 29.
15. Jeffries, *Colonial Police*, p. 84. In 1935, Sir Herbert Dowbiggin commented that the Hong Kong Police were better equipped for crowd and riot control than many of their colonial counterparts. This included transport and weaponry available. Dowbiggin, 'Notes on Police Forces visited in 1935', Rhodes House Library, Oxford (RHL) MSs. Ind. Oc. s. 288/f. 24.
16. C. L. Scobell (RHKP, Sen. Assist. Com. Rtd., 1951–78) in correspondence with the author, 22 February 2000.
17. Anthony Annieson, *The One-Eyed Dragon: The Inside Story of a Hong Kong Policeman* (Moffat: Lochar Publishing Ltd, 1989), pp. 37–64.
18. Schouten interview, 10 November 2006.
19. In 1956, each Police Tactical Squad (PTS) comprised some twenty-eight to thirty men divided into sections: baton; lock-up; rifle and gas with one non-commissioned officer (NCO) and six men per section managed by two European or Chinese officers.
20. Annieson, *One-Eyed Dragon*, pp. 39–40.

21. Sinclair and Ng Kwok-cheung, *Asia's Finest*, pp. 39–40.
22. Schouten interview, 10 November 2006; Eates interview, 23 July 2003.
23. Annieson, *One-Eyed Dragon*, p. 161.
24. Schouten interview, 10 November 2006.
25. Scobell interview, 22 February 2000, Eates interview 23 July 2003.
26. Trench to Colonial Secretary, Secret, 'Hong Kong: A Review of Principal Developments', 15 December 1966, The National Archives, London, TNA, DEFE 13/534.
27. Michael Hogan, C. K. Lo, L. T. Ride and Maurice P. K. Wong, 'Kowloon Report' (1966), TNA, FCO 40/39.
28. In the event, 93 rounds of ammunition were fired and this resulted in one dead and three injured according to the report. Report Kowloon disturbances, 1967, pp. 60–67, TNA, FCO 40/39.
29. Eates interview, 19 September 2007.
30. Report Kowloon disturbances, 1967, p. 65, TNA, FCO 40/39.
31. Report Kowloon disturbances, 1967, p. 66, TNA, FCO 40/39.
32. Trench to Commonwealth Secretary, 'Hong Kong: Principal Developments December 1966–June 1967', 25 July 1967, TNA, DEFE 25/300.
33. Eates, as deputy commissioner, replaced the commissioner of police, Edward Tyrer, in August 1967, having been acting commissioner during his six-week leave of absence in the UK. Tyrer had returned to Hong Kong in August and resumed command of the Hong Kong Police (HKP) at that time. He was said to have retired subsequently from the police for reasons of ill health; see Sinclair and Ng Kwok-cheung, *Asia's Finest*, p. 49. However, official correspondence does not provide any conclusive evidence of the reasons for his premature retirement. Eates has said that Tyrer told him that the Hong Kong government had lost confidence in him, but he did not give specific reasons for this. Rumours at the time suggested that Tyrer had been seen to have 'given the Communists too much elbow room and not taken a tough enough line', although police policy at the time was keen not to provoke Beijing in terms of HKP handling of local communist supporters. Moreover, Tyrer had told Eates on several occasions that he had disagreements with the commander of the British Forces (CBF) on how police operations should be managed; Eates interview, 15 February 2008. It could be suggested here that police commissioners had been forced into early retirement during colonial emergencies as a result of a difference of opinion with the CBF. For example, Nicol Gray in Malaya in 1952, George Robbins in Cyprus in 1956 and John Biles in Zanzibar in 1963.
34. Commissioner of Police, Annual Departmental Report, 1965 (Hong Kong, 1966), p. 1.
35. Taken from an interview with Pedro Ching (Sen. Assist. Com., RHKP, Rtd., 1963–98), 28 May 2007. Ching was recruited into the Inspectorate in 1963.
36. Trench to Commonwealth Secretary, 'Hong Kong: Principal Developments December 1966–June 1967', 25 July 1967, TNA, DEFE 25/300.
37. See, for example, Sinclair and Ng Kwok-cheung, *Asia's Finest*, pp. 45–50.
38. Eates noted that police morale 'suffered' temporarily though there were no incidents recalled when the Hong Kong Police failed to carry out their duties and responsibilities efficiently, nor were there more than a handful of resignations at that time. Eates interview, 15 February 2008.
39. Trench to Commonwealth Office, Secretary of State, 24 May 1967, TNA, FCO 2/191.
40. Hong Kong Information Office to Commonwealth Office, telegram, 23 May 1967, TNA, FCO 2/191.

41. Ching interview, 28 May 2007.
42. This was perceived as evidence that the British government were intent on remaining in Hong Kong; Eates interview, 15 February 2008 and Trench to Secretary of State, Commonwealth Office, secret telegram, 22 May 1967, TNA, FCO 2/191.
43. CINCFE to MOD UK, 22 May 1967, TNA, DEFE 25/300.
44. Ching interview, 28 May 2007.
45. 'General Situation and Policing', Hong Kong; Political Affairs, report, May 1967, TNA, FCO 21/191.
46. Hong Kong government to FCO, general report on disturbances, May 1967, TNA, DEFE 11/754.
47. 'Chinese Communist Confrontation with HK Government – Assessment of Recent Activities', Special Branch report, 15 January 1968, TNA, FCO 21/196.
48. Trench to Secretary of State, Commonwealth Office, secret telegram, 17 May 1967, TNA, FCO 2/191.
49. Eates interview, 4 February 2008.
50. Press Office Hong Kong to Press Chapelries, London, telegram, 17 May 1967, TNA, FCO 2/191.
51. Cooper, 'Hong Kong Disturbances', p. 14. Allegations were made of police violence during the 1967 disturbances, which the government then claimed to have been 'grossly exaggerated'. Five people died while in police custody. In four cases, it was claimed that these people had been arrested on 'occasions when extreme violence had been resorted to in attempts to resist the efforts of the Police to maintain law and order. The persons concerned had received injuries almost certainly incurred in the course of their arrest from which they subsequently died.' An inquiry was held into each case: two deaths due to misadventure, one accidental and one justifiable homicide. In the fifth case, three police officers were charged with murder and convicted with manslaughter. The convictions were all quashed on appeal owing to incomplete evidence. Police casualties were 10 killed and 212 injured, and for civilians, 17 people killed and 43 injured as a result of the use of firearms. Total casualties amongst the public were 39 killed and 585 injured, many as a result of bombings. TNA, FCO 40/226.
52. For example, a corporal and two constables were charged following an attack on a man held in custody from 24 June to 26 June. HK office to FCO, telegram, 1 July 1967, TNA, FCO 21/192.
53. Hong Kong Annual Report, 10 January 1968, TNA, FCO 21/193.
54. Sinclair and Ng Kwok-cheung, *Asia's Finest*, pp. 49–50, Eates interview, 22 October 2007.
55. For an in-depth overview of police/military relationship, see Samuel P. Huntington, *The Soldier and the State: The Theory and Politics of Civil-Military Relations* (Cambridge, MA: Belknap Press of Harvard University Press, 1957), pp. 1–98.
56. Thomas R. Mockaitis, *British Counterinsurgency 1919–1960* (Basingstoke: Macmillan, 1990), p. 145.
57. 'Dormant Commission for CBF, Hong Kong', Top Secret, 1967, TNA, FCO 40/98.
58. 'UK Policy towards Hong Kong', secret, TNA, FCO 21/199.
59. Police/military exercises, known as TEWT (tactical exercises without troops), were carried out yearly, but involved police and army officers working out joint manoeuvres from a theoretical rather than practical perspective.
60. Eates interview, 19 September 2007.
61. Trench to Colonial Secretary, secret telegram, 12 January 1967, TNA, DEFE 24/595.

62. Ibid.
63. Defence Report, 'Dormant Commission', 1967, TNA, FCO 40/98.
64. Secret Special Branch Report, HKP, 15 May 1967, TNA, FCO 21/192.
65. This was also in response to the number of crimes recorded, which rose by 11.8 percent that year to 24,047, being the highest reported figure for eleven years. Hong Kong Police Annual Report, 1 April 1967 – 31 March 1968, pp. 4, 8, 19.
66. Chiefs of Staff Committee Defence Planning Report, 6 October 1966, TNA, DEFE 24/519.
67. Hong Kong defence contributions, 1967, TNA, FCO 40/99.
68. Minutes of Defence Planning Meeting, 11 October 1966, TNA, DEFE 24/519.
69. Secret memorandum by Colonial Secretary to Defence Planning Committee, October 1966 entitled 'Hong Kong Garrison', TNA, DEFE 13/534.
70. Top secret, Foreign Secretary notes taken at Defence Planning meeting, 5 September 1967, TNA, DEFE 11/756.
71. K. M. Wilford, Colonial Secretariat, HK to FCO, 21 July 1967, TNA, FCO 21/209.
72. Trench to Colonial Secretary, confidential telegram, 24 June 1967, 'Bilateral Border Incidents', TNA, FCO 21/209.
73. Trench to Colonial Secretary, confidential telegram, 27 June 1967, TNA, FCO 21/209.
74. 'Aspects of Recent Chinese Dealings with Hong Kong', Special Branch Report, 10 May 1968, TNA, FCO 21/198.
75. Eates interview, 7 September 2007 and Wilford, Colonial Secretariat, HK to FCO, 21 July 1967, TNA, FCO 21/209.
76. FCO to Peking Office, cipher, 5 July 1967, TNA, FCO 21/209.
77. FCO to Peking Office, cipher, 5 August 1967, TNA, FCO 21/209.
78. FCO Confidential report, 'Border Incidents', TNA, FCO 21/193.
79. Ching interview, 28 May 2007.
80. Peking Office to FCO, telegram, 15 August 1967, TNA, FCO 21/209.
81. Chief of the Defence Staff to the Commonwealth Secretary, Top Secret Report, UK eyes only, 27 July 1967, TNA, DEFE 25/300.
82. 'Hong and Border Incidents', FCO report, 16 October 1967, TNA, FCO 21/210.
83. 'Border Agreement', FCO report, 16 October 1967, TNA, FCO 21/198.
84. Eates, in correspondence with the author, 13 October 2007.
85. Signed D. W. H., Colonial Office to Ministry of Defence, 9 June 1967, TNA, DEFE 11/756.
86. Gerry Northam, *Shooting in the Dark: Riot Police in Britain* (London: Faber and Faber, 1988), pp. 38–42. This visit by the Royal Hong Kong Police (RHKP) was never made public, nor was the decision to adopt colonial-style riot police tactics in Britain, although these riot control methods had been employed in Northern Ireland since the inception of the Royal Ulster Constabulary (RUC) in 1922.
87. Taken from an interview with Eric Blackburn (RHKP, Dep. Com., Rtd., 1954–1988), 20 October 2006.

Chapter 7

1. Part of the research for this chapter was undertaken while the author was Visiting Fellow at the Hong Kong Institute for Monetary Research. The research was funded by an ESRC research grant RES-165-25-0004.
2. C. R. Schenk, *Hong Kong as an International Financial Centre: Emergence and Development 1945–65* (London: Routledge, 2001).

Notes to pages 105–109 **199**

3. The next two sections draw on C. R. Schenk, 'The Empire Strikes Back: Hong Kong and the Decline of Sterling in the 1960s', *Economic History Review*, LVII (3) August 2004, pp. 551–80.
4. Note by Secretary of the Cabinet (Burke Trend), the Economic Situation, 18 July 1966. The National Archives, Kew, London (hereafter TNA) CAB129/126.
5. Hong Kong Legislative Council, 15 March 1967.
6. P. R. Baldwin (Principal Private Secretary to Chancellor) to F. E. Figgures (HMT), 25 October 1966, TNA, T317/1067.
7. Ministry of Defence paper, Defence Estimates 1967; draft white paper, 2 February 1967, TNA, CAB129/128.
8. Intelligence memorandum, 11 July 1967, CIA Office of Current Intelligence, 'The Situation in Hong Kong'. Lyndon B. Johnson Library.
9. Ministry of Defence (DEI) memo, 'The Economic Value of HK to China', 18 May 1967, TNA, T317/902.
10. CIA Intelligence memorandum, Office of Current Intelligence, 'The Outlook for Hong Kong', 25 August 1967, Lyndon B. Johnson Library.
11. F. E. Figgures to Sir Denis Rickett, 17 May 1967. Reporting a discussion with Sir Roger Jackling on FO opinion of HK situation, TNA, T317/902.
12. Ministry of Defence (DEI) memo, 'The Economic Value of HK to China', 18 May 1967, TNA, T317/902.
13. Note for the record of a meeting between Denis Rickett and the Chancellor, by P. R. Baldwin, 16 May 1967, TNA, T317/902.
14. H. A. Copeman to Goldman, 19 May 1967. The memo was read by the chancellor on 25 May, TNA, T317/902.
15. Cabinet Conclusions, 10 a.m., 30 May 1967, TNA, CAB128/42.
16. Cabinet Conclusions, 11 July 1967, TNA, CAB128/42.
17. The other members were the secretary of state for defence, president of board of trade, Lord Shackleton, and the minister of state for foreign affairs (Mulley).
18. S. H. Wright to Mr Houghton, Top Secret 'Ministerial Committee on Hong Kong; interim report by officials', 21 July 1967, TNA, T317/902.
19. H. Jenkyns to Sir A. Galsworthy, 19 July 1967, TNA, T317/902.
20. HMT, Board of Trade, Bank of England Paper for Rogers Committee, 'Hong Kong: Contingency Planning for an Evacuation (financial and economic)', 10 August 1967, TNA, T295/240.
21. Bank of England, Treasury, Board of Trade paper, 'Hong Kong: Contingency Planning for an Evacuation (financial and economic)', 10 August 1967, TNA, T295/240. The book value of UK FDI in Hong Kong (excluding oil, insurance and banking) at the end of 1964 was £26 million. A. Mackay to Hubback (BE), 14 September 1967, TNA, T317/903.
22. Cowperthwaite meeting at Bank of England, 15 September 1967, TNA, PRO T295/240.
23. A. Mackay (HMT) to Hubback (BE), account of Rogers Working Party meeting, 24 August 1967, TNA, T295/240.
24. S. H. Wright to Mr Lavelle, passing on Commonwealth Secretary's views to Chancellor of the Exchequer calling for an end to the contingency planning, 7 December 1967, TNA, T295/240.
25. Note by P. Nicholls of a meeting of Rogers Working Party, 6 September 1967, TNA, T317/903.

26. Schenk, *Hong Kong as an International Financial Centre*, p. 70.
27. Report on 14 July 1967. Hong Kong Public Records Office (hereafter HKRS) 163-1-2660.
28. N. H. T. Bennett memo, 7 June 1967. Chairman's papers, Carton 4, Hong Kong Disturbances 1967, HSBC Group Archive (hereafter HSBC).
29. A. Mackay to Hubback, 24 August 1967, TNA, T295/240. L. Goodstadt, 'Painful Transitions: The Impact of Economic Growth and Government Policies on Hong Kong's Chinese banks, 1945–70', HKIMR Working Paper, 16, 2006.
30. 'The Sterling Supply' by J. M. Scott. Given to Government and to Cowperthwaite (then in the UK), 6 June 1967. The Chartered Bank were also worried about the drain of sterling from the note issue. Haslam (Bank of England) to G. O. W. Stewart, 15 June 1967. Chairman's papers, Carton 4, Hong Kong Disturbances 1967, HSBC.
31. F. J. Knightly to G. O. W. Stewart in London, 7 June 1967. Chairman's papers, Carton 4, Hong Kong Disturbances 1967, HSBC.
32. Haslam (Bank of England) to G. O. W. Stewart, 15 June 1967. Chairman's papers, Carton 4, Hong Kong Disturbances 1967, HSBC.
33. F. J. Knightly to J. A. H. Saunders, 20 June 1967. Chairman's papers, Carton 4, Hong Kong Disturbances 1967, HSBC. The government also agreed that the HSBC could hold a larger reserve of un-issued Hong Kong doallar notes in London for emergencies.
34. I am grateful to Robert Bickers for drawing my attention to the following news reports: 19 May 1967, *China Mail*; 23 May 1967, *South China Morning Post*.
35. Extract from *Cheng Wu Pao*, 20 May 1967, HKH95, HSBC.
36. Telegram from Sir David Trench to the Foreign and Commonwealth Office, 19 May 1967, TNA, T295/241. Cash withdrawals had been limited to HK$100 per day during the 1965 banking crisis.
37. Memo by M. Brereton, S. S. (EM) to Financial Secretary, 29 March 1968, HKRS 163-1-3276.
38. Note by N. H. T. Bennett, 26 May 1967. Chairman's papers, Carton 4, Hong Kong Disturbances 1967, HSBC.
39. Extract from *Sing Tao Jih Pao*, 31 October 1967. HKH95, HSBC.
40. GHO 262/1, HSBC.
41. Memo, 3 May 1967, HKRS 163-1-3275.
42. For an account of the development of the Hong Kong banking system, see C. R. Schenk, 'Banking Crises and the Evolution of the Regulatory Framework in Hong Kong 1945–70', *Australian Economic History Review*, 43(2), pp. 140–54, 2003; C. R. Schenk, 'Banks and the Emergence of Hong Kong as an International Financial Centre', *Journal of International Financial Markets, Institutions and Money* 12(4–5), pp. 321–40; Catherine Schenk, 'Banking Groups in Hong Kong 1945–65', *Asia Pacific Business Review*, 2000: 7(2), pp. 131–54.
43. Leo F. Goodstadt, *Uneasy Partners: The Conflict Between Public Interest and Private Profit in Hong Kong* (Hong Kong: Hong Kong University Press, 2005), p. 186.
44. HKRS 163-1-3274.

Chapter 8

1. Thanks to The Leverhulme Trust, which provided financial assistance, the Centre of Asian Studies of the University of Hong Kong, which provided support during field work, and participants at the 'May Days' workshop.

2. Tai-lok Lui and Stephen W. K. Chiu, 'Social Movements and Public Discourse on Politics', in Tak-Wing Ngo (ed.), *Hong Kong's History, State and Society Under Colonial Rule* (London, and New York: Routledge, 1999), p. 102.
3. See Catherine Jones, *Promoting Prosperity: The Hong Kong Way of Social Policy* (Hong Kong: Chinese University Press, 1990), pp. 209–83.
4. See Joe England and John Rear, *Chinese Labour Under British Rule* (Hong Kong and Oxford: Oxford University Press, 1975), pp. 121–53; Joe England, *Industrial Relations and Law in Hong Kong* (Oxford: Oxford University Press, 1989).
5. On the strike, see John M. Carroll, *A Concise History of Hong Kong* (Latham, MD; Plymouth: Rowman and Littlefield, 2007), pp. 89–116. On trade unions, see England and Rear, *Chinese Labour*, pp. 74–85.
6. See David Clayton, 'Capitalism under Confucianism and Colonialism: The Government and Trade Unions in Hong Kong, c. 1948–60', available from the author on request.
7. See David Clayton, 'From "Free" to "Fair" trade': The Evolution of Labour Laws in Colonial Hong Kong, 1958–62', *Journal of Imperial and Commonwealth History*, 35:2 (2007), pp. 263–83.
8. Ibid.
9. England, *Industrial Relations*, p. 166.
10. Carroll, *History of Hong Kong*, pp. 158–61.
11. Steve Tsang, *A Modern History of Hong Kong* (London: I. B. Tauris, 2004), p. 171.
12. See Frank Welsh, *A History of Hong Kong* (London: Harper Collins, 1997), p. 461. On Chicago-school polemics, see Alvin Rabuska, *Hong Kong: A Study in Economic Freedom* [William H. Abbott Lectures in International Business and Economic] (Chicago: University of Chicago, Graduate School of Business, 1979).
13. See David W. Clayton, 'Industrialisation and Institutional Change in Hong Kong, 1842–1960', in John Latham and Heita Kawakatsu (eds.), *Asia Pacific Dynamism 1550–2000* (London and New York: Routledge, 2000), pp. 149–69.
14. See David W. Clayton, 'Labour-intensive Industrialization in Hong Kong, 1950–70: A Note on Sources and Methods', *Asian Pacific Business Review*, 12:3 (2006), pp. 375–88.
15. The National Archives (Kew, London), Foreign and Commonwealth Office [henceforth TNA, FCO] 40/124, telegrams to London, 18 April, no. 481, and 24 April 1967, no. 495.
16. See Jürgen Osterhammel, *Colonialism: A Theoretical Overview* [translated from German by Shelley L. Frisch] (Princeton: M. Weiner, Kingston, Ian Randle Publishers, 1997), p. 60.
17. On structures, George B. Endacott, *Government and People in Hong Kong, 1841–1962: A Constitutional History* (Hong Kong: Hong Kong University Press, 1964). On historical processes, see Steve Tsang, *Democracy Shelved* (Hong Kong and New York: Oxford University Press, 1988).
18. See Norman Miners, *Hong Kong under Imperial Rule, 1912–1941* (Hong Kong and New York: Oxford University Press, 1987), on *mui-tsai* (indentured girl servants).
19. See John M. Carroll, *Edge of Empire: Chinese Elites and British Colonials in Hong Kong* (Cambridge, MA and London: Harvard University Press, 2005).
20. England and Rear, *Chinese Labour*, p. 11.
21. Ian Scott, 'Policy-making in a Turbulent Environment: The Case of Hong Kong', *International Journal of Administrative Sciences*, 52 (1986), p. 455.

22. See Clayton, 'Free Trade'.
23. See Hong Kong Public Record Office (PRO), Hong Kong, Record Series [henceforth HKRS] 939/1/65, *Wah Kiu Yat Po*, 7 September 1960; HKRS 939/52, *Wah Kiu Yat Po*, 18 January 1961, 13 and 20 March 1959, and the *Hong Kong Times*, 14 March 1959.
24. See HKRS 270/5/60.
25. See Steven Chi Man Chow, 'Economic Growth and Income Distribution in Hong Kong' [Unpublished PhD] (Boston: University Graduate School, 1977).
26. See David W. Clayton, 'Inter-Asian Competition for the British Market in Cotton Textiles: The Political Economy of Anglo-Asian Cartels, c.1932–1960', in John Latham and Heita Kawakatsu (eds.), *Inter-Asian Competition for the World Market Since the Sixteenth Century* (London and New York: Routledge, 2006), pp. 186–209.
27. See Clayton, 'Free Trade'.
28. See Ian Scott, *Political Change and the Crisis of Legitimacy in Hong Kong* (London: Hurst, 1989), pp. 81–121.
29. England, *Industrial Relations,* pp. 12–16.
30. Grace O. M. Lee, 'Labour Protection', in Paul Wilding, Ahmed Shafiqul Huque, and Julia Tao Lai Po-wah (eds.), *Social Policy in Hong Kong* (Cheltenham, UK, and Lyme, US: Edward Elgar, 1997), pp. 128–45; and Scott, *Political Change.*
31. Lee, 'Labour Protection', p. 131.
32. For details, see Clayton, 'Free Trade'.
33. TNA, FCO 40/127, 'Labour Conditions in Hong Kong', memorandum by the Hong Kong Labour Department, July 1968.
34. See Colonial Office [henceforth, CO] CO859/1715, and note on the hours of work of women and young persons, Hong Kong, Labour Department, 16 March 1965.
35. TNA, CO 859/1715, comment by J. S. Bennett, 9 October 1964.
36. TNA, CO 859/1715, letter to Robert Black, Governor Hong Kong, 13 December 1963.
37. HKRS 1017/2/2, 'Report on Visit to Hong Kong', 4–18 January 1963, by C. G. Gibbs, 14 February 1963.
38. TNA, CO 859/1715, minute by Gibbs, 14 February 1963.
39. TNA, CO 859/1715, letter from Trafford Smith to Black, 13 December 1963.
40. HKRS 1017/2/2, telegram to Hong Kong, 5 June 1963.
41. TNA, CO 59/1715, telegram to Hong Kong, 14 January 1964.
42. TNA, CO 8859/1715, minute by Bennett, 13 December 1963.
43. TNA, CO 859/1715, minute of meeting with Hong Kong officials, 9 October 1964; TNA, FCO 40/27, 'Labour Conditions in Hong Kong', July 1968; HKRS 1017/2/2, report on Visit, Gibbs, 14 February 1963.
44. TNA, CO 859/1715, minute by J. W. Vernon, 5 October 1964; TNA, CO 859/1715, minute of meeting with Hong Kong officials, 9 October 1964.
45. HKRS 1017/2/2, report by Gibbs, 14 February 1963.
46. TNA, CO 859 1715, minute of meeting with Hong Kong officials, 9 October 1964.
47. HKRS 1017/2/2, report by Gibbs, 14 February 1963.
48. Ibid.
49. TNA, CO 859/1715, note by P. C. M. Sedgwick, 9 October 1964.
50. TNA, CO 859/1715, minute by Vernon, 5 October 1964.
51. TNA, CO 859/1715, minute by Bennett, 14 August 1964.

52. HKRS 1017/2/2, report by Gibbs, 14 February 1963.
53. TNA, CO 859/1715, minute by Bennett, 14 August 1964.
54. TNA, CO 859/1715, minute by Shelia. A. Ogilvie, 13 August 1964.
55. TNA, FCO 40/266, Hong Kong, Visit of Labour Advisor, 11–16 October 1967, G. Foggon, 17 November 1967.
56. TNA, FCO 40/124, telegrams from Hong Kong, 18 April, no. 481, and 24 April 1967, no. 495.
57. TNA, FCO 40/127, 'Hong Kong's Labour Legislation Programme: The Commissioner of Labour's Address to the Legislative Council on 14th February, 1968'.
58. TNA, FCO 125, telegram from Hong Kong, 19 June 1967.
59. TNA, FCO 40/125, telegram from Hong Kong, no. 668, 23 May 1967; telegram from Hong Kong, 19 June 1967, no. 1138.
60. TNA, FCO 40/125, telegram to Hong Kong, no. 1017, 23 May 1967.
61. On lobbying, TNA, FCO 40/124, letter from J. Greenhalgh [General Secretary of the International Textile and Garment Workers Federation, London] to Judith Hart, Secretary of State for Colonial Affairs, 23 November 1967; TNA, FCO 40/125, letter from Greenhalgh to Hart, 5 May 1967; letter from Greenhalgh to Foggon, 4 May 1967; letter from Ernest Thornton to Hart, 18 May 1967.
62. TNA, FCO 40/266, report on visit, Foggon, 17 November 1967.
63. TNA, FCO 40/267, Extract from a report by the Special Branch, Hong Kong Police, 27 February 1970.
64. Ibid.
65. See Clayton 'Capitalism under Confucianism'.
66. TNA, FCO 40/267, minute by Foggon, 19 February 1970; and TNA, FCO 40/266, minute by Foggon, 19 January 1970.
67. TNA, FCO 40/267, note for a 'visit by Mr Anthony Royle', October 1970.
68. TNA, FCO 40/267, minute by Foggon, 15 May 1970.
69. TNA, FCO 40/333, telegram from Hong Kong, no. 361, 11 May 1971; minutes by K. M. Wilford, 7 January 1970.
70. TNA, FCO 40/266, letter from David Trench to Lord Malcolm Newton Shephard, Minister of State, 26 February 1970.
71. TNA, FCO 40/333, telegram from Hong Kong, no. 380, 25 May 1971; minutes by E. O. Laird, [undated].
72. TNA, FCO 40/267, letter from D. R. Holmes to E. O. Laird, 10 August 1970.
73. TNA, FCO 40/266: note of meeting with Lord Shephard, 19 March 1970; letter to *The Guardian*, 11 March 1970.
74. TNA, FCO 40/266, comment by Greenhalgh, cited in minutes of meeting with Shephard, 17 March 1970.
75. TNA, FCO 40/266, *The Guardian*, 3 March 1970; Confidential Memorandum on 'Conditions of Employment in Hong Kong'.
76. TNA, FCO 40/266, letter from Greenhalgh to Lord Shephard, 23 February 1970.
77. TNA, FCO 40/333, Telegram from the Governor of Hong Kong, no. 402, 27 May 1971.
78. TNA, FCO 40/333, minute by E. O. Laird, May 1971.
79. TNA, FCO 40/267, extract from a Special Branch, Hong Kong Police, report, 27 February 1970.
80. Ibid.

Chapter 9

1. John D. Young, 'The Building Years: Maintaining a China-Hong Kong-Britain Equilibrium, 1950–71', in M. K. Chan (ed.), *The Precarious Balance: Hong Kong Between Britain and China, 1842–1992* (Armonk, NY: M.E. Sharpe, 1994), p. 139; Ian C. Jarvie, 'A Postscript on Riots and the Future of Hong Kong', in Ian C. Jarvie and Joseph Agassi (eds.), *Hong Kong: A Society in Transition* (London: Routledge and Kegan Paul, 1969), p. 361; Keith Hopkins (ed.), *Hong Kong: The Industrial Colony* (Hong Kong: Oxford University Press, 1971), p. xiii.
2. David Faure (ed.), *Society: A Documentary History of Hong Kong* (Hong Kong: Hong Kong University Press, 1997), p. 287.
3. Doug McAdam, Sidney Tarrow and Charles Tilly, *The Dynamics of Contention* (Cambridge: Cambridge University Press, 2001), p. 13.
4. Alan Smart and Josephine Smart, 'Learning from Disaster? Mad Cows, Squatter Fires, and Temporality in Repeated Cases', in Eric Jones and Arthur D. Murphy (eds.), *The Political Economy of Hazards and Disasters* (Lanham, MD: Altamira Press, 2009), pp. 267–93.
5. Alan Smart, 'Unreliable Chinese: Internal Security and the Devaluation and Expansion of Citizenship in Postwar Hong Kong', in Deborah Cowen and Emily Gilbert (eds.), *War, Citizenship, Territory* (New York: Routledge, 2007), pp. 219–40.
6. Steve Tsang, *A Modern History of Hong Kong, 1841–1997* (Hong Kong: Hong Kong University Press, 2004), p. 205.
7. For a brief survey of changing government policies on social services, see Catherine Jones, *Promoting Prosperity: The Hong Kong Way of Social Policy* (Hong Kong: The Chinese University Press, 1990), Chapter 6.
8. Gertrude Williams, *Report on the Feasibility of a Survey into Social Welfare Provision and Allied Topics in Hong Kong* (Hong Kong: Government Printer, 1966), p. 1.
9. Young, 'The Building Years', p. 143.
10. Commission of Inquiry on Kowloon Disturbances 1966, *Report of Commission of Inquiry: Kowloon Disturbances 1966* (Hong Kong: Government Printer, 1967).
11. Quoted in Faure, *Society,* p. 308.
12. Commission of Inquiry on Kowloon Disturbances 1966, *Report of Commission of Inquiry,* p. 125.
13. Ambrose Yeo-chi King, 'Administrative Absorption of Politics in Hong Kong', *Asian Survey,* 15:5 (1975), pp. 422–39; Elizabeth Sinn, *Power and Charity: The Early History of the Tung Wah Hospital* (Hong Kong: Oxford University Press, 1989); John M. Carroll, *Edge of Empires: Chinese Elites and British Colonials in Hong Kong* (Cambridge, MA: Harvard University Press, 2005).
14. Tak-wing Ngo, 'Industrial History and the Artifice of Laissez-Faire Colonialism', in Tak-wing Ngo (ed.), *Hong Kong's History: State and Society under Colonial Rule* (London: Routledge, 1999), pp. 119–40.
15. Stephen W. K. Chiu, 'Unravelling Hong Kong's Exceptionalism: The Politics of Laissez-faire in the Industrial Takeoff', *Political Power and Social Theory,* 10 (1996), pp. 229–56.
16. Leo F. Goodstadt, *Uneasy Partners: The Conflict Between Public Interest and Private Profit in Hong Kong* (Hong Kong: Hong Kong University Press, 2005).
17. Ibid., p. 120.
18. Ibid., p. 26.

19. Tsang, *Modern History of Hong Kong*, p. 142.
20. James Hayes, *Friends and Teachers: Hong Kong and Its People 1953–1987* (Hong Kong: Hong Kong University Press, 1996), p. 9.
21. Siu-kai Lau, 'Utilitarianistic Familism: The Basis of Political Stability', in Ambrose Y. C. King and Rance P. L. Lee (eds.), *Social Life and Development in Hong Kong* (Hong Kong: The Chinese University Press, 1981), pp. 195–216; *Society and Politics in Hong Kong* (Hong Kong: The Chinese University Press, 1982).
22. Denis J. Dwyer, 'The Problems of In-migration and Squatter Settlement in Asian Cities: Two Case Studies, Manila and Victoria, Hong Kong', *Asian Studies*, 2 (1965), pp. 145–69.
23. Alan Smart, *Making Room: Squatter Clearance in Hong Kong* (Hong Kong: Centre of Asian Studies, the University of Hong Kong, 1992); *The Shek Kip Mei Myth: Squatters, Fires and Colonial Rule in Hong Kong, 1950–63* (Hong Kong: Hong Kong University Press, 2006).
24. Wai-man Lam, *Understanding the Political Culture of Hong Kong: The Paradox of Activism and Depoliticization* (Armonk, NY: M.E. Sharpe, 2004).
25. Ibid., p. 80.
26. Goodstadt, *Uneasy Partners*.
27. Smart, *Making Room*, p. 151.
28. Lam, *Understanding the Political Culture of Hong Kong*, p. 105.
29. Ibid., p. 105.
30. Smart, *The Shek Kip Mei Myth*; 'Unreliable Chinese.'
31. HKRS 920-1-2. This file includes a compilation of societies denied registration and it is a fascinating list ranging from a drivers' instructors association to the Hong Kong Chinese Basket-ball Society.
32. Steve Tsang, 'Strategy for Survival: The Cold War and Hong Kong's Policy towards Kuomintang and Chinese Communist Activities in the 1950s', *The Journal of Imperial and Commonwealth History*, 25:2 (1997), p. 317.
33. Ibid.
34. HKRS (Hong Kong Record Series) 163-3-87.
35. Manuel Castells, L. Goh and Reginald Kwok, *The Shekkipmei Syndrome: Economic Development and Public Housing in Hong Kong and Singapore* (London: Pion, 1990); James Lee, *Housing, Home Ownership and Social Change in Hong Kong* (Aldershot: Ashgate, 1999).
36. Smart, *The Shek Kip Mei Myth*, pp. 95–116.
37. Iam-chong Ip, 'Welfare Good or Colonial Citizenship? A Case Study of Early Resettlement Housing', in Agnes S. Ku and Ngai Pun (eds.), *Remaking Citizenship in Hong Kong: Community, Nation and the Global City* (London: Routledge Curzon, 2004), pp. 37–53.
38. Christopher John Mackay, 'Housing Management and the Comprehensive Housing Model in Hong Kong: A Case Study of Colonial Influence', *Journal of Contemporary China*, 9:25 (2000), pp. 449–66.
39. McAdam, Tarrow and Tilly, *Dynamics of Contention*.
40. Smart, *The Shek Kip Mei Myth*.
41. Lam, *Understanding the Political Culture of Hong Kong*, p. 124.
42. Trench's last valedictory despatch, written shortly before his departure from Hong Kong, was considered 'little more than a covering letter to a copy of . . . [his] final address to the Hong Kong Legislative Council on 1 October 1971.' TNA, FCO 40/385, A. W. Gaminara to Mr Clewley and Mr Laird, 17 February 1972.

43. TNA, FCO 40/292, Governor to the Right Honourable Michael Stewart, C.H., M.P., Secretary of State for Foreign and Commonwealth Affairs, 23 April 1970.
44. Ibid.
45. Ibid.
46. TNA, FCO 40/323, J. R. A. Bottomley to Sir L. Monson, 17 February 1971.
47. See Yep's chapter in this volume, for a detailed analysis of Governor Trench's interactions with the Foreign Office during and in the immediate aftermath of the 1967 riots.
48. TNA, FCO 40/439, Governor to the Rt. Hon. Sir Alec Douglas-Home, K.T., M.P., 1 January 1973.
49. Ibid.
50. TNA, FCO 40/329, C. M. MacLehose to Sir Leslie Monson, Mr Wilford, Mr Morgan and Mr Laird, 16 October 1971.
51. Ibid.
52. TNA, FCO 40/439, Governor to the Rt. Hon. Sir Alec Douglas-Home, K.T., M.P., 1 January 1973.
53. Ibid.
54. Ibid.
55. See, for example, Kwong-leung Tang, *Colonial State and Social Policy: Social Welfare Development in Hong Kong 1842–1997* (Lanham, NY: University Press of America, 1998), Chapter 5. Social welfare under MacLehose is described as a 'big bang'.
56. Tai-lok Lui, 'Between Metropole and Colony: Reflecting on Hong Kong's Coloniality.' Keynote speech delivered at the 9th Annual Conference of Hong Kong Sociological Association, 8 December 2007, City University of Hong Kong.
57. TNA, FCO 40/439, Governor to the Rt. Hon. Sir Alec Douglas-Home, K.T., M.P., 1 January 1973.

1967: Witnesses remember

1. Oxford, Rhodes House Library, Mss.Ind.Ocn.s.337, Transcript of interviews, 23 and 24 April 1987, given by Sir David Trench, Governor of Hong Kong (1964–71), to Dr Steve Tsang, and edited by Sir David Trench.
2. Gary Cheung (2000), *Xianggang liuqi baodong neiqing* (Inside story of the 1967 riots in Hong Kong) (Hong Kong: Pacific Century Press).
3. *Women Bisheng Gangying Bibie* (We will win! The British will lose!) (Hong Kong: Ta Kung Pao, 1967).
4. Chow Yik (Zhou Yi), *Xianggang zuopai douzheng shi* (A History of Leftist Struggle) (Hong Kong: Liwen chuban, 2002).
5. This was a detention centre used by the Hong Kong Police Special Branch during the riots.
6. Li Yee, 'Canjia fanying kangbao di rizi' (Days of involvement in the anti-colonial struggle) *Apple Daily,* 6 May 2007, A. 14.

Bibliography

Anderson, David. *Histories of the Hanged: Britain's Dirty War in Kenya and the End of Empire*. London: Weidenfeld and Nicolson, 2005.

Annieson, Anthony. *The One-Eyed Dragon: The Inside Story of a Hong Kong Policeman*. Moffat: Lochar, 1989.

Ashton, S. R. 'Keeping a foot in the door: Britain's China policy, 1945–50', *Diplomacy and Statecraft*, 15:1 (2004), pp. 79–94.

Benton, Gregor. 'Chinatown UK v. Colonial Hong Kong: An early exercise in transnational militancy and manipulation, 1967–1969', *Ethnic and Racial Studies* 28:2 (2005), pp. 331–47.

——. *The Chinese in Britain: Economy, Transnationalism, Identity* (with Edmund Terence Gomez). Basingstoke: Palgrave MacMillan, 2007.

Bickers, Robert. *Britain in China: Community, Culture and Colonialism, 1900–49*. Manchester: Manchester University Press, 1999.

——. 'The colony's shifting position in the British informal empire in China.' In *Hong Kong's Transitions, 1842–1997*, edited by Judith Brown and Rosemary Foot, pp. 33–61. London: MacMillan, 1997.

Boxer, C. R. *Fidalgos in the Far East, 1550–1770: Fact and Fancy in the History of Macao*. The Hague: Martinus Nijhoff, 1948.

Carroll, John M. *A Concise History of Hong Kong*. Lanham: Rowman and Littlefield, 2007.

——. *Edge of Empires: Chinese Elites and British Colonials in Hong Kong*. Cambridge, MA: Harvard University Press, 2005.

Castells, Manuel, L. Goh and Reginald Kwok. *The Shek Kip Mei Syndrome: Economic Development and Public Housing in Hong Kong and Singapore*. London: Pion, 1990.

Cater, Sir Jack. 'The 1967 riots.' In *Hong Kong Remembers,* edited by Sally Blyth and Ian Wotherspoon, pp. 108–9. Hong Kong: Oxford University Press, 1996.

Catron, Gary Wayne. 'China and Hong Kong, 1945–1967'. Unpublished PhD thesis, Harvard University, 1971.

Chan, Ming K. 'Labour vs. Crown: Aspects of society-state interactions in the Hong Kong Labour Movement before World War II.' In *Between East and West: Aspects of Social and Political Development in Hong Kong*, edited by Elizabeth Sinn. Hong Kong: Centre of Asian Studies, the University of Hong Kong, 1990.

Chen Yangyong. *Kucheng Weiju: Zhou Enlai zai 1967* (Shoring up a shaky situation: Zhou Enlai in 1967). Beijing: Zhongyang wenxian chubanshe, 1999.

Cheung Ka-wai (Gary Cheung). *Xianggang liuqi baodong neiqing* (Inside story of the 1967 riot in Hong Kong). Hong Kong: Pacific Century Press, 2000.

Chiu, Stephen W. K. 'Unravelling Hong Kong's exceptionalism: The politics of laissez-faire in the industrial takeoff', *Political Power and Social Theory,* 10 (1996), pp. 229–56.

Chow, Steven Chi Man. 'Economic growth and income distribution in Hong Kong'. Unpublished PhD thesis, Boston University, 1977.

Clayton, David. 'Capitalism under Confucianism and Colonialism: The government and trade unions in Hong Kong, c. 1948–60'.

——. 'From "free" to "fair" trade: The evolution of labour laws in colonial Hong Kong, 1958–62', *Journal of Imperial and Commonwealth History*, 35:2 (2007), pp. 263–283.

——. 'Industrialisation and institutional change in Hong Kong, 1842–1960.' In *Asia Pacific Dynamism 1550–2000,* edited by A. J. H. Latham and Heita Kawakatsu, pp. 149–169. London: Routledge 2000.

——. 'Institutions, demography and development: A survey and some speculations on the Hong Kong case', unpublished manuscript.

——. 'Inter-Asian competition for the British market in cotton textiles: The political economy of Anglo-Asian cartels, c.1932–1960.' In *Inter-Asian Competition for the World Market Since the Sixteenth Century,* edited by A. J. H. Latham and Heita Kawakatsu, pp. 186–209. London: Routledge, 2006.

——. 'Labour-intensive industrialization in Hong Kong, 1950–70: A note on sources and methods', *Asian Pacific Business Review*, 12:3 (2006), pp. 375–388.

Clutterbuck, Richard. *Riots and Revolution in Singapore and Malaya 1945–1963.* London: Faber and Faber, 1972.

Commission of Inquiry on Kowloon Disturbances 1966, *Report of Commission of Inquiry: Kowloon Disturbances 1966.* Hong Kong: Government Printer, 1967.

Committee of Hong Kong Kowloon Chinese Compatriots of All Circles for the Struggle Against Persecution by the British Authorities in Hong Kong. *The May Upheaval in Hong Kong*. Hong Kong: Committee of Hong Kong Kowloon Chinese Compatriots of All Circles for the Struggle Against Persecution by the British Authorities in Hong Kong, 1967.

Cohen, Paul A. 'Remembering and forgetting: National humiliation in twentieth-century China.' In *China Unbound: Evolving Perspectives on the Chinese Past*, pp.148–84. London and New York: RoutledgeCurzon, 2003.

Cooper, John. *Colony in Conflict: The Hong Kong Disturbances May 1967–January 1968.* Hong Kong: Swindon Book Company, 1970.

Cradock, Percy. *Experiences of China.* London: John Murray, 1994.

Crisswell, Colin and Mike Watson. *The Royal Hong Kong Police, 1841–1945.* Hong Kong: MacMillan, 1982.

Darwin, John. 'Hong Kong in British decolonisation.' In *Hong Kong's Transitions, 1842–1997,* edited by Judith M. Brown and Rosemary Foot. Basingstoke: MacMillan, 1997.

Davies, Hugh. '1967: An undiplomatic foray in Macau', *Journal of the Hong Kong Branch of the Royal Asiatic Society* 47 (2008), pp. 115–26.

De Leeuw, Hendrik. *Cities of Sin.* London: Noel Douglas, 1934.

De Pina-Cabral, Joao. *Between China and Europe: Person, Culture and Emotion in Macao.* London: Berg Publishers, 2000.

Dicks, Anthony R. 'Macau: Legal fiction and gunboat diplomacy.' In *Leadership on the China Coast,* edited by Goran Aijmer, pp. 90–128. London: Curzon Press, 1984.

Dockrill, Saki. *Britain's Retreat from East of Suez: The Choice between Europe and the World?* London: Palgrave Macmillan, 2002.

Dwyer, Denis J. 'The problems of in-migration and squatter settlement in Asian cities: Two case studies, Manila and Victoria, Hong Kong', *Asian Studies*, 2 (1965), pp. 145–169.
Edmonds, Richard Louis, and Herbert S. Yee. 'Macau: From Portuguese autonomous territory to Chinese special administrative region', *The China Quarterly*, No. 160 (1999), pp. 801–17.
Endacott, G. B. *Government and People in Hong Kong, 1841–1962: A Constitutional History*. Hong Kong: Hong Kong University Press, 1964.
England, Joe. *Industrial Relations and Law in Hong Kong*. Hong Kong: Oxford University Press, 1989.
England, Joe, and John Rear. *Chinese Labour Under British Rule*. Hong Kong: Oxford University Press, 1975.
Fang, Karen. 'Britain's finest.' In *After the Imperial Turn: Thinking with and through the Nation*, edited by Antoinette Burton. Durham, NC: Duke University Press, 2003.
Faure, David. *Colonialism and the Hong Kong Mentality*. Hong Kong: Centre of Asian Studies, the University of Hong Kong, 2003.
—— (ed.). *Society: A Documentary History of Hong Kong*. Hong Kong: Hong Kong University Press, 1997.
Fernandes, Moisés Silva. 'As prostrações das instituições britânicas em Macau durante a "revolução cultural" chinesa em Maio de 1967 e algumas das suas consequências' ('The prostration of British institutions in Macau during the Chinese "Cultural Revolution" in May 1967 and some of its repercussions'). In *Confluência de Interesses: Macau nas Relações Luso-Chinesas Contemporâneas 1945–2005*, pp. 305–44. Lisbon: Ministério dos Negócios Estrangeiros, Colecção Biblioteca Diplomática Série A No. 9, 2008.
——. *Macau na Política Externa Chinesa, 1949–1979*. Lisboa: Imprensa de Ciências Sociais, 2006.
——. *Sinopse de Macau nas Relações Luso-Chinesas, 1945–1995*. Lisboa: Fundação Oriente, 2000.
Gao Wenqian, *Wannian Zhou Enlai* (Twilight years of Zhou Enlai). Hong Kong: Mirror Books, 2003.
Gaylord, Mark S., and Harold Traver. 'Colonial policing and the demise of British rule in Hong Kong', *International Journal of the Sociology of Law*, 23:1 (1995), pp. 23–43.
Goodstadt, Leo F. *Uneasy Partners: The Conflict Between Public Interest and Private Profit in Hong Kong*. Hong Kong: Hong Kong University Press, 2005.
Hamilton, K. A. '"A week that changed the world": Britain and Nixon's China visit of 21–28 February 1972', *Diplomacy and Statecraft*, 15:1, (2004), pp. 117–35.
Hayes, James. *Friends and Teachers: Hong Kong and Its People 1953–1987*. Hong Kong: Hong Kong University Press, 1996.
Heaton, William, 'Maoist revolutionary strategy and modern colonialism: The Cultural Revolution in Hong Kong', *Asian Survey*, 10:9 (1970), pp. 840–57.
Hinchcliffe, Peter, John T. Ducker and Maria Holt. *Without Glory in Arabia: The British Retreat from Aden*. London: I. B. Tauris, 2006.
Hopkins, Keith (ed.). *Hong Kong: The Industrial Colony*. Hong Kong: Oxford University Press, 1971.
Hooper, Beverley. *China Stands Up: Ending the Western Presence, 1948–50*. London and New York: Allen and Unwin, 1986.
Huntington, Samuel P. *The Soldier and the State: The Theory and Politics of Civil-Military Relations*. Cambridge, MA: Belknap Press of Harvard University Press, 1957.
——. *The Third Wave: Democratization in the Late Twentieth Century*. Norman: University of Oklahoma Press, 1991.

Ip, Lam-chong, 'Welfare good or colonial citizenship? A case study of early resettlement housing.' In *Remaking Citizenship in Hong Kong: Community, Nation and the Global City,* edited by Agnes S. Ku and Ngai Pun, pp. 37–53. London: Routledge Curzon, 2004.

Jarvie, Ian C. 'A postscript on riots and the future of Hong Kong.' In *Hong Kong: A Society in Transition*, edited by Ian C. Jarvie and Joseph Agassi, pp. 361–69. London: Routledge and Kegan Paul, 1969.

Jeffries, Charles. *The Colonial Police*. London: Max Parrish, 1952.

Jin Yiuru. *Xiangjiang wushinian yiwang* (50 years in Hong Kong). Hong Kong: Jin Yiuru Memorial Foundation, 2005.

Jin Yaoru. *Zhonggong Xianggang zhengce miwen shilu* (Secrets and facts of the Chinese Communist Party's Hong Kong policy). Hong Kong: Tinyuan Press, 1998.

Jones, Catherine. *Promoting Prosperity: The Hong Kong Way of Social Policy*. Hong Kong: The Chinese University Press, 1990.

King, Ambrose Yeo-chi. 'Administrative absorption of politics in Hong Kong', *Asian Survey*, 15:5 (1975), pp. 422–39.

Kongsu Gangying diguozhuyi faxisi baoxing (Complaint against the Fascist violence of British colonialism). Hong Kong: Sanlian, 1967.

Lam, Wai-man. *Understanding the Political Culture of Hong Kong: The Paradox of Activism and Depoliticization*. Armonk, NY: M.E. Sharpe, 2004.

Lau, Siu-kai. 'Utilitarianistic familism: The basis of political stability.' In *Social Life and Development in Hong Kong,* edited by Ambrose Y. C. King and Rance P. L. Lee, pp. 195–216. Hong Kong: The Chinese University Press, 1981.

——. *Society and Politics in Hong Kong*. Hong Kong: The Chinese University Press, 1982.

Lee, James. *Housing, Home Ownership and Social Change in Hong Kong*. Aldershot: Ashgate, 1999.

Legislative Council, Hong Kong. *Reports of the Meeting of the Legislative Council of Hong Kong, sessions 1968*. Hong Kong: Government Printer, 1968.

Lethbridge, Henry J. *Hong Kong: Stability and Change: A Collection of Essays*. Hong Kong: Oxford University Press, 1978.

Liang Jiaqun et al. *Baodong mixin* (Secret stories of the riots). Hong Kong: Hong Kong Economic Press, 2001.

Lilley, James. *China Hands: Nine Decades of Adventure, Espionage and Diplomacy in Asia*. New York: Public Affairs, 2004.

Louis, Wm Roger. 'Hong Kong: The critical phase, 1945–1949', *American Historical Review* 102:4 (1997), pp. 1052–84.

Lui, Tai-lok, and Stephen W. K. Chiu, 'Social movements and public discourse on politics.' In *Hong Kong's History, State and Society under Colonial Rule,* edited by Tak-Wing Ngo. London and New York, 1999.

McAdam, Doug, Sidney Tarrow, and Charles Tilly. *The Dynamics of Contention*. Cambridge: Cambridge University Press, 2001.

MacFarquhar, Roderick, and Michael Schoenhals. *Mao's Last Revolution*. Cambridge, MA: London: Belknap Press of Harvard University Press, 2006.

Mark, Chi-kwan. *Hong Kong and the Cold War: Anglo-American Relations 1949–1957*. Oxford: Oxford University Press, 2004.

Miners, Norman. *Hong Kong under Imperial Rule, 1912–1941*. Hong Kong: Oxford University Press, 1987.

Mockaitis, Thomas R. *British Counterinsurgency 1919–1960*. Basingstoke: MacMillan, 1990.

Ngo, Tak-Wing. 'Industrial history and the artifice of laissez-faire colonialism.' In *Hong Kong's History: State and Society under Colonial Rule*, edited by Tak-Wing Ngo, pp. 119–140. London: Routledge, 1999.
Northam, Gerry. *Shooting in the Dark: Riot Police in Britain*. London: Faber, 1988.
Osterhammel, Jürgen. *Colonialism: A Theoretical Overview*. Princeton: Princeton University Press, 1997.
Porter, Jonathan. *Macau: The Imaginary City. Culture and Society, 1557 to the Present.* Boulder, CO: Westview Press, 2000.
Qi Pengfei. *Deng Xiaoping yu Xianggang huigui* (Deng Xiaoping and the return of Hong Kong), pp. 19–52. Beijing: Xinhua Chubanshe, 2004.
Rabushka, A. *Hong Kong: A Study in Economic Freedom*. Chicago: Graduate School of Business, University of Chicago, 1979.
Rear, John. 'One brand of politics.' In *Hong Kong: The Industrial Colony*, edited by Keith Hopkins, pp. 55–125. Hong Kong: Oxford University Press, 1971.
Reynolds, David. 'A "special relationship"? America, Britain and the international order since the Second World War,' *International Affairs*, 62:1 (1986), pp. 1–20.
Rice, Edward E. *Mao's Way*. Berkeley: University of California Press, 1972.
Ross, Richard, and Phillip Davies. *Inheritance in Public Policy: Change without Choice in Britain*. New Haven: Yale University Press, 1994.
Schenk, C. R. 'Banking crises and the evolution of the regulatory framework in Hong Kong 1945–70', *Australian Economic History Review*, 43:2 (2003), pp. 140–154.
———. 'Banking groups in Hong Kong 1945–65', *Asia Pacific Business Review*, 7:2 (2000), pp. 131–54.
———. 'Banks and the emergence of Hong Kong as an international financial centre', *Journal of International Financial Markets, Institutions and Money* 12:4–5 (2002), pp. 321–40.
———. 'The empire strikes back: Hong Kong and the decline of sterling in the 1960s', *Economic History Review* 57:3 (2004), pp. 551–80.
———. *Hong Kong as an International Financial Centre: Emergence and Development 1945–65*. London: Routledge, 2001.
Scott, Ian. 'Policy-making in a turbulent environment: The case of Hong Kong', *International Journal of Administrative Sciences*, 52:4 (1986), pp. 447–69.
———. *Political Change and the Crisis of Legitimacy in Hong Kong*. Hong Kong: Oxford University Press, 1989.
Sinclair, Georgina. *At the End of the Line: Colonial Policing and the Imperial Endgame, 1945–1980*. Manchester: Manchester University Press, 2006.
Sinclair, Kevin, and Nelson Ng Kwok-cheung. *Asia's Finest Marches On: Policing Hong Kong from 1841 into the 21st Century*. Hong Kong: Kevin Sinclair Associates Ltd, 1997.
Smart, Alan. *Making Room: Squatter Clearance in Hong Kong*. Hong Kong: Centre of Asian Studies, the University of Hong Kong, 1992.
———. *The Shek Kip Mei Myth: Squatters, Fires and Colonial Rule in Hong Kong, 1950–63*. Hong Kong: Hong Kong University Press, 2006.
———. 'Unreliable Chinese: Internal security and the devaluation and expansion of citizenship in postwar Hong Kong.' In *War, Citizenship, Territory*, edited by Deborah Cowen and Emily Gilbert, pp. 219–240. New York: Routledge, 2007.
Smart, Alan, and Josephine Smart. 'Learning from disaster? Mad cows, squatter fires, and temporality in repeated cases.' In *The Political Economy of Hazards and Disasters*,

edited by Eric Jones and Arthur D. Murphy, pp. 267–93. Lanham, MD: Altamira Press, 2009.
Shipp, Steve. *Macau, China: A Political History of the Portuguese Colony's Transition to Chinese Rule.* Jefferson: McFarland and Company, 1997.
Sinn, Elizabeth, *Power and Charity: The Early History of the Tung Wah Hospital.* Hong Kong: Oxford University Press, 1989.
Tang, James T. H. 'World War to Cold War: Hong Kong's future and Anglo-Chinese interactions, 1941–55.' In *Precarious Balance: Hong Kong Between China and Britain 1842–1992*, edited by Ming K. Chan, pp. 107–30. New York: M.E. Sharpe: 1994.
Tang, Kwong-leung. *Colonial State and Social Policy: Social Welfare Development in Hong Kong 1842–1997.* Lanham: University Press of America, 1998.
'The Hong Kong University Students' Union Council on the recent riot' (17/5/1967). In *The Riot in Hong Kong,* edited by Ma Ming. Hong Kong: Sky Horse Book Company, 1967.
Thompson, Thomas N. *China's Nationalisation of Foreign Firms: The Politics of Hostage Capitalism, 1949–57.* Baltimore: School of Law, University of Maryland Occasional papers, 1979.
Tongxuemen, tuanjie qilai! (Students, organize and rise up!) Hong Kong: Sanlian, 1967.
Tsang Steve. *Democracy Shelved: Great Britain, China, and Attempts at Constitutional Reform in Hong Kong, 1945–1952.* Hong Kong: Oxford University Press, 1988.
———. *A Modern History of Hong Kong, 1841–1997.* Hong Kong: Hong Kong University Press, 2004.
———. 'Strategy for survival: The cold war and Hong Kong's policy towards Kuomintang and Chinese communist activities in the 1950s,' *Journal of Imperial and Commonwealth History,* 25:2 (1997), 294–317.
Tsang, Steve (ed.). *Government and Politics: A Documentary History of Hong Kong.* Hong Kong: Hong Kong University Press, 1995.
Tucker, Nancy Bernkopf (ed.). *China Confidential: American Diplomats and Sino-American Relations, 1945–1996.* New York: Columbia University Press, 2001.
Turner, H. A., et al. *The Last Colony: But Whose? A Study of the Labour Movement, Labour Market and Labour Relations in Hong Kong.* Cambridge: Cambridge University Press, 1980.
Waldron, Stephen Edward. 'Fire on the rim: A study in contradictions in left-wing mobilization.' (Unpublished Ph.D. Thesis, Syracuse University, 1976).
Walden, George. *Lucky George: Memoirs of an Anti-politician.* London: Allen Lane, 1999.
Wang Zhicheng, *Portuguese in Shanghai.* Macao: Macau Foundation, 2004.
We Shall Win! British Imperialism in Hong Kong Will be Defeated! Hong Kong: Ta Kung Pao, 1967.
Welsh, Frank. *A History of Hong Kong.* London: HarperCollins, 1997.
Who Is Guilty of These Atrocities? Hong Kong: Ta Kung Pao, 1967.
Whiting, Allen S. 'The use of force in foreign policy by the People's Republic of China', *Annals of the American Academy of Political and Social Science,* 402:1 (1972), pp. 55–66.
Williams, Gertrude. *Report on the Feasibility of a Survey into Social Welfare Provision and Allied Topics in Hong Kong.* Hong Kong: Government Printer, 1966.
Wong, Cheuk-yin. 'The communist-inspired riots in Hong Kong, 1967: A multi-actors approach' (unpublished M.Phil. Thesis, the University of Hong Kong, 2001).
Yang Jianhua et al. *Xianggang chong beizhan dao huigui* (Hong Kong: From colonial rule to reunification). Fuzhou: Fujian Renmin Chubanshe, 1997.

Yep, Ray. 'The 1967 riot in Hong Kong: Autonomy under imperial rule', *The China Quarterly* No. 193 (2008), pp. 122–39.
Ying diguozhuyi zai wanhuo (British colonialism is playing with fire). Hong Kong: Sanlian, 1967.
Yong, C. F., and R. B. McKenna. *The Kuomintang Movement in British Malaya, 1912–1949*. Singapore: Singapore University Press, 1990.
Young, John D. 'The building years: Maintaining a China-Hong Kong-Britain equilibrium, 1950–71.' In *Precarious Balance: Hong Kong between China and Britain, 1842–1992*, edited by Ming K. Chan, pp. 131–47. Armonk, NY: M.E. Sharpe, 1994.
———. 'Towards a Hong Kong identity: The riots of 1966 and 1967.' Paper presented at the Twelfth Conference of the International Association of Historians, the University of Hong Kong, June 1991,
Yuan Bangjian (ed.). *Xianggang shilue* (A concise history of Hong Kong). Hong Kong: Mainstream Publisher, 1987.
Xu Jiatun. *Xu Jiatun Xianggang huiyilu* (Xu Jiatun's reflection on Hong Kong Affairs), Vol. 1. Taipei: United Press, 1994.
Zhang Xichang et al., *Fengluan dieqi gongheguo de sanci jianjiao gaochao* (Twists and turns: The third wave of diplomacy of the Republic), pp. 95–120. Beijing: Shijie Zhishi Chubanshe, 1998.
Zhou Yi, *Xianggang zuopai douzhengshi* (History of left-wing struggle in Hong Kong. Hong Kong: Leeman Press, 2002.

Index

User's Note:

The arrangement of entries is word-by-word. Entries comprising numbers are alphabetized and placed in the appropriate alphabetical sequence, e.g. '1967' is read as 'nineteen sixty-seven' and placed after 'Ngo'.

Where references are made to subject matter in the endnotes, the page number is followed by 'n' and then the number of the note, viz: 189n59.

Tables and charts have also been indexed where the subject matter does not appear in the text on the same page. References to tables and charts comprise the page number followed by the table or figure number in parentheses, viz: 124 (Figure 7.14).

Afternoon News, 9, 31
Akers-Jones, Sir David, 50
All Circles Anti-Persecution Struggle Committee, 4, 6, 9, 22
American Chamber of Commerce, 27
Americans, *see* United States
Annieson, Anthony, 93
Anti-British Struggle Committee, 70
anti-colonial campaign, 6–8, 22
anti-riot policy, 41–2
archives, 16, 21, 74, 105, 148, 153
arrests, 1, 9
    editors and publishers, 9, 31, 40
Auxiliary Police Force, *see* Hong Kong Auxiliary Police Force

Bank of China, 121, 122
Bank of England, 113
bank deposits, 118–20
    mainland banks, 122–3, 124 (Figure 7.14)
banking system, impact of 1967 riots on, 115–26
banknote issue, 113, 115
banks, *see* Chinese mainland banks, foreign banks, and names of individual banks
Beijing, demonstrations in, 6, 22
Bennett, N. H. T., 113, 116
Benton, Gregor, 13
Bernacchi, Brook, 28, 45
Black, Sir Robert Brown, 13, 130, 132
bombs, 11, 30, 41, 81,177
    bombing campaign, 3, 8, 97–8
    statistics, 6, 7 (Table 1.1)
Bonavia, David, 63, 89
border, Hong Kong-China
    'border screen' security, 100–2
    incidents, 100–1
Bottomley, J. R. A., 154
boycotts, against British goods, 71, 76
Bray, Denis, 38, 39, 41
    on crisis of legitimacy, 50, 189n59
    on use of emergency powers, 42, 43
Britain (*see also* Sino-British relationship)
    policy towards China, 74

216 *Index*

position on Hong Kong, 63–4, 66, 108
relations with Hong Kong as sovereign power, 5, 15–6, 74, 105, 107, 133, 158
British concessions in China, 74
British consulate, Macao, 55
  abandonment of, 53, 59–61
  demonstrations against, 57–9
British garrison, 13, 26, 90, 98, 100
  deployment of, 40, 93
'British interests'
  defence of, 25, 36, 74
  interpretation of, 15
British Mission, Beijing, attack on, 9, 31, 41
British Mission, Shanghai, 31
Bulwark, HMS, 10, 77, 96
business community, opposition to labour reforms, 136, 137, 138, 139, 143

Cabinet Ministerial Committee on Hong Kong, 27
Callaghan, James (later Lord Callaghan of Cardiff), 106
Canton (*see also* Guangzhou), 54
Canton Trade Fair, 32
capital, financial, *see* financial capital
Carvalho, Nobre de, 54, 57
Carver, General Sir Michael, 3
Cater, Sir Jack, 30, 31, 38, 40
  quoted, 39, 48, 80, 83
Catron, Gary, 69, 70, 72
Central Intelligence Agency (CIA), 107
Centre of Contemporary British History, London University, 164
Chamberlain, Joseph, 84
Chan Chi Kong, 176–7
Chartered Bank, 116, 117
Chatham Road detention centre, 176
Chen Yi, 24, 187n25
Cheng Wu Pao, 116
Cheung Ka-wai, 75, 165
Chiang Kai-shek, 74, 92
China (*see also* Sino-British relationship), 23, 35, 74
  importance of Hong Kong to, 107–8
  policy towards Hong Kong, 73
  support for Hong Kong disturbances, 41, 70, 71–2, 73, 74
  threat from, 8, 107
China factor, 11–2, 70–4
  views on, 49, 155
China Motor Bus, 69
Chinese (language), as official language, 83, 151
Chinese (people), government attitude towards, 148, 151, 152
Chinese Communist Party, 13, 36, 72, 107, 128
Chinese communities
  in Britain, 10, 13
  overseas, 79
Chinese mainland banks
  in Hong Kong, 105, 117, 118, 119, 120–5, 126
  liquidity of, 124–5
Chinese Manufacturers' Association (CMA), 130–1
Chinese Mechanics Institute, 76
Chinese militia, 101
Chinese nationalism, 74, 76
Chinese News Agency, *see* Xinhua News Agency
Chinese Seamen's Union, 76, 78
Chinese Students Weekly, 173
Ching, Pedro, 101
Chiu, Stephen W K, 149
Chow, Shouson, 12, 72, 79, 82, 84
Chow Yik, 165–6, 167
Chung Kwok San Man Po (China News), 72–3
Chung Wah Middle School, 10, 32, 34, 176
city district offices system, 148
City University of Hong Kong, 'May Days' workshop, 163–4
Clementi, Sir Cecil, 71, 73, 77, 78, 84
Cole, Leo, 116
colonial administration, *see* Hong Kong government
colonial administrators, British, 5
colonial governance, 5, 12, 15, 155
Colonial Office, 4, 5, 133, 135, 137, 155
colonial police forces, 89–90
Colonial Police Service, 90

colonial policy, conflict with diplomatic policy, 5
colonial state, the, see Hong Kong government
Commonwealth Relations Office, 4, 30
communist schools
    closure of, 10, 32, 77, 185n51
    proposed de-registration of, 34
communists, Hong Kong, 23, 152
    raids on premises of, 9
'confrontation', use of term, 3
confrontation prisoners, 34, 36
constitutional reforms, plans for, 84
Cooper, John, 1, 75
corruption, 84, 103, 175, 178
Counter-Propaganda Bureau, 79
Cowperthwaite, Sir John J., 109, 115, 130
'crisis', definition of, 49
crowd control, 'newer' methods of, 96
Cultural Revolution, 3, 33, 38, 75, 79
    impact on Hong Kong, 69, 95
    1967 riots seen as result of, 37, 167, 171
curfew, 178

Darwin, John, 4
Davies, Emrys, 53, 60
Davies, Hugh, 53, 60
death threats, 82
deaths, 1, 71, 81, 93, 94, 98, 101
Defence and Overseas Policy Committee, 62
Defence Review, British, 10, 13, 26, 100, 105
    Working Pary, 64
demonstrations, 6–7, 22, 39
detention centres, 168, 176
Dicks, Anthony R., 190n15
District Watch Force, 79
disturbances, see riots
Double Ten riots (1956), 14, 90, 92–4, 146, 152, 158, 178
Dowbiggin, Sir Herbert, 195n15
Dwyer, Denis, 150

Eates, Edward (Ted), 29, 92, 94, 95, 102
economy, 71, 76, 133
education, 10, 77
    communist influence in, 32, 33

eight-hour day, 127, 132, 135, 137, 139
Elliot, Elsie, 45, 75
'emergency', use of term, 3
emergency legislation, 9, 42
Emergency Regulations Ordinance, 42, 77
employers, see business community
Employment Ordinance, 129, 148
Ernst, Fritz, 93
Ernst, Ursula, 93
evacuation
    of Hong Kong, 15, 27, 34, 65–6
    of Macao, 56
Ewins, Fred, 98
Executive Council, 12, 14, 28, 30, 32, 84, 137

Factories and Industrial Undertakings Ordinance, 134–5
    amendment of, 137, 138, 139, 141, 142
    enforcement of, 139–41
factory inspectorate, 139–40, 141
Faure, David, 81, 146
Federation of Hong Kong Industries (FED), 29, 130–1
Federation of Students, 79
Ferdinand, Peter, 188n56
financial capital, flight of, 110–1
5.22 incident (1967), see Garden Road incident
Foggon, G., 139
food rationing, 39
Ford, (later Sir) David, 38
foreign banks, in Hong Kong, 117, 118, 119
Foreign and Commonwealth Office, 4, 142
Foreign Office, 4, 5, 15, 74, 155
Fu Ki, 168
Fung Kam Shui, 166

Galsworthy, Sir Arthur, 3, 62, 64
Garden Road incident (1967), 165, 167, 169, 172
garrison, British, see British garrison
Gass, Michael, 5, 42
Gibbs, C. G., 135
Godber, Peter, 84, 93
Goodstadt, Leo, 13, 15, 84, 150, 151
Government Communications Headquarters (GCHQ), 98

Government Information Service, 38
Government-Military and Medical Staff Union, 174
governors, Hong Kong (*see also* names of individual governors), 74, 77–8
Grandy, Air Chief Marshal Sir John, 100
Grantham, Sir Alexander, 182n19
Greenhalgh, J., 138, 142
Grey, Anthony, 24
Guangzhou, 71, 73, 76, 78
   demonstrations in, 6, 22
Guomindang, 39, 57, 72, 92, 128, 152
Guyatt, Les, 93

'hair water', 176, 177, 179
Hang Seng Bank, 118
Hankou, 74
Hase, Dr Patrick, 48, 189n59
hawkers, 172
Hayes, Dr James
Heaton, William, 16
Hermes, HMS, 82, 97
Hewitt, Peter, 41, 70
Hill, Norman 'Bomber', 98
Ho Yin, 30
Hon Wah Middle School, 185n51
Hong Kong Auxiliary Police Force, 79, 99, 169, 195n6
Hong Kong, colony of, 4–5
   China factor in, 11–2, 70–4
   economy, 71, 76, 133
   as financial centre, 105
   future of, 107, 156, 158
   relationship with sovereign power, 5, 15–6, 74, 105, 107, 133, 158
   strategic interests of United States in, 26–7
   value of, to mainland China, 107–8
   withdrawal of British sovereignty from, 108
Hong Kong Commercial Daily, 176
Hong Kong Daily News, 31
Hong Kong Evening News, 9
Hong Kong Federation of Trade Unions, 6, 22
Hong Kong government
   action against local leftists, 9–10
   anti-riot policy, 41–2
   attitude towards Chinese, 148, 151, 152
   capacity of, 12–4, 132, 146
   contribution to defence costs, 106, 107
   crisis in legitimacy of, 46–50
   interaction between, and local population, 147, 149, 152, 157
   local disturbances, policy response to, 21–2, 43–4
   public support for, 4, 11, 12, 28–9, 49, 159
   response to the Macao crisis, 62, 107
Hong Kong Government Office, London, 10
Hong Kong Government Permit Office, Macao, 57–8
Hong Museum of History, 1
Hong Kong Plastic Workers' Union, 165, 166
Hong Kong Police Force (*see also* Police Tactical Units, Police Tactical Squads
   Police Training Contingent, Special Branch), 13, 90–2, 93, 97, 102–3, 169–70
   Chinese members of, 8, 29
   international reputation of, 89
   localization, 103
   loyalty of, 10, 80, 195n12
   morale of, 29, 80, 96–7
   relations with military forces, 98–100
   treatment of prisoners by, 97, 166, 168, 171, 178, 179
   use of weapons by, 175–6
Hong Kong population (*see also* local population), 75
Hong Kong Seamen's Union, 73, 95, 171
Hong Kong Telephone Company, 151
Hong Kong Tramways Company, 151
Hopson, Donald, 34, 40, 41, 70
   attitude of, to crisis, 24–5, 30, 33
Housing Authority, 147
HSBC (Hongkong and Shanghai Banking Corporation 113, 115, 116, 117, 118
humiliation,
   of British in Macao, 61
   of China, 62
Huntingdon, Samuel, 47–8

identity, Hong Kong, growth of, 80–1, 147
Illegal Strike and Lockout Ordinance, 85
India, police recruits from, 91
intelligence services, 98
International Textile and Garment Workers' Federation 138
interviews, with left-wing leaders, 16
Ions, Norman, 53, 55, 57–60, 66

Irish Constabulary, *see* Royal Irish
    Constabulary

Jenkyns, Henry, 64, 65, 108
Jin Yaoru, 1
Jiujiang, 74

Kan, Sir Yuet-Keung, 28–9, 106
Kemble, John, 55, 58, 60
Kiu Koon Mansion, 43
Kiu Kwan Building, 169
Knight, Frank, 102
Kotewall, Robert, 12, 72, 79, 80, 82
Kowloon disturbances (1966), *see* Star
    Ferry riots
Kowloon Motor Bus, 69
Kowloon Walled City incident (1948), 14,
    146
Kung Sheung Yat Po (Industrial and
    Commercial Daily Press), 79
Kwangtung Provincial Bank, 122

labour advisors, British, 133, 135, 139, 142
Labour Advisory Board (LAB), 132, 138
labour laws, 127, 129, 148
    enterprises not subject to, 131
    making of, 134–9
    views of workers towards, 131
labour policy, making of, 130–4
Labour Protection Bureau, 79, 80
labour unions, *see* trade unions
laissez-faire, 150
    principles not applied, 151
Lam Bun, attack on, 81
Lam, Wai-man, 150, 151, 152
Lam Yuet Tin, 175–6
Lam, Siu-kai, 150
Laughton, David, 60
law and order, maintenance of, 39, 96, 152
Lee, Grace O. M., 134, 143
Leese, John, 93
leftists, local, 37, 79, 169
    alienation of population by, 8, 70
    anti-colonial campaign, 6–8
    government action against, 9–10, 43–4,
        167
    'guerrilla' campaign, 81
    leaders, interviews with, 16

legitimacy, concept of, 47–8
'legitimacy crisis', debate on, 46–50
Lethbridge, Henry, 81
Li Cheng Uk Estate, 152, 174
Liang Jiaqun, 2
Liang Wailin, 23
Liang Weichen, General, 79–80
Ling Man Hoi, 166–8
Liu, Alan P. L., 48, 188n56
local population
    alienation of, by leftists, 8, 70
    interaction between government and,
        147, 149, 152, 157
    support for colonial government by, 11,
        12, 28–9, 44, 49, 79, 96
    values of, 150
Locking, Robert, 38
Louis, William Roger, 5
Lui, Tai-lok, 14
Luk Kai Lau, 169–70
Luk Tak Shing, 170–2
Luo Guibo, 70

Ma Man-fei, 188n49
Macao, 26, 54–5
    12.3 incident, 11–2, 54, 55, 56–7, 165,
        167, 171
    lessons from, 62–3
Macao demonstrations (1967), 55–61, 63,
    107
Macartney, Lord, 54
MacFarquhar, Roderick, 62
McGregor, Jimmy, 77
MacLehose, Sir Murray (later Lord
    MacLehose of Beoch), 36, 77, 83, 146,
        149, 153–8, 159
    annual reporting by, 155, 156
    reputation of, as social reformer, 127,
        142, 147
Macmillan, Harold (1st Earl of Stockton),
    26
Maddocks, Arthur Frederick, 17
Mao Zedong, 35
market forces
    self-regulation by, 144
    social justice and, 143
Marine Police, *see* Water Police
May, Charles, 91

mechanics' strike (1920), 76
Metropolitan Police, 89, 91, 103
military forces, British (*see also* British garrison), 10, 13
    expenditure on, 106–7
    relations with police force, 98–100
    withdrawal of, 16, 106
Miners, Norman, 49
Ming Chan, 76, 78
Ming Pao, 29
Ministry of Foreign Affairs, China (MFA), 6, 22, 24, 41
Mount Davis Road detention centre, 168, 176
Mutual Aid Committees, 147, 149

Nanyang Commercial Bank, 121, 122
National Commercial Bank, 122
Nationalists, Chinese, *see* Guomindang
New China News Agency, *see* Xinhua News Agency
New Evening News, 176
'New Territories Action Group', 81
New Youth, 172, 173
newspapers
    left-wing, 72
    'mosquito newspaper', 6, 172
    suppression of pro-communist, 9, 29–32, 40, 176
Ng Huen Yan, 172–4
Ng Kin Piu, 177
Ngo, Tak-wing, 149
1967 riots, 21, 144
    banking system, impact on, 115–26
    context of, 2, 5–6
    contrasting accounts of, 1–2
    domestic character of, 164
    financial impact of, 109–15
    lessons of, 14
    origins, 6, 22, 37, 95, 171
    phases of, 37–46
    policy making, impact on, 127, 129, 134, 143
    public representation of, 1
    renewed interest in, 2
    research on, required, 16, 17
    social reforms, impact on, 14–5, 83, 143, 158, 159
    statistics, 7 (Table 1.1)
    victims, 167, 168, 179
    'witness accounts' of, 17, 163–80

official language, Chinese as, 83
Oil Paint Union, 171
overtime, 138, 139, 140–1

Peel, Sir Robert, 89
Peking, *see* Beijing
People's Daily, editorials, 6, 7, 8, 22
People's Liberation Army (PLA), 23, 40, 41, 57
People's Republic of China, *see* China
Perth, Lord, 135
police, *see* Hong Kong Auxiliary Police Force, Hong Kong Police Force
police raids, 9, 42–3, 71, 82, 97, 171
Police Tactical Squads (PTSs) (*see also* riot squads), 195n19
Police Tactical Units (PTUs), 94, 95, 102, 169
Police Training Contingent (PTC), 93
policing models, 89–90, 91–2
political apathy, 150
population, *see* Hong Kong population, local population
Portugal, relations with China, 63
Portuguese, response to demonstrations in Macao, 56, 57, 58, 61
posters, 72, 77
Printers and Publishers Ordinance, 85
propaganda, 7–8, 10, 29, 72, 79
public confidence, maintenance of, 96, 154–5, 157
public opinion, 4, 97, 146
Pui Kiu Middle School, 185n51

Qiaoguan Building, raid on, 9
Quine, Richard, 103

Radio Hong Kong (now Radio Television Hong Kong), 38
Red Guards, 16, 21, 28, 56, 57, 73
    attack on British mission, 9, 41
reforms, *see* social reforms
'refugee crisis', 133
    mentality, 134, 137, 141

remittances, from overseas Chinese, 111–2
Requisitioning of Ships Order, 34
research, on 1967 events, required, 16, 17
Resettlement Department, 147
resettlement estates, 92, 152, 174
'Reunion Incident' (1952), 174
riot squads, 93, 94
'riots', use of term, 3, 4, 167
riots, *see* Double Ten riots (1956), 1967 riots, Star Ferry riots (1966), Tung Tau Comfort Mission riot (1952)
Robinson, Sir William, 84
Rogers, Philip, 5
Rose, Richard, 11
Royal Hong Kong Police Force, *see* Hong Kong Police Force
Royal Interocean Line, 95
Royal Irish Constabulary, 89, 91
Royal Ulster Constabulary, 103, 198n86
Rubber Labourers' Union, 177
Rusk, Dean, 27
Ruttonjee, Dhun Jehangir, 28

San Po Kong, 74–6
San Po Kong Artificial Flower Factory incident, 6, 95, 165, 169, 170, 172, 175–6
schools, *see* communist schools
Schouten, Peter, 93
Scott, Ian, 14, 51, 134, 143
    on colonial state, 12, 132
    'legitimacy crisis', case for, 37, 46–9
Scott, Ivan, 91
seamen's strike (1922), 76, 78
Secret Intelligence Service (MI6), 98
security, of Hong Kong, *see* law and order
Sedgwick, P. C. M., 138
Sha Tau Kok Anti-Persecution Committee, 177
Sha Tau Kok (Shatoujiao) incident, 23, 97, 101
    impact on local population, 9, 81
    policemen killed in, 9, 40, 71, 176
Shackleton, Lord, 199n17
Shamian Massacre (1925), 71
Shanghai, 31, 70
Shanghai Municipal Police, 77
Shek Kip Mei, 174
Shek Wai, 168

Shock, The, 172, 173
Sin Hua Trust, 122
Sino-British relationship, 22, 24, 33, 36, 63
Smart, Alan, 14
So Sau-chung, 75, 94
social conditions, 75, 149–52, 175
social reforms, 145, 147–9, 154, 156
    demand for, 44–6
    impact of 1967 riots on, 14–5, 83, 143
Societies Ordinance, 151
South China Morning Post, 115
Special Branch, Police, 38, 62, 65, 167
'Special Group', establishment of, 38
Squatter Resettlement Programme, 146
squatters, 150, 151, 152
Stanley Prison, 179–80
Star Ferry riots (1966), 14, 75, 84, 94–5, 146, 151, 165
statistics, of disturbances, 7 (Table 1.1)
sterling
    balances, 109
    devaluation of, 65
    sale of, 114 (Figures 7.5–7.6)
    shortage of, 113
sterling area, 25, 105
strike-boycott (1925–26), 69, 76–7, 78, 82, 83
    impact of, 84, 85, 128
    influence of forces in China on, 71–2, 73, 74
strike pickets, violence by, 82
strikers, dismissal of, 39
strikes, 7, 69, 76, 78, 165
Stubbs, Sir Reginald Edward, 71, 72, 73, 78
Sun Fo, 76
Swire Automobile Union, 171
Swire Dockyard Union, 171

Ta Ku Ling, attack on, 101
Tam Chi Keung, 167
testimonies, of 1967 riots, 163–80
Thornton, Ernest, 138, 141
Tin Fung Yat Po (Tin Fung Daily), 9, 31, 176
trade associations, 130–1
Tram Workers' Union, 167
trade unions (*see also* names of individual unions), 38, 85, 128, 132, 140, 144, 175

Trench, Sir David, 13, 16, 33–4, 38, 77, 130, 132, 136, 142, 153
  career of, 5
  colonial governance, 155
  communist newspapers, proposed action against, 30, 31
  diagnosis of disturbances, 23, 62, 70, 71
  'flea-bite' quote, 164
  labour law, amendment of, 137, 138, 139, 141
  public confidence, concern for, 97, 154, 155
  quoted, 2, 9, 17, 44
  strategic response to local disturbances, 21–2, 28, 35
triads, 92, 93
Tsang, Steve, 147, 150
Tsuen Wan riot (1956), 93, 174
Tu, Elsie, *see* Elliot, Elsie
Tu, Parker, 185n51
Tung Tau Comfort Mission riot (1952), 14, 146, 155, 158
Tung Wah Hospital Committee, 79
Tung Wah Hospitals, 12
Tyrer, Edward, 196n33

'unfair' competition, 133
unions, labour, *see* trade unions
United Nations Association, 44, 188n49
United States
  as factor in British strategy, 16
  strategic interest in Hong Kong, 26–7
University of Hong Kong Students' Union, 79

violence, 6, 7 (Table 1.1), 31, 81–2, 164, 167, 172
volunteers, 79

Walden, George, 60
Waldron, Stephen, 83
Wan Kwok Hang, 177

Wang Li, 40, 41
Water Police (later Marine Police), 90
water supply, 73, 170
Weihaiwei, 74, 91
Wan Wei Po, 30, 72, 165, 167, 173, 176
Whampoa Dockyard Union, 176
'white terror', allegation of,167
Williams, Lady Gertrude, 148
Wodehouse, Captain Superintendent P. P. J., 80
women, working hours of, 127, 129, 134, 137, 139, 140, 143
workers, 177
  customary regulation by, 144
  erosion of customary protection, 128
  in public utilities, 8 (Table 1.2)
  unco-ordinated bargaining by, 140
  views of, towards labour laws, 131
working hours, factory women, 127, 129, 134, 137, 139, 140, 143
World Trade Organisation (WTO), demonstration at meeting of, 169, 170
Worseley, Lieutenant-General Sir John, 99
Wu Kang-min, 187n30
Wu Tin Leung, 177–9

Xinhua News Agency, 4, 23, 43, 44, 72, 77, 108, 176
Xu Jiatun, 4

Yang Jiang (Yeung Kwong), 4
Yao Dengshan, 40, 41
Yau Yue Commercial Bank, 120
Yeung Kwong, *see* Yang Jiang
Yip Mo Chiu, 179–80
Young, John, 80, 146
Youth Garden, 173
youth movement, 173

Zhenjiang, 74
Zhou Enlai, 40, 70
Zhou Yi, 2

www.ingramcontent.com/pod-product-compliance
Ingram Content Group UK Ltd.
Pitfield, Milton Keynes, MK11 3LW, UK
UKHW021833210426
5322IPUK00012B/201/J